VIKRAM SARABHAI

Amrita Shah is a journalist and writer. She has worked for *Time* magazine, edited *Debonair* and *Elle*, and been a contributing editor with *Indian Express*. She is the author of *Hype, Hypocrisy and Television in Urban India* and *Ahmedabad: A City in the World*. She is an alumna of the Institute for Public Knowledge, New York University, and visiting faculty at the Centre for Contemporary Studies, Indian Institute of Science, Bengaluru.

Let the life of Vikram Sarabhai ji inspire us.

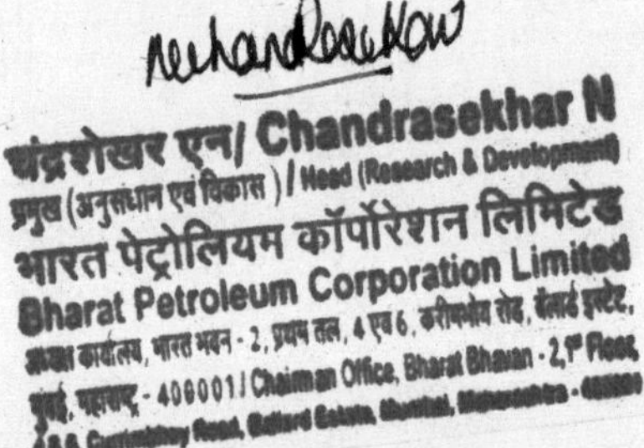

VIKRAM SARABHAI
A LIFE

Amrita Shah

PENGUIN BOOKS
An imprint of Penguin Random House

PENGUIN BOOKS

USA | Canada | UK | Ireland | Australia
New Zealand | India | South Africa | China

Penguin Books is part of the Penguin Random House group of companies whose addresses can be found at global.penguinrandomhouse.com

Published by Penguin Random House India Pvt. Ltd
4th Floor, Capital Tower 1, MG Road,
Gurugram 122 002, Haryana, India

First published in Viking by Penguin Books India 2007
Published in Penguin Books 2016

10 9 8 7 6 5 4 3 2

The views and opinions expressed in this book are the author's own and the facts are as reported by her which have been verified to the extent possible, and the publishers are not in any way liable for the same.

ISBN 9780143426745

Typeset in Minion Regular by SÜRYA, New Delhi
Printed at Repro India Limited

www.penguin.co.in

For my late mother, Kirtida

Ah, but a man's reach should exceed his grasp,
Or what's a heaven for?

—Robert Browning

CONTENTS

LIST OF ABBREVIATIONS

AEC	Atomic Energy Commission
AMA	Ahmedabad Management Association
AMA	Ahmedabad Millowners Association
ATIRA	Ahmedabad Textile Industry's Research Association
BARC	Bhabha Atomic Research Centre
CEO	chief executive officer
CNES	Centre National d'Etudes Spatiales
COSPAR	Committee for Space Research
CSIR	Council of Scientific and Industrial Research
DAE	Department of Atomic Energy
DRDO	Defence Research and Development Organisation
ECIL	Electronics Corporation of India Limited
GISE	Group for the Improvement of Science Education
IAEA	International Atomic Energy Agency
IISc	Indian Institute of Science
IIM-A	Indian Institute of Management, Ahmedabad
IGY	International Geophysical Year
INCOSPAR	Indian National Committee for Space Research
ISI	Indian Statistical Institute
ISRO	Indian Space Research Organisation
MIT	Massachusetts Institute of Technology
NID	National Institute of Design
NPL	National Physical Laboratory
NPT	Non-Proliferation Treaty
ORG	Operations Research Group
PRL	Physical Research Laboratory
RATO	rocket-assisted take-off

SITE	Satellite Instructional Television Experiment
SLV	satellite launch vehicle
SNEPP	Study of Nuclear Explosions for Peaceful Purposes
SSTC	Space Science and Technology Centre
TERLS	Thumba Equatorial Rocket Launching Station
TIFR	Tata Institute of Fundamental Research
VSSC	Vikram Sarabhai Space Centre

AUTHOR'S NOTE

I was nine when Vikram Sarabhai died. I remember very clearly the arrival of the newspaper one cold winter morning—31 December 1971, it must have been—and my mother's audible gasp.

'What happened?' I asked, trying to get a peek at the headlines.

'A great scientist died,' she said, visibly moved.

With a reverence I had never before witnessed in her attitude either to science or to the daily news, she showed me the photograph. And she told me something about his life. She told me about the illustrious business family he had belonged to, a family which had been close to Gandhi and deeply involved in the freedom struggle. She told me about his great contributions to the country, the nature of which she appeared to have only a vague understanding of, but the idea of which clearly inspired in her a deep regard. She also told me, with an animation I could more easily connect to her interest in the classical arts, of his marriage as a young, handsome man to a distinguished Bharatanatyam dancer from the south.

Intrigued, I joined her in tracking the news over the next few days, marvelling at the long list of dignitaries who offered tribute and applauding when the teenage daughter took the place of the absent son in lighting the funeral pyre. And so it was that Vikram Sarabhai came to occupy a fuzzy space in my head, an idea of a progressive and romantic figure, a leading light of the intensely idealistic post-independence generation, who had died young and full of promise.

I next encountered Vikram Sarabhai more than two decades later in a book by mass communication scholars Arvind Singhal and Everett M. Rogers. Or perhaps it was a little before then. I had been working on a book on the proliferation of the audio-visual media starting in the mid-1980s and my research had inevitably led to the ideological concerns that guided the introduction of television in India. I had come across references to Vikram Sarabhai's passionate advocacy of a space programme and its application, through television and other means, for socio-economic upliftment. Somewhere along the way I had also gleaned that he had run a business enterprise and that he had succeeded the charismatic Homi Bhabha as head of the Atomic Energy Commission in the 1960s. And that he may have had, unusually for a person in his position at the time, grave reservations about India's move towards nuclear weaponization.

Singhal and Rogers's book, *India's Information Revolution*, provided other details. From a brief profile in its pages I learned for the first time that Vikram Sarabhai had established a large number of diverse institutions. Among those listed were the Indian Space Research Organisation, the Physical Research Laboratory, the Operations Research Group, the Indian Institute of Management, Ahmedabad, and the National Institute of Design. The book itself was dedicated to the memory of Vikram Sarabhai: 'who saw a revolution coming, and helped to make it happen'.

These revelations, following upon the other bits of information that had come my way, evoked a strangely unsettling feeling in me. I began to wonder what kind of mind could envisage developments of such long-term impact. What kind of man could encompass such a wide range of activities? And what had he really thought of the bomb?

These then were the questions that propelled the writing of this book.

'Did you get paid well?' is a question I have found myself faced with each time I have had occasion to mention that I was writing a biography of Vikram Sarabhai. I find the question and its underlying assumptions disturbing. There is something profoundly sad about an environment in which people naturally assume that a biography—of howsoever significant a personality—can only come about, and that a writer will only undertake it, because he or she has been commissioned by a family or institution interested in perpetuating the memory of the subject.

I have no aversion to money. But I have not and would not accept funding from any source which would curb my objectivity and my freedom to write the truth as I find it. In the circumstances I feel the need to clearly state that this is an independent work undertaken by me for the simple reason that it was a story that I felt had to be told and I very much wished to tell it.

That said, I cannot pretend that the conditions under which the non-fiction writer in India operates are not dire. In this case I confess my meagre resources did not allow me to travel as widely and as often as I felt I needed to. The paucity of archival material was another major handicap: no personal effects, letters or diaries were available, and documents involving Sarabhai's last years at the Department of Atomic Energy were out of bounds for reasons of official secrecy. This being the first-ever full-fledged biography of Vikram Sarabhai, I had to be mindful of the need both to introduce Sarabhai and the sheer magnitude of his achievements as well as discuss the more controversial aspects of his personality and career. And lastly, there was the problem, for someone with my limited expertise, of grappling with the varied nature of Sarabhai's interests: physics, management psychology, space technology, atomic power and architecture to name just a few.

I was fortunate, though, to have been helped in my endeavours by a number of people.

Mayank Chhaya appreciated the need for this book and his

enthusiasm and support were extremely encouraging. Padmanabh K. Joshi made available to me speeches made by Sarabhai, tributes by distinguished colleagues and other material collected painstakingly by him for the Dr Vikram Sarabhai Archives at the Nehru Foundation for Development. Vikram Sarabhai's wife Mrinalini, and children, Kartikeya and Mallika, made time for me, were generous with permissions for photographs and quotations, and shared their insights and memories.

Binit Modi and Urvish Kothari sent me cuttings from Ahmedabad. S. Krishnamurthy at ISRO helped out with relevant material. Praful Bhavsar patiently answered my extensive queries about the early years at PRL. Both he and S.M. Chitre were kind enough to offer comments on the sections dealing with Sarabhai's physics while Itty Abraham cast a perceptive eye over the chapters on nuclear power. The responsibility for lapses in these and other areas, though, is mine alone.

Maitreyi Lakhia, Kumudini Lakhia, Shishir Hattangadi, Ayisha Abraham, Satyajit Mayor, Seema Guha, Meenakshi Ganguly and Annie Mathews were warmly hospitable and sustained me greatly with their companionship. Shekhar Gupta introduced me to the world of strategic studies and encouraged me to continue writing about the present even while I worked on long-term projects about the past. Shiraz Rustomjee and Ajay Sharma gave generously of their legal expertise. My father Nalin and my brother Hemal were affectionately supportive. Sumita Hattangadi was a friend I could always count on. At Penguin Books, Krishan Chopra provided benevolent and supportive guardianship while Shantanu Ray Chaudhuri made valuable suggestions and skilfully ironed out rough edges in the manuscript.

To all these, my sincere thanks.

1

THE CRUCIBLE

When you land in Ahmedabad you see smoke from all the chimneys blowing one way and smoke from the Calico Mills blowing the other way.

—Old Ahmedabad saying

Thrust deep into the armpit of western India, close to the Gulf of Cambay, and yet not close enough to protect it from the severe desert wind sweeping down from Kathiawar, is the city of Ahmedabad. With no natural beauty to boast of save for the Sabarmati slicing through it, the city Vikram Sarabhai called home has a reputation, nevertheless, of being a hardy city.

How hardy can be judged from the legend that surrounds its origins. Way back in the fifteenth century, the story goes, Sultan Ahmed Shah I, who had taken over Gujarat following the internecine wars that overthrew the Tughlak dynasty, was passing through the area then known as Ashavali. When he paused to rest at a river bank, he noticed a strange sight: a rabbit giving chase to his hound dogs. Overwhelmed by this show of bravery on the part of the smallest of its creatures, Ahmed Shah immediately decided upon the fertile soil as the site for his new capital.[1]

It was no ordinary city that Ahmed Shah went on to build,

but one that rivalled the glory of Anhilvad Patan, capital of the erstwhile Solanki rulers of Gujarat. It had walls, gates, palaces and mosques in the Indo-Saracenic style alongside wide streets, marketplaces and artificial lakes that evoked fulsome praise from diverse quarters. The sixteenth-century Persian work *Haft Iqlim*, for instance, gushed over Ahmedabad's 'neatness', the 'excellence of its monuments' and called it a '... grand beautiful town'.[2] The British traveller John Jourdain who, in 1611, looked in on his travels through Arabia, India and the Malay Archipelago, described it as 'one of the fairest cities in all the Indies'.

It was a prosperous city. A popular stopover for travellers—from the Pandavas who were said to have paused there on their way to Draupadi's swayamvar to Hajis on their way to Mecca—Ahmedabad flourished due to the foresight of Ahmed Shah who had invited merchants, weavers and craftsmen to settle there. The industriousness and thrift of its people turned the inland city into a pulsing centre for trade. Cotton, smooth velvet, silks, silver and gold brocade, saltpetre and indigo flowed from it through the port of Cambay to the Middle East, Europe, Africa and South-east Asia. Western imports stocked in Ahmedabad's warehouses moved on the backs of donkeys and camels to the courts of Delhi, Agra, Rajasthan and Malwa. In 1638, the European traveller Mandelslo, trudging through western India, remarked on the ease with which foreign bills of exchange could be obtained in the city as local merchants had correspondents in places as distant as Constantinople.

Over the centuries, Ahmedabad changed hands. The Mughals came in the sixteenth century. Akbar, the third Mughal emperor, considered this south-western province of such importance that, on hearing of a plot being hatched by its governor, he rode out immediately all the way from Agra to the city's north gate to shame the treacherous governor into submission. With the decline of the Mughals, however, the city too declined. The period between 1738 and 1753 saw the Marathas establish a foothold in the region. And in 1817 the East India Company took charge.

At the advent of the twentieth century, then, Ahmedabad had seen more than a fair share of tumult. Yet, the trauma of conquest and natural calamities had not caused the sort of upheaval in the ordinary life of the townsfolk as could have been expected. Even the ravages perpetrated by the British elsewhere, such as in the flourishing manufacturing towns of Murshidabad and Dacca, had not dented Ahmedabad's ebullience.[3] The city not only survived but emerged with its social ethos intact.

Those who have studied the city's evolution through the ages attribute its stubbornness to two main factors: the influence of Jainism and the commercial mindset of the Gujarati people.

Jainism, the religion popularized by Mahavira in the sixth century BC, had strong roots in Gujarat and had endured over time with the patronage of dynasties such as the Maitrakas, the Solankis and the Vaghelas. Known to be among the world's most rigorously ascetic faiths, the religion enjoined its followers to adhere strictly to its tenets of nonviolence and public duty. Ahmedabad's Jains, for instance, were fervent vegetarians and refused to deal in firearms, alcohol and animal hides. They were, at the same time, the city's leading traders and, either due to their immense wealth or the natural inclination of others, they exercised a disproportionately strong influence on the city's social life. The Jain ethic was the shared ethic of the city.[4]

The other source of Ahmedabad's survival was money. 'The Gujaratis,' points out Kenneth L. Gillion, in his book *Ahmedabad*, 'are perhaps the least otherworldly of all the Indian peoples.'[5] This is not a view likely to be much contested, least of all by the Gujaratis themselves. According to Muni Jinvijayji, head of the historical research section of the Gujarati Sahitya Parishad in the 1930s, 'The main aim of the people here is to figure out ways to make the most amount of money.'[6]

Commerce proved to be an effective binder. The single-minded purposefulness of the community fostered harmony between Muslim weavers and Jain and Hindu vania merchants. According to the Danish psychoanalyst Erik Erikson who visited the city in the 1960s, this was what gave Ahmedabad 'a character both solid and limited, both strong and ingrown, both alive and isolated, by which it had been able to household through the centuries a remarkable energy...'[7]

Vikram's ancestors were rich merchants belonging to the Dasa Srimali Jain sect. The family business house or *pedhi*, as it was called, was named after Karamchand Premchand who lived in the early 1800s and amassed his fortune by advancing loans to local chieftains and trading in Chinese opium and silk. Most of the city's merchants at the time were involved in similar pursuits jointly operating as a pan-India network with offices in Bombay, Malwa, Baroda, Poona, Calcutta, Jaipur and Delhi.

By the middle of the nineteenth century, however, competition from the Chinese and other Indian traders forced Ahmedabad's merchants to consider new avenues of generating wealth. In 1861, Ranchodlal Chotalal, a Nagar Brahmin entrepreneur, showed the way by establishing the first modern steam-driven cotton mill.

The event that was to significantly alter the prospects of the city and its people was, by all accounts, a risky enterprise. Cotton, it was true, was an indigenous crop. The quality of Indian spinning had been once so admired by the weavers of Blackburn and Bolton that the East India Company had set up *karkhanas* all over Gujarat. But that was in the past. The invention of the power loom, the arrival of the railways, and protective tariffs had tilted the balance in favour of British goods. The time, thus, was not propitious, and Ahmedabad, with no port close by and an inhospitably dry climate, was not particularly suited for the manufacture of cotton textiles.

Yet Ranchodlal, stubborn Ahmedabadi that he was, was

determined to set up his textile mill. And after many setbacks—the first lot of machinery was shipwrecked, the first technician died of cholera—he set up the Ahmedabad Spinning and Weaving Company in 1861, a joint stock company one of whose shareholders was Karamchand Premchand's son, Maganbhai Karamchand.

By all accounts Maganbhai was a flamboyant personality. Stories of his prodigious wealth abound. He had coins showered on the streets in the wake of his *palki* and, in 1877, when a portion of his house collapsed in a major fire that destroyed Sarangpur and Zaveri Vad, ornaments were found embedded in the broken bits of wall.[8]

Some of the money was put to public use though. Maganbhai Sheth set up a Jain *pathshala*, Jain temples and donated money towards founding Ahmedabad's first girls' school, the Maganbhai Karamchand Girls' School. The last had a ring of prescience about it for his own Vaishnavite daughter-in-law, Godavariba, turned out to be a great reader and kept, or so it is said, a copy of *Hamlet* under her pillow.

Though Maganbhai had acquired a stake in the pioneering company, he and his fellow Jains were hesitant to enter the new business directly. The hesitation stemmed from a fear of social ostracism. The opening of a mill by a Visa Porwad Jain in 1878, for instance, had evoked protest from the community on the grounds that insects could get caught in the raw cotton as it passed through the machines.[9]

In time, however, commercial interests effectively overruled religious objections. By the time Sarabhai, Maganbhai's grandson and heir, came of age, a number of textile mills had come up in Ahmedabad, many of them owned by Jains. So, in 1880, when the city's first mechanized cloth printing factory, the Ahmedabad Calico Printing Company Limited, failed and was offered to its largest lender, the pedhi of Karamchand Premchand, Sarabhai saw no reason to decline. He bought the mill and set about expanding it. He added the functions of spinning and weaving, thus laying the foundation for what was to become the family's flagship concern, Calico.

He did not live to see it flourish. Both Sarabhai and his wife died young, leaving three small children: Ansuya, eleven, an infant, Kanta, and the boy who would grow up to be Vikram's father, the five-year-old Ambalal.

In the tall, grey building constructed by the acclaimed French architect Le Corbusier in 1954, which houses the Ahmedabad Millowners Association (AMA), is a room in which, under a lofted ceiling, hang portraits of past presidents of the AMA. It is easy to spot Ambalal Sarabhai among them. He is the only one in a Western-style suit. His dark hair is slicked back from a broad forehead. His jaw is florid and the eyes behind round glasses convey the impression of sternness or reserve—it is hard to tell which.

If a photograph of Vikram were to be put next to his, it would be difficult to tell they were father and son. For, apart from his fair complexion, Vikram did not resemble his father, having inherited his mother's bright eyes and sharp features. Yet, the impact of the man with the unfathomable expression on his life and that of his siblings' would be immense.

'Ambalal set up the Sarabhai identity,' claims Vikram's son Kartikeya. 'The kind of contemplation that went into the making of Vikram's eclectic personality was actually done by his father a generation before.'

Ambalal was a remarkable man. And an unusual one for his times. He was well read and had a wide variety of interests, leading Erikson to describe him as 'a Renaissance man, Indian style'.[10] He was also an extremely complex man with many contradictory shades to his personality.

Precocity was perhaps the most striking one. Following the death of his parents, Ambalal was brought up by a paternal uncle. A likeness of him painted by the foremost portraitist of the times, Raja Ravi Varma, captures him in a loose cloak, embroidered cap and a chain of pearls, fist resting lightly on a globe. It is an exaggeratedly pompous pose, more so for a twelve-year-old. But it gives an indication of the exalted perception Ambalal, heir to the Sarabhai wealth, had of himself even as a child.

When his uncle Chimanbhai Nagindas passed away, Ambalal, barely eighteen at the time, was left in charge of two mills, Calico and Jubilee, the pedhi of Karamchand Premchand and a significant fortune. In addition, he was at the head of a household of women which included his two young sisters, a widowed aunt and three cousins.

His grandson, Kartikeya, claims that it was this early onset of responsibility that led him to 'distance himself from the world and look within'. It is likely, however, that Ambalal's introspective bent had also much to do with his religion. The Sarabhais were not only devout Jains but, being heads of their sect, also enjoyed a position of leadership in the community, a position inherited by Ambalal when he came of age.

In time, Ambalal would opt out of both sect and community but it is reasonable to assume that the philosophical aspect of Jainism exerted a strong influence on him, regardless. A passage in Lawrence A. Babb's *Ascetics and Kings in a Jain Ritual Culture* that describes the role of a Tirthankar or 'an extraordinary human being' accurately conveys the kind of striving both Ambalal and later Vikram seemed inclined towards:

> [A Tirthankar is one] who has conquered the attachments and aversions that stand in the way of liberation from worldly bondage. By means of his own efforts and entirely without the benefit of being taught by others, he has achieved that state of omniscience in which all things are known to him—past,

> present and future. But, before final attainment of his own liberation, the Tirthankar imparts his self-gained liberating knowledge to others so that they might become victors too. Thus, he establishes a crossing place for other beings.[11]

If Ambalal's propensity for 'looking within' came from his religious background, his ideas were drawn from his exposure, through reading, of Western liberal thought. What emerged was a curious mixture of East and West, modernism and tradition. In her book *Akhand Divo*, his daughter Leena Mangaldas describes her father's priorities as 'self-respect', 'self-reliance' and 'self-evolution'.

He was always acutely conscious, proud even, of his philosophical yearnings. Many years later he was to tell Ted Standing, a Britisher who had been employed as a teacher for his children, that he did not like to be immersed in business all day. 'I would like to be able to get away from it all for a few minutes to meditate on something deeper and more permanent.'[12]

In his sudden elevation to family patriarch on the death of his uncle, the teenage Ambalal perceived an opportunity to put some of his experimental ideas into practice. The personal front offered the most potential since both he and his sister Kanta were yet to marry. In both cases, the budding idealist decided to choose spouses who were at variance in terms of status and wealth with their own. In Kanta's case, the decision was motivated by a wishful belief in the virtues of education over wealth. Kanta's husband was a mechanical engineer of modest means; the marriage was not successful and she was to die unhappily soon after, to Ambalal's everlasting regret.

The unequal matches (in Ambalal's case the situation was aggravated by the fact that his bride-to-be was not, like him, a Dasa Srimali Jain) caused a furore within the community. Angry Jains threatened to stone the marriage processions. The threats did not deter young Ambalal in the least. He went on to take the even bolder step of helping his elder sister Ansuya escape the confines of her child marriage and, at her wish, put her on a boat to England.

For a callow youth to flout social convention and go against the wishes of his assertive community was no small matter and Ambalal's courage and firmness was an unequivocal signal of his intention to live life on his own terms.

Strikingly though, it did not occur to Ambalal to bring his strongly progressive ideas to the arena of business. By the turn of the century there were almost 20,000 millhands in the city. Most of the men who worked in these mills, which included Ambalal's two, came from the villages around Ahmedabad. They flocked to the city and set up homes in grimy shacks till the sheths built *chawls* where they lived in better, but equally cramped, conditions. Work was strenuous. The hours were long and there was little time off; workers came even on Sundays to clean the machines. The artificially induced dampness inside the mills was unhealthy but there was no protection in the form of sick leave or medical cover. The manufacturers had come together to form the Millowners Association as far back as 1891, but the workers were not unionized and had little awareness of their rights.[13]

Ambalal, it is claimed by the publicity material put out by Ambalal Sarabhai Enterprises, was one of the first employers to favour recognition of trade unions, and to build a hospital for employees and a crèche 'long before these services were statutorily required'. Yet, he did not make a path-breaking intervention to change the sorry plight of the workers, nor did he appear to have contemplated any such move.

A challenge to his conservatism, however, was in the offing. And it was to come from within his home. In 1914, Ambalal's sister Ansuya returned from England. Originally intending to study medicine, she had found herself unable to stand the sight of blood and had become involved in the suffragette movement instead. Back in Ahmedabad she cut a shocking figure, smoking cigarettes and moving about with her head uncovered. She had started a school for the children of millworkers and was appalled by their squalid living conditions.

The following year, coincidentally, saw the arrival of the man who was to become the city's most distinguished resident, Mohandas Karamchand Gandhi. Tales of the slight, bespectacled, England-trained advocate and his crusade against racism in South Africa had preceded his return to India and he was given a tumultuous welcome on his travels round the country. While he toyed with possible options for locating a new settlement, he had accepted the temporary offer of a house in Kochrab on the outskirts of Ahmedabad. Almost immediately, however, he had found himself up against a wall. His decision to take in untouchables had provoked indignation in the caste-ridden town and funds had dried up. It was then, in a story that has passed into legend, that an unidentified man came by in a car and dropped off a generous contribution. The anonymous donor turned out to be Ambalal.[14]

The gesture probably aroused Gandhi's hopes, for he eventually settled upon Ahmedabad as a permanent home, listing among his reasons the expectation that 'monetary help from its wealthy citizens' would be forthcoming.[15] Just as he hoped, help indeed would be forthcoming. In fact, the rich mill owners of Ahmedabad would not only extend financial support but would become fervent followers of the Mahatma. Gandhi's values of 'non-violence, frugality, honesty, integrity, self-reliance and peace', so like their own, as business historian Dwijendra Tripathi points out, would endear him to the sheths.[16] But Gandhi would also, unexpectedly, be good for commerce. His campaign for 'swadeshi' would have the effect of protecting local mill owners from the need to compete with imported cloth. His influence on the workforce would also ensure harmonious labour conditions for decades to come.

But it would happen only after a fight—the most bitter fight between employer and employee that Ahmedabad had ever witnessed. And it was Ansuya who started it all by complaining to Gandhi that the mill owners had reneged on a proposed wage increase. Gandhi heard her out and called for a strike.

A strike was a rare phenomenon for the mild-mannered Ahmedabadi. And this one went on for many weeks. The mill owners, banding together under the leadership of Ambalal, remained intransigent. The workers weakened. Some returned to work. Sensing loss, Gandhi went on a fast. His stand was simple. A solution that satisfied only one side could not last, he reasoned. He urged the mill owners to compromise. The latter were embarrassed but adamant. Prominent figures such as Annie Besant, president of the Indian National Congress, stepped in. As Gandhi's fast wore on, there was pressure on the owners to accept Gandhi's demand for an impartial arbitrator. Eventually, a satisfactory compromise was arrived at and Gandhi broke his fast. Gandhi, Ambalal and Ansuya were driven around in a buggy in a victory procession.

The episode passed into folklore for a variety of reasons, not the least of which was the fact that it was here, in this face-off, that Gandhi first practised the use of what was to become his most potent negotiating weapon against the British, the hunger strike. Erik Erikson, who explored the incident in its various aspects in his 1970 Pulitzer prize-winning book *Gandhi's Truth*, described the outcome, in the words of an observer, as 'the emergence and the investment of an almost spiritual belief in reconciliation as a ritual'.[17]

The impact on Vikram of this piece of family history seems to have been considerable. In a speech in 1969 he was to define the experience in scientific terms as recognizing the importance of 'frames of reference'. 'Gandhiji,' he said, 'would constantly try to ensure in a conflict situation that a solution had to be perceived as a right and a reasonable one from the point of view of both the opposing sides.'[18] Reconciliation was to be a significant theme in Vikram's life. It was to be both his strength and his nemesis.

The episode was also much remarked upon for the mutual respect displayed by all sides to the dispute. Many found what they perceived as Ambalal's forbearance towards his sister incomprehensible and even suggested he stop her allowance. But Ambalal had already shown he was not susceptible to social pressure. Vikram was to refer to this trait in a 1970 interview with the BBC: 'My family was very unconventional. All through my childhood, I was brought up on doing what one felt was right rather than what necessarily society thought was appropriate.'[19]

For Ambalal the doing of 'right', whatever his personal definition of 'right', had the ring of an imperative. In doing right, he was, as he told Erikson, merely observing his dharma. It was an attitude that also inculcated a quality of understatement in the doer. Erikson found both Ambalal and Ansuya reluctant to talk about their individual roles in the historic episode. Years later, the writer Khushwant Singh was to note a similar quality in Ambalal's daughter, the fiery freedom fighter, Mridula: '...she was the living example of *nishkama karma*; performing the task given to her was all the reward she ever needed or wanted.'

It might have been expected that Ambalal's iconoclastic bent and religious inclinations would keep him from enjoying material pleasures. On the contrary, Ambalal's personal philosophy urged an almost studied embrace of the good life. Photographs of the 1910s and 1920s show the family fitted out in the height of fashion: Ambalal in a Saville Row suit; his wife Sarla in a high-collared blouse and sari with an embroidered border, both surrounded by their children in frocks, socks and sailor suits; watched over by a formidable-looking English governess, large-boned and stylishly dressed with lace at her neck and a hat.

Up to 1920, the Sarabhais shuttled between various cities. For a while they moved into a three-storeyed house called Malden Hall on Marine Lines in Bombay, furnishing it with furniture from the fashionable European stores Wimbric and Benjamin, and living it up with rides on the beach and evenings at the clubs. Business often took Ambalal to England and the whole family accompanied him, setting up house in Hampstead with two cars and silver tableware. Schooling for the fast-expanding family was a problem as none of the educational institutions in any of the places they stayed in fitted in with Ambalal's idealistic notions. Nor those of his wife's.

Sarla Devi (born Rewa) was the daughter of a widower, Harilal Ghosalia, an advocate, a 'self-made man', somewhat Victorian in outlook and influenced by Kant and Hegel. Frugal, deeply pious—her role model was Rama's faithful consort Sita—and slight in build, Rewa nevertheless had a streak of independence and, unusually for the times, was schooled in English. It is believed that Ambalal was impressed by the boldness of her responses at their first meeting and settled on her despite the obvious differences in their material circumstances.[20]

The two, however, had a lot in common. Like Ambalal, Rewa had had to accept early responsibility. She had to adopt a parental role with regard to her siblings, run a home and be a friend to her lonely father. It was this combination of maturity and idealism perhaps that enabled her to respond with what seems like surprising ease to Ambalal's unusual courtship. During the period of their engagement, the couple exchanged letters covering various expectations of their married life with what was for the times an astonishing frankness. In Rewa, or Sarla as she was to be known after her marriage, Ambalal had found a partner in his enterprise of constructing the 'ideal' life.

Given their joint inclinations it seems amazingly propitious that the review of a new book on childrearing in the *Times Literary Supplement* should have fallen into their hands at the exact time that they were pondering the future of their growing brood. The book was written by Maria Montessori, the Italian physicist who had structured a revolutionary system of primary education that had as its motto: 'First the education of the senses, then the education of the intellect.' The emphasis in her system was on self-determination and self-realization, ideas she tested by establishing a children's home (Casa dei Bambini) in Rome in 1907.

The Sarabhais read it on a ship sailing back from England. And what they saw filled them with elation. Everything in it seemed to correspond to their vague yearnings and half-expressed thoughts on education. The discovery filled them with a determination to put its ideas 'so radical and yet so convincing'[21] into practice. They would, they decided, start a school, their own Casa dei Bambini in Ahmedabad.

Money was no object. They were financially able to do as they pleased. Ambalal was one of the most prominent figures in the community of mill owners; by then he had also established himself as a shrewd businessman. The machinery and techniques he had imported after his frequent trips to Lancashire had made Calico a pioneer in the production of fine cloth. Apart from textiles he had also promoted a host of enterprises that included a sugar factory in Bihar, a railway line in East Bengal, the import of borax from Tibet on yaks, cotton ginning factories in East Africa and a trading office in London. Some of these were in partnership with his cousin's husband and close friend, Babubhai. With his broad shoulders, fine suits and 555 cigarettes which had his name embossed in gold, Ambalal cut an imposing figure. He was the proud owner of the city's first car and had just moved his family to a twenty-one-acre home in Shahibaug called, in suitably colonial style, The Retreat.

Shahibaug, the royal garden palace, had been built in the seventeenth century by Shah Jahan when he was viceroy of Ahmedabad. Providing a glimpse of the aesthetic temperament that was to make him famous throughout the world as the creator of the Taj, Prince Khurram, as he was known at the time, had ordered a royal garden, a traditional Mughal char-baug, to be built around his new palace on the outskirts of the town. It came to be known as the best garden of seventeenth-century India.

Two hundred years later the garden palace had fallen into decay. The emperors were gone and the commoners lived, as they always had, within the city walls in intricately carved, warren-like *pols*. It was then that the sheths with the vast fortunes generated by their mills, looking for alternatives to the crowded pols, stumbled upon Shahibaug. The vast open space outside the walled city where once royalty sauntered seemed to offer a fitting ambience for their changing lifestyles. And one by one, they began to gravitate to Shahibaug to build palatial homes in the architectural style of the princely clans of Gujarat and Saurashtra.

Ambalal's uncle, Chimanbhai, had built a bungalow there as far back as 1904 on twenty-one acres of farmland. After his marriage, Ambalal moved from Shantisadan, the joint family house in the city, to the new house, The Retreat.

Most of the Shahibaug sheths were bound to each other by marriage or other ties. The Parsi Vakils who lived on the left of The Retreat over the police lines had come to Shahibaug even before the Sarabhais. Cowasjee Vakil made bricks with which much of old Ahmedabad, including the Calico Mills, had been built. On the other side of The Retreat was Chimanbhai Lalbhai's abode, Lalbaug. The Lalbhai family had close relations with the Sarabhais. Chimanbhai's beautiful daughter, Manorama, was to marry Ambalal's eldest son, Suhrid, while his brother, the well-known philanthropist–industrialist Kasturbhai was to be Vikram's most loyal and flamboyant collaborator.

In 1919, despite the arrival of its new inhabitants, Shahibaug was still a dark, rambling stretch of land abutting the Sabarmati which was dry most of the year except for the monsoon when it would swell into a flood and burst its embankments. Wells from Mughal times dotted the shady dirt paths. Every evening a man came by to light the street lamps. And every morning at six, the air was filled with the sound of a siren summoning workers to the factories. The sheths' properties were strung out along the road that led to the palace and the cantonment, passing a decrepit Hanuman mandir overrun by chattering monkeys. In this wilderness Ambalal Sarabhai mapped out his Eden.

The entrance to his property was marked by tall gates. A long driveway led to a squat, three-storeyed structure, topped by a turret surrounded by acre upon acre of verdant space. The simple lines and tastefully appointed interiors reflected a mix of Indian and European influences. Each of the fifty-odd rooms was fitted with electric pankhas and shutters to combat the searing summer heat. Adjoining the main house or scattered about the property were outhouses, garages, a swimming pool, and courts for badminton, croquet and cricket. Twenty *hamal*s, six bais, two cooks, thirty gardeners, ten guards and an army of drivers and cleaners looked after this mini township which also had a dhobi ghat, a cowshed and stables with a horse for every member of the family. Exotic creatures and birds roamed the extensive grounds which were planted with all manner of trees and flowers and punctuated here and there with Greek statues, including a copy of the Venus De Milo, and serene lily ponds.

This was The Retreat in which, on 12 August 1919, Vikram was born. In *Akhand Divo*, his sister Leena Mangaldas describes the event.

> We [by this time there were five siblings: Mridula, Bharti, Suhrid, Gautam and Leena] were out on a drive when we heard hoof beats. It was our syce Salim Khan on a horse signalling us to return. He said a baby brother had been born. We rushed home and climbed eagerly to the third floor. He was a fair baby in a cradle with a large forehead and big ears like Gandhi. We wanted to fold his ears and make paans out of them.

As a toddler Vikram turned out to be noticeably energetic, disappearing on a steamer trip once to surface in the hold at Port

Said. Ted Standing recalls his 'large head and big beautiful brown eyes'. In a diary he maintained of his time in Ahmedabad, Standing writes:

> Vikram has just acquired the art of walking on two legs and is determined to take full advantage of it, filled with the spirit of adventure he is constantly going off on voyages of discovery, followed by his faithful angel, a pretty and gracious creature of much dignity but very few words. She just follows him around like his shadow: and whenever he falls into any serious difficulty, she appears like a goddess in a great tragedy—a deux et machina and puts him on his feet again, literally or metaphorically or both.[22]

Standing also drew brief portraits of the other children. Mridula, the eldest, was 'too old for her age'; Bharti 'precocious' with 'a touch of genius'; Suhrid was a 'real boy' full of curious questions unlike Gautam who was 'quiet', 'very enterprising' and determined 'not to be left out at anything'. Leena, he wrote, had beautiful 'dark eyes' and was 'full of mischievous pranks'. The last two, Gita and Gira, were then yet to be born. Also in the house was Tippie, a bull terrier of 'imperturbable temperament and charitable disposition', and puppies with names like Robin, Gipsy and Charlie Chaplin.

The humans on the list formed the entire student community of the new school at The Retreat. The decision to limit the school to their own children was not spontaneous. After the moment of discovery on the boat, the Sarabhais had apparently given considerable thought to their dream project, particularly as to its composition. For a while they had toyed with the idea of inviting outsiders. The growing power of the British had wrought many changes in Ahmedabad. Schools and colleges had opened, social reform movements had taken root, a thriving press and publications brought out by institutions such as the Buddhi Prakash Mandal or the society for intellectual enlightenment discussed women's education, scientific discoveries and other similar subjects. As a result of these developments and the opening up of new avenues of employment such as with the East India Company, a moderate-sized middle and intellectual class had come into existence.

Whether this new upwardly mobile class would have considered sending its children to school at The Retreat was not entirely certain. Though grudgingly respectful after the textile strike, the townspeople were still sceptical of Ambalal's radicalism. When he named a hospital wing after his wife in 1918, the local magazine *Praja Bandh*, for instance, had observed: 'A young Hindu gentleman does not thus parade the name and fame of his wife. But Mr Ambalal is nothing if not thoroughly modern in all his ideas.'

It was not just his ideas that the townspeople found difficult to digest. In his bluntness and avowed individuality Ambalal did not come across as a likeable person to those outside his immediate circle. Ushaben, daughter of the writer Dhumketu, maintains that the Sarabhais were the 'pride of Ahmedabad' but admits that they were a whimsical family. Pranlal Patel, a photographer who was routinely invited to shoot pictures of family celebrations in Shahibaug, had a similarly ambivalent response.

As it happened, the question of inviting outsiders never came up. After thinking it through, the Sarabhais decided to run the school exclusively for their own eight children. Leena claims the decision was based on the conclusion that it would have been unfair to subject others to an experiment. After all as C.J. Bhatt, a teacher at The Retreat, pointed out: '[It required] no small amount of faith and courage to build up such a school, apparently without any personnel trained in the new way. There was no clear-cut blueprint. It was like sailing on uncharted seas...'[23]

On the other hand, it is not unlikely that the Sarabhais felt they could do best on their own. In their obsessive search for the ideal both Ambalal and Sarla often displayed an intolerance for anything that fell short of their high expectations. For their cherished offspring a hothouse is what they appeared to have in mind. And it was one they filled with every stimulus they could think of.

'Not in books have I read, nor in dreams have I dreamed of parents so devoted to their children and to their education,' wrote Miss Williams, a young woman—identified in records simply by her second name—who came down from London to teach at The Retreat.[24] Indeed the scale on which the school was mounted reveals that no expense was spared and no doubt or faint-heartedness entertained. The kind of teachers hired was a startlingly clear indication of the seriousness with which the Sarabhais, and Sarla in particular (Maria Montessori called her the 'ideal Montessori mother'), viewed their mission.

Of the dozen-odd teachers, three were PhDs, three were graduates from various European universities and the rest were respected local stalwarts such as Karuna Shanker who taught Sanskrit, the Cambridge-trained mathematician S.H. Gidwani, and the poet Dhumketu. There were teachers for music and sports. And when Sarla found herself dissatisfied with the local dancing teacher, she had little hesitation in getting a new one dispatched from the acclaimed Bengali cultural centre Santiniketan.

The curriculum included Gujarati, Sanskrit, Hindi, English, Bengali, history, geography, mathematics, physics, chemistry, drawing, painting, dancing, music, pottery, handicrafts and sculpture. For the athletically inclined there were lessons in badminton, tennis, riding, archery and yoga. For the artistic, instruments such as the sitar, the veena, the dilruba, the violin and the tabla were provided. No distinctions were made between work and play. The children were encouraged to help in the aviary, the kitchen and the cowshed, to manage cash and to look after guests.

The guiding principle of this system of education was the

absence of force. J.S. Badami, a teacher at The Retreat, explained that the primary function of a teacher was considered 'not so much the imparting of knowledge as stimulating in the pupil its love and pursuit'.[25] Examinations were taken through the government-run R.C. High School but only when it was felt that the child was ready for matriculation.

Life at The Retreat then had a fairly esoteric quality generated by the combination of a Protestant discipline and a wholehearted embrace of sensual delights. Days began early. By six, everybody would be up and preparing for some activity—singing, painting, spinning, weaving, archery or heading for the library or the workshop. School would begin by seven with glasses of cocoa. If Ambalal had just returned from Bombay where he was engaged in setting up a new factory, the Swastik Oil Mills, he would drop by to say hello. Toys would arrive periodically in fat cloth parcels and on Saturdays the comics would be delivered from England. On Sundays, guests would be invited for a dip in the pool.

Among the only other children the Sarabhai siblings met on a regular basis were the Lalbhai children who lived next door. Vikram and Gautam were frequent visitors to the shed that had been designated their playhouse. The boys would set up cricket matches with the gardeners' sons and the teachers. Arvind Lalbhai recalls a small-built teacher with a strapping wife who was particularly good. Occasionally, there would be garden parties with bands and strawberry drinks. And for special events, such as a performance by the Russian dancer Anna Pavlova, the children would be taken to Bombay.

Periodically, and this was considered an essential part of the children's education, the family would embark on long vacations accompanied by a retinue of servants, pets and the entire team of teachers. Mussoorie, Simla, Shillong, Kashmir, Ooty, Ceylon, Mount Abu and Matheran were some of the places they visited. These trips necessitated a great deal of organization, with an advance party going ahead to make arrangements. Ambalal apparently took the lead in planning these trips. He was a resourceful organizer, having signs painted in yellow on the family's luggage for easy identification and drawing up lists of vegetarian meals to be sent to restaurants they were likely to visit.

'The parents kept the children above everything. They were utterly cared for, completely cherished,' observes Vikram's wife Mrinalini. For a man in a patriarchal society, Ambalal displayed an unusually acute sensitivity towards his children. On his frequent absences he took care to stay in touch with the family, even writing a comical daily newsletter called *Tirangi Samachar*. Leena recalls the time her pet mongrel disappeared on a train journey and Ambalal not only deputed a servant to hunt for it but also put out an advertisement offering a reward for its safe recovery.

It was probably from Ambalal and the gentleness and security with which he was surrounded in his early life that Vikram inherited his exceptional ability to trust. The social theorist Ashis Nandy, who knew the family, is of the opinion that 'Vikram must have been a very wanted child'.

Yet, there was also a sense of disproportion about Ambalal's extreme solicitude for his family. That a man of his vast responsibilities should bother himself with trivial travel details suggests an obsessive fastidiousness that Vikram was also to be accused of. Even more disconcerting were the unquestioned assumptions underlining Ambalal's relationship with his children. This story related by Mrinalini provides a vivid example of the same.

The family was holidaying in England when Vikram, probably six or seven, saw a toy he liked and asked for it. Ambalal explained that he was running short of money and that if he had enough left over at the end of the trip he would buy it. The promise clearly satisfied the boy for no more was said and the matter was forgotten till they had departed from England. When the ship stopped at the Italian port Brindisi for refuelling, Vikram remembered the toy and asked his father if he had had money left over. 'Oh God,' Ambalal said, 'I did.' At this point, Mrinalini says, Ambalal in all seriousness offered to take Vikram back to England to purchase the toy but Vikram declined and the family carried on.

From the way Mrinalini tells the story it is clear that it is offered as evidence of how solemnly Ambalal would regard a promise given even to his small son. From a mundane perspective, however, it is an astonishing revelation of the kind of behaviour that was considered appropriate in the Sarabhai household. For a father, having forgotten his promise, to make an offer that could only be deemed childish in its extravagance; and for the child, instead of screaming his head off, to decline with adult-like maturity suggests a reversal of roles here that was perhaps an echo of Ambalal's own childhood experience. It also goes a long way in explaining Vikram's own early maturity.

Ambalal's nurturing quality, however, also derived partly from his Jain roots. The Sarabhais were not overtly religious. The children's schooldays, in deference to the mixed composition of the faculty, would begin with a few minutes of silent meditation rather than prayers. In a letter to Mrinalini in the late 1950s, Vikram makes a rare reference to his beliefs—'[I pray] *in my way*'—revealing that in religion, as in all other matters, the stress at The Retreat was on individual choice.

As far as the life-preserving rituals of Jainism were concerned, however, these were scrupulously observed. In the Sarabhai household even the dogs were vegetarian and every day a servant was instructed to put a saucer of milk out for ants. Vikram was to remain a lifelong vegetarian 'out of choice'. 'We are not religious at all,' he was to say in a television interview. 'To me it is a question of aesthetics. Aesthetics because it is repugnant to kill.'[26]

It was in many ways an idyllic existence. Refined, purposeful and filled with aesthetic satisfaction. Yet, it made some uncomfortable. Standing, for instance, while clearly impressed with his hosts and their ideals, wrote that the compound with its fairy lights and its alabaster statues reminded him 'of the endosure described in the *Light of Asia* where the young prince Siddhartha was immured in order to be shielded from everything which would suggest disease or death'. Standing professed to feelings of guilt about the thousands living in a state of 'incredible squalor' outside the high walls.[27]

Indeed it was not just poverty; in the early days, nothing as crude as violence ever entered the sylvan surroundings of The Retreat. 'In our family,' says Leena, 'there was no shouting, no abuse. No fighting.' Visitors commented with surprise on the polite behaviour of the children towards elders and each other. There were individual tastes such as Bharti's penchant for silks and brogues and Gira's tomboy predilections. There may have been differences of view as well. Yet, it is claimed and apparently true that eight children fairly close in years passed into adulthood with no memories of quarrels, jostling or fisticuffs that would have been a regular feature in almost every family half the size.

'My grandmother instilled in her children the feeling that the Sarabhais were different from others: there was to be no jealousy, no hatred,' Kartikeya explains. There were problems with this attitude, he admits. 'For those who really didn't have these emotions it worked okay but those who did, did not know what to do with them.'

Suppression of the more destructive childish urges was possibly one consequence. Leena, for instance, writes about how she once deliberately smacked her aunt with a poisonous weed and threw sand into the piano on which Ambalal regaled the children with tunes from Gujarati musicals every evening. Both incidents are narrated with remorse but also with a genuinely puzzled air as if the narrator has no clue how such things could happen.

Unspoken taboos hung heavy in the dry air of The Retreat. Sex was not alluded to until the children had crossed adolescence and even then, Leena is at pains to point out, no coarseness was permitted. Mrinalini's sister, the well-known freedom fighter Captain Lakshmi Sehgal, recalls with acute clarity the lack of humour and boisterousness around the dinner table.

Fear came in natural forms as well. Despite the presence of two gardeners entrusted with the specific task of shooing away monkeys, the long-tailed creatures assailed the silence with their noisy chatter and pattering on the roof. The large cold house was also full of lizards and bugs. One bit Vikram on the eyelid as a child and he went around for days with a swollen, black eye. More significantly, death came calling.

If Kanta, after her demise, remained a shadowy presence in the Sarabhai household, kept alive by Ambalal's remorse, then, a few years later, he had to contend with the loss of his closest friend and business partner, Babubhai. Babubhai was also married to his cousin, his deceased uncle Chimanbhai's daughter, Nirmala. The couple lived at The Retreat and the two men had been, in Standing's words, 'almost inseparable'. Babubhai's death must have been a blow. But, with outward displays of grief being firmly discouraged, Ambalal had to keep his tears in check.

The trait was passed on to the children. Leena's son Kamal Mangaldas, an architect, recalls how Leena reacted to the news of her mother's death many years later. 'It happened at night. I woke her up. There was a sob and then immediately she was controlled and ready to do what had to be done.'

In retrospect, it seems possible to say that for many of the Sarabhai siblings the experiment yielded mixed results. As adults, each was to excel in various pursuits. Bharti wrote a play that won praise from T.S. Eliot, among others. Gautam set up the National Institute of Design and the B.M. Institute of Mental Health. Leena started the Shreyas School, Gita pursued her interest in music and drama while Gira put together the much acclaimed Textile Museum. On a personal level though, their lives seemed far from happy, with instances of broken marriages, alcoholism (in a family of near teetotallers) and a reputation for eccentricity surrounding them.

Kamal Mangaldas candidly admits that, but for a couple of exceptions, 'the rest of us are selfish, self-centred and not very good at human relationships'. In the years that followed the school experiment, the family business was to collapse and the division of assets to cause extreme bitterness. The Retreat, once a bustling home, was to turn into a museum for a collection of paintings and antiques, open only by appointment. And further down, in the secluded darkness of the rambling grounds, several members of the Sarabhai family were to build large, beautiful and separate houses, immersing themselves in what appeared to many outsiders as solitary and elitist preoccupations. Khushwant Singh's description of a visit to The Retreat offers an insight into this private domain:

> It was a dense jungle. They all had their own cottages. Gautam's I think was the most elaborate: mud with lavish Gujarati carvings and earthenware animals. Gira's was more modest with exotic trees. Leena reared unusual animals, I believe. The Retreat was full of peacocks. When you stayed with them you were billed to different members of the family. My wife was Gautam's guest, I was Gira's. Once a week there would be a family meal for which everyone would turn up. But when they split they were not even on talking terms. And the business rapidly went down.

Two of the siblings did not quite fit the bill. Mridula, the eldest, and Vikram, though many years apart, were to pursue a very different course. Unlike the others, they were to leave the family nest early and stay away. They were to throw themselves into public life and work towards their more mass-based ideals, their overpowering commitment to which would owe much to their unconventional upbringing.

There appeared to be little similarity between Vikram and the short-haired, gruff-voiced Mridula, however. Ambalal and

Sarla's eldest born, called 'boss' by the family and 'pathan' by awestruck Ahmedabadis, was a tough rebel. As a child she would eat with poor Harijans and frequent the cheap seats in cinema halls, refusing to move even when the embarrassed owner recognized her and offered an upgrade. Her strong sense of injustice led her fairly early into an involvement with the freedom struggle where she displayed what Khushwant Singh calls 'a kind of fearlessness and courage that defied description'.[28]

Following independence though, her defiance was to become a source of embarrassment for her friends. Nehru's private secretary, M.O. Mathai, would describe her as having both the courage and the stupidity of a wild boar.[29] There were even allegations of cruelty towards refugees of the Partition. Undoubtedly, there was a touch of the manic about her; a neighbour remembers her coming out of the house with a whip to scare off a taxi driver who had cheated on the fare. As a young girl though, Mridula, according to her teachers, mothered her brothers and sisters and was particularly protective of baby Vikram.

Baby Vikram was a good-looking infant with an enormous forehead, delicate features and stuck-out ears. Pictures of him as a boy show him dressed variously in shorts, a sailor suit and a white *jabho* with *mojdis*, his long, straight hair falling over his eyes. There is a suggestion of easy compliance in his readiness to pose. He is rarely smiling in his photographs as a child but looking intently into the camera with a faint wrinkle above the nose that hints at silent preoccupations. His younger sister Gita corroborates the impression. 'Vicky seemed to have a little existence, a private life of his own. He was with us but always a little apart.' Years later, his daughter Mallika was to describe him as 'always thinking', with his chin on his hands, 'like Rodin's "Thinker"'.

Vikram's elder sister Leena vividly recalls his passion for his toy train as a child. 'He would eat with it, take it to bed and even on the potty he would be saying "choo choo",' she says. Gita has memories of him learning the Manipuri dance and the sitar. 'My aunt Ansuya also told me that he used to tease me mercilessly by reciting verses from the Ramayana at top speed.'

His brilliance was noted early. J.S. Badami observes in his diary: 'I could see in him a mind with an intellectual awareness and a flowering of integrated personality which is rare even among men of genius.... Even at that young age Vikram's pursuit of knowledge was all-embracing.' On 10 January 1936, he adds: 'In some of the questions he asked me, he showed a keenness of observation and originality in his thinking which is very gratifying.'[30]

Despite the atmosphere of refinement at The Retreat, Vikram seems to have been a fairly robust boy playing cricket, boating on the estate's lake and cheerfully taking a tumble in the water. He was an expert cyclist and there was a circus trick he was fond of performing much to the terror of the servants. He would pedal at high speed, lift up his hands and feet, cross his hands and put his feet on the handlebars, sometimes even closing his eyes if the road was straight.

In hagiographical accounts of Vikram Sarabhai's life much is made of two incidents that are supposed to have occurred in his childhood. One was in the nature of a prediction said to have been made by Rabindranath Tagore. Tagore visited Ahmedabad in 1920, a fact duly noted by all city records. He stayed with the Sarabhais not only on this trip but spent a month as their guest in Shillong. At some time during his stay, the poet laureate, also an amateur phrenologist, observed baby Vikram's large and unusually shaped forehead, and reportedly said to Sarla: 'This boy will achieve great things.'

The other incident took place on a family holiday. Ambalal, apparently noticing that his son was receiving mail every day on the family stationery asked him who was writing to him so regularly. Vikram is said to have innocently replied, 'I write to myself.'[31]

While the tenor of both anecdotes suggests the potential for an overbearing precocity, as a child there was no evidence of it. It is likely, of course, that in a family of strong individuals each, as Erikson was to later describe them, with 'overweening causes', it would have been difficult, if not impossible, for one child to stand out. And Vikram, if anything, appears to have been a quiet child with Ambalal's introspective leanings.

An affectionate son, Vikram was close to his mother, and his sisters remember that even as a grown-up he would put his head in her lap and behave with her as 'a boy did with his mother'. The physical demonstrativeness might have been unusual. Most people felt inhibited by a certain coldness about Sarla. Kamal Mangaldas, for instance, recalls that he 'never touched' his grandmother while he remembers clambering up his grandfather's shoulders, patting his bald head. In general, Ambalal seems to have been less puritanical and possessing a greater sense of fun than his wife. Navroz Contractor who lived next door and was a friend of Kartikeya's remembers asking him to donate money for a cricket pitch. 'He wrote us a cheque right away and then he would come and watch us play and ask us "why are you losing?"'

Outwardly at least, Vikram appeared to have less of his mother's simple rigidity and more of his father's complex approach to life. In matters of ritual, for instance, Sarla behaved as any devout Gujarati housewife of means would, worshipping daily and organizing a Satyanarayan puja—a ritual inherited from her mother—every fortnight. Ambalal, though he kept a private shrine in his room, was more steeped in the philosophical aspects of his religion. And contrary to his fastidiousness in other matters, he was not averse to breaking rules if practicality demanded.

In 1915, for instance, when a rabid dog started biting passers-by in the Calico Mills compound, Ambalal had all the stray dogs in the compound shot. His action predictably sparked off an uproar in the community. Ambalal was unmoved by the public condemnation. Four years later when Gandhi asked him for help in killing a young calf with smallpox in Sabarmati Ashram, he obliged, leading furious Jains to compare him to Brigadier-General Reginald Dyer, the man responsible for the Jallianwala Bagh massacre.

The episode is particularly significant in view of Vikram's later involvement with matters of security. It has been suggested that he was a pacifist, a Gandhian and someone who abhorred violence. In fact, this was only a partial view. Vikram, like his father, was also a pragmatist who could see shades of grey in the choices presented to him.

Part of Vikram's education also consisted of an exposure to the best minds of the times. Ambalal and Sarla were appreciative of art, culture and intellect, and threw their doors open to a host of luminaries. Tagore was just one of the many talented and significant individuals who passed through The Retreat. Jagadish Chandra Bose, the physicist reputed to have given the world's first public demonstration of electromagnetic waves; Jadunath Sarkar, a historian with a specialization in the Mughal period; Nobel-winning scientist C.V. Raman who was later to take Vikram under his wing; the Bombay lawyer–politician Bhulabhai Desai; the pioneering Bharatanatyam dancer Rukmini Arundale; philosopher–guru J. Krishnamurti; and stage and film actor Prithviraj Kapoor were some other well-known personages to enjoy the Sarabhais' hospitality. Drawn by Gandhi's presence many political luminaries also came to Ahmedabad and stopped at The Retreat. Dadasaheb Mavlankar, Madan Mohan Malaviya, Sardar Patel, Maulana Azad, Sarojini Naidu, C.F. Andrews, Muhammad Ali Jinnah, and Dr S. Radhakrishnan, some of the leading lights of the pre-independence era, were among them. The family was particularly close to the Nehrus. Motilal and Jawaharlal both stayed at The Retreat and when Jawaharlal's daughter Indira moved to Poona for her studies, Ambalal and Sarla looked in on her. These connections were to prove invaluable for Vikram later.

From the list of distinguished guests it may seem as if the Sarabhais had the penchant of the rich for collecting the famous, but in truth the Sarabhais were no mere parlour hosts. The family was actively involved in the freedom movement.

Gandhi was the primary inspiration. The confrontation with Gandhi at the time of the textile strike had not diminished Ambalal's admiration for the revolutionary. In 1918, he and Sarla had even brought him home to be treated for a serious illness. Gandhi was to comment: 'It was impossible for anyone to receive more loving and selfless service than I had the privilege of having during this illness.'[32]

Sarla, with her craving for simplicity (she was to give up her silks for white cotton; some say it was in response to the death of her eldest son, others maintain it was the influence of Gandhi) and her religiosity, was especially drawn to the Mahatma who called her his 'sister' and proposed her name as a trustee of the All-India Spinning Association. His proposal was opposed on the ground that she was unfit by virtue of being the wife of a 'textile king'.[33] He then put her in charge of the Kasturba Gandhi National Memorial Trust in Gujarat. And before long the family was swept up in the struggle for freedom.

In 1920, a year after Vikram's birth, on the eve of the Prince of Wales's visit, Gandhi had called for the Non-cooperation Movement. His fiery words ('If you feel for the country, if the fire which has been raging in me also rages in you…take to non-cooperation as I have been doing'[34]) had stirred the nation to a passion. As Raj Thapar, wife of journalist Romesh Thapar, who grew up in the Punjab, wrote: 'Our minds were unburdened and eager to devour…arguing…on the tyranny of British rule, longing to grow up and plunge into battle, to redeem our "national honour", having as yet no idea of what the concept meant and what the battle would be all about.'[35]

At The Retreat, however, the shadow loomed ominous and very real. The Sarabhai women were totally involved in the various activities and were frequently arrested. Vikram's aunts Indumati and Nirmalaben organized the city's first khadi bhandar. Sarla and Mridula handled the boycott of foreign cloth and the picketing of liquor shops. This was dangerous work given the sort of people they were dealing with. But Mridula was fearless. She is said to have stopped the passage of a liquor consignment by grasping the reins of a horse, an act that was to make her famous and inspire many young girls to join the satyagraha.[36]

The movement entered the home. In the house of the foremost textile manufacturer of the city, khaddar became a fabric of choice. Mridula and Ansuya even had curtains and bedclothes made of the coarse material. Vikram and Gita also adopted khaddar, influenced by the charged atmosphere and copies of the *Harijan*, Gandhi's magazine, that they read.

One of the most striking experiences Vikram was to go through was probably the Dandi March. He was eleven at the time Gandhi decided to challenge the salt law by marching to the sea and 'making' salt, and the whole Sarabhai brood, with 10,000 others, descended upon Sabarmati Ashram the evening before. The prayer meeting was said to have been especially stirring on that occasion and nobody slept much. The next morning, Gandhi set off on the 200-mile walk, through gaily festooned villages with a swelling crowd of thousands, which would end in a powerful symbolic gesture against the colonial rulers.

The growing confrontation and the sight of relatives being hauled off to jail had a tremendous effect on the Sarabhai children. In a documentary for French television Vikram was to recall how the police would come to the house to confiscate a car or some other piece of moveable property because a relative was in jail and Ambalal, in keeping with the spirit of non-cooperation, had refused to pay the fine. He relates it in a neutral tone but Gita, two years his junior, is more forthcoming about the feeling of loss these incidents generated. 'I was desperately miserable,' she says, 'when the police took my mother away. Everything changed, from playfulness into something more grim.'

The family's association with Gandhi threw Vikram into close proximity with the great man. Most of his colleagues would later presume that, like his parents, Vikram too was deeply influenced by Gandhi. One colleague recalls discussing Gandhian economics in depth with him. Vikram's own response in the French television documentary, when asked about Gandhi, is marked by an earnestness that indicates a certain degree of hero worship. In the interview he recalls the prayer meetings at Sabarmati Ashram, the chanting 'in beautiful Sanskrit' which made a 'deep impression' on him. He also refers to a long discussion on 'how to solve the communal problem' and how touched he was that Gandhi would spend time talking with someone of his age, a mere boy. 'He never made me feel immature or that I was talking nonsense.'[37]

It is intriguing that with so much happening around him, Vikram did not get drawn into the freedom movement. When the struggle intensified in the 1930s, drawing ordinary men, women and children from all over the country into its fold, Vikram was a teenager. For a young man growing up in this environment, it would have been hard to escape the headiness of the times. In fact, the movement had created a special place for children; they were the 'vanar senas', Hanuman's monkeys, who would spy for the crusaders and take to the streets every morning singing patriotic songs. Even Prabhaben who was to marry Vikram's neighbour and friend Chinubhai, and who grew up in a Bombay diamond merchant's family, recalls indulging in childish stunts such as painting Gandhi's face on posters and hiding the paint brushes fearing possible police raids. But there was no suggestion, not in Ahmedabad, at Cambridge, nor on his return, that the thought of participating in the freedom struggle had even crossed Vikram's mind.

There are several possible explanations. The most likely one seems to be that he had his sights clearly fixed on the post-independence period. He was aware of his strengths and realized he could make a greater contribution in the building of institutions of education and technology instead of frittering away his energies in the rough and tumble of political activism. It is significant that though he was to make a number of public speeches on a host of issues throughout his life, he never alluded to current events or controversies of the time. His vision was always for the long term. And in his childhood he had already chosen the subject that would not only be his object of passion but also the vehicle for everything he was to do.

He had fallen in love with science. 'His first preference was for the pure sciences…these subjects claimed his attention much more than any other,' wrote his schoolteacher, C.J. Bhatt.[38] Early indications of his interest were manifested in his absorption with a toy set called Junero which consisted of metal strips which a child could cut, punch and mould into designs. The game seems to have whetted his appetite, for at some point he enlisted the assistance of Khimjibhai Mistry, a carpenter, to make a steam engine. The engine they built, complete with tracks, was large enough for a child to sit on and there are pictures of a young Vikram posing with his adult collaborators sitting astride the model.

His parents, recognizing Vikram's predilection for the mechanical, and in keeping with the Montessori method, had a workshop set up on the premises of The Retreat. It was a full-fledged operation with lathes, drills, a foundry and a mechanical instructor. Later, a physics and chemistry laboratory was added, providing the budding scientist with all the facilities required to indulge his growing interest. By all accounts, Vikram spent a lot of time pottering about in the workshop, acquiring experience that would prove invaluable when he later had to make instruments for his experiments.

He was familiar with the works of popular science writers of the time or so it would seem from later conversations with his students. He would also have been aware of the mind-boggling advances in physics and rocketry through the local papers.

Ahmedabad, like many Indian cities, had a lively press, and public interest in science at the time was high. Poona-bred physicist Pramod Kale, for instance, had built his own radio while still in school and had read all of Jules Verne, serialized in a Marathi children's magazine. Magazines and technical journals such as *Nature*, *Popular Science*, *Popular Mechanics* and *Wireless World* were available in school libraries. Vikram, with his resources, would most certainly have had far wider access including access to the latest scientific magazines from the West.

It was a wildly exciting time for physics. The discovery of the electron at the turn of the twentieth century had sparked off a series of rapid advances in what had come to be known as atomic physics. In 1932, British scientists John Douglas Cockcroft and Ernest Thomas Sinton Walton had invented a controlled process to split the atom, a step forward from Ernest Rutherford and James Chadwick's attempts to bombard elements with alpha particles. Across the channel, Irene Curie and her husband Frederic Joliot had produced artificial radioactivity. New atomic particles were being discovered.

The airplane was still a novelty, yet people were already talking about space travel. Werner Von Braun, later to be the builder of Germany's V2 rockets, was shooting missiles into fruit stalls in the 1920s and was overwhelmed by Hermann Oberth's 1923 book *The Rocket into Interplanetary Space* which had ninety-two pages of formulae and equations and a vivid exposition of the physics of rocketry.[39] The interest in space was so intense that the German film-maker, Fritz Lang, made a film called *Frau im Mond* ('Woman in the Moon'). In the US, an engineer, Robert Goddard, had already launched the first liquid-fuelled rocket, and by 1931, a medical student, Constantin Generales, was doing experiments on the effects of space on mice.

These then were the events that might have whetted Vikram's appetite for science. But Vikram was not to lead the life of the conventional scientist. To comprehend the sweep of his achievements it is important to understand that it was not merely a specific area of physics or a particular question alone that was to fascinate him. He was passionate about science itself: its premises, its attitudes, its rigour, its aims. 'Many people suppose,' he was to say in a 1966 talk, 'that there is the absence of the imaginative and intuitive element in the pursuit of science in contrast to philosophy, literary or artistic endeavour. This surely is a fallacy. What distinguishes the scientist is his compelling urge to test his concepts in terms of observations. He is ready to *let his castle crumble to dust* on the results of experiments.'[40]

He could see aestheticism in its search for patterns ('if only one listens to the music in the [apparent] noise, the work becomes very rewarding indeed').[41] He was to apply the scientific approach successfully to a host of unrelated activities: business, the teaching of management studies, market research. But above all, it was in science that he saw a way of satisfying the urges that seemed to naturally attend the blend of his lineage, upbringing and personality and which included a sense of duty, a love of beauty and a deeply felt patriotism.

In a speech at the International Symposium on Science and Society in South Asia at Rockefeller University, New York, in May 1966, he was to expound on the last theme. His words explain, to some extent, what drove him to become the person he did:

> A person who has imbibed the ways of science injects into a situation a new way of looking at it, hopefully perhaps a degree of enlightenment with regard to the approach to problems and this provides leadership which is very valuable.... Through experience we know that conditions of work in India within our own specialized scientific fields rarely match the facilities available in several other countries...some get frustrated striving against heavy odds. Others leave the country. But those that can apply their insights to the problems of the community and of the nation discover an exciting area of activity where effort is rewarding even while the results show slowly.[42]

2

'STARTING PROCESSES'

On the lawns of The Retreat they assembled. The children, the teachers, the parents. Gautam and Vikram had garlands on their arms, Vikram was smiling. Instructed by the photographer, all of them took their places, posing stiffly for the formal picture that would mark the occasion of the two young men of the family setting out for their education. They would not be the first to leave. Their two older siblings, Suhrid and Bharti, had left for Oxford four years before. It was the done thing in those days for Indian families of a certain class to send their children to England for further studies.

In Ahmedabad, though, where business acumen was prized over scholastic achievement, not everyone sailed abroad. Arvind Lalbhai and Chinubhai Lalbhai, Vikram's close friends and neighbours, for one would stay home and learn to manage the family's mills and, in the case of the latter, become the city's mayor. For a while, after completing his basic education at The Retreat and clearing his matriculation through the R.C. High School, Vikram had joined them at the Gujarat College.

Gujarat College, the region's first college built by the British in 1887, was a classical colonial structure with stone walls, three-point arches and a wooden truss roof. It was located in the middle of a dense forest on the other side of the Sabarmati. The

Ellis Bridge provided a link to what would become the new city but which at the time had only a town hall and a library as its main attractions.

Vikram spent two years there after his matriculation, probably the closest he ever came to living the life of an average Indian. He had cleared the intermediate exam, distinguishing himself in his chosen subjects, physics and chemistry. J.S. Badami, who had taught him earlier at The Retreat, was one of his teachers at the college. Badami's diary informs us that in the 1936 college terminals his prize student stood first in chemistry and just missed the top position in physics due to an 'oversight' by the examiner.[1] But apart from pursuing his studies in science, Vikram had enjoyed learning Sanskrit poetry—there would be many occasions in the future when he would quote Kalidasa's *Meghadootam* and *Vikramorvasiyam*. He also had cycled and played cricket with the college team.

But now it was time for him to move on. To Cambridge. Family friend Rabindranath Tagore had written him a letter of recommendation: 'He is a young man with a keen interest in science.... He comes from a wealthy cultured family...he is a fit and proper person for admission to the university.'[2] St John's College had responded that it was happy to grant him admission.

So one sunny day in the summer of 1937, Vikram and Gautam set sail for England. A pretty, young woman, Raj, who was to later marry Khushwant Singh, was travelling on the same ship and the three struck up a friendship. Her husband recalls her remarking on the fact that the Sarabhai boys spoke to their father in Ahmedabad on the telephone every single day—an unheard of luxury in the days of expensive long-distance communication. The respected Bombay art trader Kekoo Gandhy was also in Cambridge at the time, studying economics, and has memories of some 'great cocktail parties' given by the brothers, though he adds wryly, 'they never drank themselves'.

Vikram was at Cambridge from 1937 to 1940. Photographs

show him resembling a waif in a Christmas tale, with prominent ears, his fragile form almost swallowed up in a set of dandy clothes: a waist-length jacket with exaggerated lapels over a high-collared shirt and tie, ankle-length trousers and gleaming, leather round-toed shoes. St John's lies around him draped in snow while he leads a giant-size dog that reaches his hips. Professor S.M. Chitre, who was to meet Vikram while the latter was visiting Cambridge a decade-and-a-half later, claims that Vikram was in his element amidst the mellow stone buildings, tree-lined avenues and picturesque cafés of the town. He is of the opinion that a person of Vikram's curious temperament would have thrived in the university's eclectic ambience.

There is, however, little evidence of an active extra-curricular life. Records show that he was a fellow of the Cambridge Philosophical Society[3] but little else. Unlike others like Jawaharlal Nehru's daughter Indira who was at Oxford around the same time, and who was active politically, enrolling volunteers for the International Brigade for Spain and being part of Krishna Menon's India League, Vikram stayed glued to his scientific studies. Gita visited him and found him 'terribly busy'.

In film footage of the time, Vikram can be seen darting through the shrubbery, a shadow-like figure, as if not yet fully formed. There was an ethereal quality about him in his student days: the skin smooth, the features sharp, almost effeminate but for the determined set of mouth, the eyes alternately soft and piercing, the lower lip full and jutting out, and the hair, plentiful then, swept off his wide forehead.

It was not the best time for a physicist to be in Cambridge. The Cavendish and Mond laboratories were no longer leading centres of physics as they had been in the early 1930s when Chadwick had discovered the neutron, Walton and Cockcroft had caused light elements to transmute by bombarding them with high-speed protons, and Patrick Maynard Stuart Blackett and Giuseppe Occhialini had demonstrated electron–positron pairs and showers through their remarkable photographs taken in a cloud chamber developed by Charles Thomson Rees Wilson. In fact, months after Vikram arrived, Ernest Rutherford, the brilliant and charismatic New Zealander who had presided over these remarkable discoveries, died.

With his death, the Cavendish and Mond laboratories seemed to have truly reached the end of an era. Vikram, whose interests leaned firmly towards the experimental study of cosmic rays rather than atomic fission, may not have felt the loss as keenly as some of his peers, but he could not fail to have been affected by the general feeling of desolation that was building up around him. Hitler's star was on the ascendant. And Jewish scientists, fearing for their lives, were fleeing Europe; many were headed for America, which would subsequently emerge as the dominant centre for science. By summer that year, the news that a certain amount of Uranium-235 could create an immense explosion was known all over the scientific world. In September 1939, war broke out.

Ambalal was frantic with worry. He insisted both brothers come home immediately. It was some months into the war, however, that Vikram actually made his way back to India. The interruption in his studies was a matter of concern. He had by then completed his undergraduate studies in physics and mathematics. He made inquiries with the authorities at Cambridge about the possibility of continuing his work back home and was informed that he could work on his postgraduate research in India as long as it was under the supervision of C.V. Raman. So, in 1940, Vikram, armed with a tripos in the natural sciences, returned to India and headed for the Indian Institute of Science (IISc) in Bangalore.

In 1898, the far-sighted Bombay industrialist, Jamsetji Tata, had announced his intention of establishing an institute to impart education in science, technology, medicine, psychology and philosophy. However, it was only in 1911, after his death, that the institute he hoped would 'lift up the best and most gifted so as to make them of the greatest service to the country'[4] came into being. The IISc is a sprawl of colonial-style grey stone buildings set amidst a vast swathe of greenery. It was started as a centre for applied sciences with departments of chemistry and electrical engineering. By the time Vikram arrived in 1940, a department of physics had been added and it was headed by the formidable C.V. Raman.

Born in 1888 in the rural south, C.V. Raman had worked as a government servant for a decade, practising physics on the side. Through his investigations into the scattering of light, he discovered what came to be known as the 'Raman effect' that won him the Nobel Prize in 1930. Thin, sallow-complexioned, with doleful eyes and a distinctive turban, Raman had an air of certainty about his genius that, as a fellow scientist put it, 'would have got him a Nobel even if he had worked in Antarctica'.[5]

It is likely that Raman received Vikram with a certain degree of warmth. He knew the Sarabhais well; Ambalal had written to him, requesting him to take his son on as a student. He was also responsible for nudging Vikram towards the area of research in which he was to work for the rest of his life.

The area in broad terms was cosmic rays, the penetrating radiations coming from outer space, the existence of which was suggested by C.T.R. Wilson, best known as the inventor of the cloud chamber in 1911. At the time, little was known about these radiations though investigations at high altitudes (notably by Father Wulf, a Jesuit priest, and the Austrian scientist, Victor Hess) had confirmed their origin from an extra-terrestrial source. Further studies (by Clay and Störmer, of Dutch and Swedish origin respectively) had revealed the effects of latitude and longitude on the intensity of radiation.

Though cosmic rays had enjoyed a spot in the limelight—

mainly for their highly charged state, which, in the days before giant accelerators, made them a poor man's laboratory—the specific area of Vikram's research does not appear to have been in vogue. In fact, when the time came for him to submit his PhD thesis, 'Cosmic Ray Investigations in Tropical Latitudes', Cambridge had to look for an oral examiner with the requisite expertise outside the university.

Given these circumstances and Raman's own markedly different preoccupations (by then the Nobel winner was immersed in the study of sound waves and in 1940 he had also begun his collection of crystals[6]), Vikram's selection seems a trifle puzzling. A possible explanation, and one Vikram suggests in his thesis, is the effect of Millikan's visit. Robert Millikan, an American scientist and winner of the Nobel Prize in 1923 for his work on the electron charge, was the man who had actually coined the term 'cosmic rays'. In 1937, he had come to India to acquire data for his world survey of cosmic ray intensity, during which time he visited Raman. In 1940, he came again to carry out stratospheric balloon ascents.

In his PhD thesis,[7] Vikram points out that most cosmic ray research at the time was being carried out in laboratories in the temperate region; south India, on the other hand, located right on the path of the magnetic equator, was of particular significance for cosmic ray investigations. The conjunction of these facts, amply demonstrated by Millikan's visits, possibly led Raman to suggest, as Vikram goes on to claim, 'the initiation of experimental research in this field at Bangalore'. 'It was hoped at first,' Vikram adds, 'to make a more detailed high-altitude survey at various latitudes in India in order to supplement Professor Millikan's results, but wartime difficulties in the procuring of the necessary balloons and other radio apparatus prevented embarking on this.'[8]

The apparatus Vikram picked instead was the Geiger counter. From a story narrated by Raman's nephew, S. Ramaseshan, also an established scientist, this was not Raman's preference. Raman, Ramaseshan recalls Vikram telling him, had suggested that he make photographic emulsion plates like Marietta Blau and Herta Wambacher had done in 1937, and take them to a height to observe the star-like tracks formed by fragments of photo plate emulsion nucleus blown apart by cosmic rays. 'You may find something new,' Raman had apparently urged, 'and win the Nobel Prize.' Vikram opted for a Geiger counter instead of the photo plate, preferring the former for its adaptability and precision. Many years later, claims Ramaseshan, when Vikram told him about Raman's advice he also added that C.F. Powell did indeed succeed in finding a new particle with a photo plate and won the Nobel for it. 'He laughed and said if he had listened to Raman it might have been his discovery,' Ramaseshan says.

Vikram's early experiments led to his first paper 'The Time Distribution of Cosmic Rays' which he presented to the Indian Academy of Sciences in 1942. Introducing him, Raman said, 'Young Vikram Sarabhai has been brought up with a silver spoon in his mouth. He has started to do original experiments and is presenting his first paper to a scientific audience. I have great faith in him—that he will contribute much to India and to the growth of science in our country.'[9]

Whether this speech reflected Raman's genuine belief in Vikram's abilities or whether the hyperbole had more to do with the family's track record is not known. Vikram for his part had genuine regard for his supervisor. A few years later, when Raman wanted to break away from the IISc and form his own Raman Institute, it was Vikram who put him in touch with Ahmedabad-based industrialists and helped him collect a tidy capital.[10] There is a picture of the two men in later years, sitting side by side on cane chairs on a lawn. The relaxed setting and the engrossed manner in which they are looking over some papers reveal a degree of fondness and ease.

A relationship he formed with another formidable name in

Indian science at the IISc was to be an even more significant part of his life. Homi Bhabha, the man who was to found India's atomic energy programme and loom like a Colossus over Indian science until his death in the mid-1960s, had gone to Cambridge a decade before Vikram. Winning several fellowships, including the prestigious Isaac Newton studentship, he had worked with top-ranking scientists in Europe such as Wolfgang Pauli and Enrico Fermi and distinguished himself with two startling papers on positron physics and the cascade theory of cosmic showers.[11]

He had been holidaying in India when the war broke out. The IISc had offered him a readership which he had accepted. When Vikram arrived in Bangalore, he was using his enforced hiatus to fine-tune the theoretical work he had initiated in Cambridge and conduct experiments on the so-called 'hard component' of cosmic rays. (Like many of his colleagues in nuclear physics, Bhabha was interested in cosmic rays for the atomic particles thrown up by them, while Vikram was to see cosmic rays eventually as a tool to study outer space.)

It was an extraordinary circumstance then that brought these two gifted individuals together. In time, the intriguing similarities and the differences of their approach would become clear; they would also develop a close professional rapport of great significance for the country's technological development. As young men in Bangalore, however, there were other, more superficial common factors to draw them to each other's company.

In the first place, both were men of means. Bhabha's grandfather had been an inspector general of education in the state of Mysore but he was related through his aunt to the Bombay-based industrial family, the Tatas, that rivalled the Sarabhais in wealth. Both hailed from western India, an anomaly at a time when most scientists tended to come from the south or the east. They were sophisticated, though Bhabha was the more westernized of the two. They were good looking—Bhabha with his dark, brooding mien and Vikram with his delicate features and complexion so translucent that Ramaseshan was moved to describe it as *paal vazhiarathu*, meaning a baby's skin with the appearance of milk flowing below the surface. Both men also had passions outside science and a taste for the good life.

Many evenings, after work, they would head off to the posh West End Hotel, to meet with friends, mainly local, self-styled intellectuals, one of whom was an attractive Sri Lankan woman called Anil D'Silva. These apparently playboy-type excursions scandalized their co-students who were mostly middle-class, conservative Tamil Brahmins. Ramaseshan recalls wryly, 'We used to look at them with envy.'

Money certainly gave Vikram an enviable lifestyle. Not for him the cramped quarters of a student hostel. Even at twenty-one he had fine taste and found for himself a house with a view on a leafy slope in the northern part of the city called Malleswaram. The veteran Congress leader S. Nijalingappa is rumoured to have lived for a while in this house which was called Premalaya. In the little house with its stone floor and sharp-angled rooms, Vikram set up home supervised by his devoted man Friday, Lala Inkayya.

Sometimes, when he was not meeting Bhabha and the others, Vikram would wander down the road from Premalaya to the Vedanta College run by the Ramakrishna Mission. He would seek out the priest there and chat with him about Hindu philosophy. These conversations clearly had an impact on him, for he was to refer to them in a public lecture in 1962, describing how 'struck' he had been 'by the great concern of ancient Indian philosophers with questions about the nature of knowledge, of the role of the observer and of the qualitative recognition of aspects of relativity'.[12] And, as always, he was to draw a connection with science. 'I believe,' he would add, 'that modern physics owes much of its remarkable progress through the recognition of the same concepts and through the discovery of a mathematical framework within which they could be quantitatively formulated.'

Vikram worked hard on his research in Bangalore. Bruno Rossi, a pioneer in X-ray astronomy and space plasma physics, to whose laboratory at the Massachusetts Institute of Technology (MIT) Vikram was later to go every year, would maintain that Vikram had 'an almost uncanny capability to absorb and store in his mind a vast amount of experimental and theoretical data. Having done that, and guided by what I am tempted to call an artistic intuition, he would then proceed to arrange these data into a self-consistent picture, bringing out hidden regularities and relationships; a picture which, through the years, would progressively evolve and become more precise.... For him scientific research was an act of love towards nature.'[13]

Scientific research was and would always be Vikram's first love, a source of sustenance in his increasingly frenetic life. Yet, it was not for the practice of science that he was to become known—he never achieved the distinction as a scientist that Bhabha had in his early life, for instance—but for building institutions and putting into motion ideas that dovetailed into a deeply humane vision. And, as his trips to the Vedanta College indicate, his focus during his student days in Bangalore was not just on science but also on personal growth.

Like Ambalal, Vikram was given to reflecting on the nature of life and on the self. Unlike his father, however, his cogitations appear to have been more action oriented. 'When you grow up,' he was to tell friend and fellow scientist M.G.K. Menon, 'you don't have to walk step by step like a toddler; you can leap, run, you can take short cuts across the fields. That means you have to start processes, not like a gambler but like a prophet infallibly accurate as to what the consequences will be.'[14] Given the self-assuredness with which he was to start these processes a couple of years later, it seems likely that it was in Bangalore, during his student days, that he refined the ideas they would be based on.

Some of these ideas are to be found in talks he gave in his later life. In a paper presented in October 1969, for instance, he would claim that 'the physical and biological characteristics of an ecological balance based on the relationship of living organisms to their environment, as translated by Gandhiji in the social context, meant the bringing together of responsibilities with rights...'[15]

In a talk on 'Leadership in Science' for All India Radio in August 1965 he would expound on the assumption which underlay his approach to management, whether of companies or of large institutions: 'There is no leader and no led. A leader, if one chooses to identify one, has to be a cultivator rather than a manufacturer. He has to provide the soil and the overall climate and environment in which the seed can grow.'[16]

Bangalore, then, was a period of incubation. It was as if, having successfully scouted satisfactory terrain, he was sniffing around, testing the water sources, exploring ideas, making alliances to secure the new settlement that he planned to establish. It was also the most hedonistic phase in his life. If self-reflection was a Jain legacy, then Madame Montessori's emphasis on the senses had not gone unlearnt. Throughout his life Vikram was to combine hard work and sensual delights. His student days in Bangalore, however, was when he was able to make the most time for ordinary pleasures—something he was to do less and less of in subsequent years. It was a last fling before he got down to a more structured life.

The performing arts was one such indulgence. Music had and would always be his most passionate hobby. Kirit Parikh, a colleague at the Department of Atomic Energy (DAE), recalls how he once happened to mention the possibility of taking a trip abroad to meet friends and Vikram responded with a spontaneous plea: 'Oh, but you can get a good hi-fi system for the price of a ticket!'

This enthusiasm took him to the *kutcheris* of the south where he soon became a familiar face. In the tightly knit circle of connoisseurs, his good looks and charm attracted attention and he became friends with many local musicians including the venerated M.S. Subbulakshmi, who was to later perform at one of his conferences.

Bhabha, though his tastes ran more towards symphonies and ballet, was also fond of the performing arts. At some point he and Vikram decided to host a dance performance to raise funds for charity. Vikram approached the acclaimed Bharatanatyam dancer, Ram Gopal, for help. And that was when he met Mrinalini Swaminathan.

It was not the first time they had met. The Swaminathans were a well-known clan in the south. Swaminadhan, Mrinalini's father, had been a respected advocate of the Madras High Court. A man of liberal persuasions, he had encouraged his wife, Ammu, to adopt a glamorous, modern lifestyle which she retained after his death, a bold move for a time when widows were condemned to a marginal existence. She had also entered politics and one of the people she had met in the course of her public work was Sarla Sarabhai. The two women had much in common: Like Mridula, Ammu's elder daughter, Lakshmi, too, was a fervent idealist and would become well known as Captain Lakshmi Sehgal of Subhash Chandra Bose's Indian National Army, the squad of volunteers that planned to liberate India through military means.

Mrinalini was nothing like her sister. When Vikram first encountered her—the Sarabhais had stopped in Madras on their way to the hill station, Ooty—she was in tennis shorts and looking the picture of the emerging socialite. He asked her out for a film. The invitation appears to have been perfunctory, for he later confessed to having been put off by her apparent frivolity.[17] Meeting her again as an adult, in Bangalore, however, he was struck by the transformation in her personality. The frisky teenager, he realized, had grown into an elegant young woman and one quite different from the tennis-bingo-ballroom dancing-obsessed creature he had met. In fact, Mrinalini had taken a leap in quite another direction: she had become passionately involved in the study of Bharatanatyam. The interest had led her from a stint at Tagore's Santiniketan to Ram Gopal's school in Bangalore. She had even sworn, she told him, to stay unmarried in order to give herself completely to her art. Her engagement, so akin, it seemed, to his own involvement in science touched a chord in Vikram. He asked her out. They began to date.

There were long, romantic drives in Vikram's Bantam and endless conversations. They munched on fresh *makkai* and recited poetry to each other, Mrinalini breaking into lyrical Bengali recalling Tagore and Santiniketan, Vikram quoting Kalidasa. Both professed repeatedly to have no inclination for marriage and yet they were moving relentlessly closer. In her autobiography, Mrinalini writes:

> His [Vikram's] intellectual ability interested me deeply and he seemed far more mature than his age. His vision and knowledge astounded me.... We had so many things in common: our love for beauty, for honesty, for tradition, and for the country and at the same time our excitement about new developments in civilization.... Science is so similar to Art...both spiritually aware of the indivisible wholeness of the cosmos.... Vikram as a scientist, and I as a dancer, shared a 'togetherness' that was hard to define.... Vikram showed me, not so much by words but by his manner, that he loved me.[18]

Vikram's family had noticed the change coming over him. Gita remembers a holiday in the south at the time and the siblings' impulsive decision to rush up a hill, much to Sarla's concern. The air of juvenility perhaps sharpened the difference in her brother's behaviour. 'Suddenly he was a young man,' she says. 'Very affectionate, telling us how nice we looked in saris, giving us books with stuff on "what a young woman must know". It was like he was educating us sisters. But he was also relying on us. He confided in me about Mrinal, asked for my opinion, even requested me to get a sari for her. It was a sudden shift.'

Vikram was an ardent lover. Vinodini Mayor, Mrinalini's cousin who spent some time with the couple soon after their wedding, claims: 'It was quite something to see them together. He had eyes only for Mrinal. He was completely in love.' When Mrinalini went to Madras to train, Vikram phoned every night and visited her every weekend. His manner of wooing was not entirely conventional though. 'I never received one normal gift from him,' Mrinalini laughs. For their engagement, her millionaire fiancé gave her a turquoise Tibetan ring. Another time he sent her a dark-eyed slender loris which she vehemently refused to accept.

Vikram's determined pursuit was remarkable for two reasons. One, Mrinalini, though she admits she was in love, at the time claimed she was 'unsure' of her feelings.[19] She was concerned, or so she said, about 'the north–south difference', and the prospect of marriage (Vikram had proposed to her) affecting her dancing. The other factor was the whiff of discouragement from his family. In keeping with their closeness, the Sarabhais had all been introduced to the object of Vikram's affections. His eldest brother Suhrid and his wife Manorama came to Bangalore and Vikram asked Mrinalini to join them for dinner. When his parents came to Madras, Mrinalini went with them for a picnic to Mahabalipuram.

On hearing of his son's intention to marry Mrinalini, Ambalal wrote a long letter expressing his reservations. 'She is young, inexperienced, ambitious,' it said. 'Do decide as you think proper.'[20] It is not known how the young man responded to this cold critique but it clearly did not sway him from his purpose. He persisted, and with some help from her own family, Mrinalini was finally persuaded to agree.

For a man in his early twenties faced with such obstacles, the haste to marry seems a trifle puzzling. To place it in context, however, some explanation is required about the background against which it occurred. Early that year, a mission led by Stafford Cripps, a member of the War Cabinet, had attempted to canvass the Indian National Congress's support for the British war effort in return for full dominion status. Congress had refused. Instead, at a meeting in Gandhi's Sevagram Ashram in July 1942, it had passed a resolution that the British should 'quit' India. Signs of an approaching storm were ominously clear. In the Sarabhai household, a series of personal crises only exacerbated the situation. Loath to have one of his beloved children away at such a time, Ambalal pleaded with Vikram to come home.

On 8 August 1942, Jawaharlal Nehru moved the Quit India resolution at the historic Gowalia Tank meet in Bombay. The resolution was passed resoundingly. 'Do or die!' said Gandhi. Nehru called it the 'zero hour of the world'. The phone calls from Ahmedabad grew more insistent. And Vikram's urge to marry even stronger. Mrinalini claims he was worried that they would part and he would lose her. Such insecurity seems uncharacteristic and one can ascribe it either to the doomsday atmosphere of the times or his understandable reluctance to be parted from his beloved for what could have been an indefinite period. In any case, his persistence won and the wedding was fixed for the last week of August 1942.

It had to be a small wedding. Mrinalini's sister, Lakshmi, was in a Singapore jail along with other members of the Indian National Army. With rail links disturbed, none of the Sarabhais could attend. Vikram's only representative was his major domo, Lala. A young man in his plight could have been expected to experience last-minute jitters. Vikram's thoughts, however, seemed to have been focused more on his anxious bride. The morning of the wedding, he scoured the bazaar for blue lotuses which he placed on a beautiful brass tray and sent up to her room. Any remaining doubts she may have had, melted away. 'No other expression of his love could have moved me so deeply,' she says.[21]

The wedding, simple Vedic rituals followed by a civil ceremony, took place in the Swaminathan drawing room. Mrinalini wore a white khadi sari with flowers instead of jewellery. Her *thali* was a Lakshmi pendant Vikram had bought in Bangalore. A musician friend played the veena. And later, at Vikram's request, Mrinalini and a dancer friend performed the deer scene from the Ramayana. They left for Ahmedabad the same night.

They moved through a harrowing landscape. In the days following the Quit India call, the country had been engulfed by strikes and demonstrations. Telegraph and telephone lines had been cut, public buildings torched and bridges blown up. 'India,' writes Katherine Frank, 'seemed on the verge of insurrection and anarchy.'[22] For Vikram and his bride, the journey to Bombay, where they would take a connecting train to Ahmedabad, took sixty long hours because the tracks on the way had been blown up. As Mrinalini recalls, 'It was a strange honeymoon indeed in a first-class coupe.'

They reached home to find The Retreat in a state of gloom. Four of Vikram's sisters and his two aunts were in jail; Mridula was serving an eighteen-month term. More worryingly, Suhrid, the eldest Sarabhai son, had fallen ill with a mysterious ailment thought to have been contracted on a business trip to Africa. Ambalal requested the authorities to release his daughters so that they could meet their ailing brother. The governor, Sir Roger Lumley, agreed. But Mridula refused to accept parole.

The crises continued for months. It is natural to assume that Vikram must have shared the family's anxiety about Suhrid's health. Yet, he was to demonstrate, in this case, as in the future, a remarkable ability—one that could lend itself to opposite interpretations of extreme focus or a lack of ordinary feeling—to keep his eye on the long term through periods of personal and external turbulence. So, despite his brother's failing health and the mounting agitations, he continued to work on his scientific research.

He first travelled to Poona to seek help in making the elaborate set of Geiger counters he required for his experiments from the Poona Observatory of the India Meteorological Department (IMD), one of the few places in the country where the requisite expertise was available. The deputy director general of the IMD, Dr K.R. Ramanathan, a kindly-faced man, received the young physicist from Ahmedabad and his wife with warm hospitality.

It is likely that Raman, whose student Ramanathan had been, was responsible for making the introduction. And evidently the latter provided Vikram the help he needed, for at a later date Vikram was to shift his apparatus to IMD's research laboratory to avail of its more accurate meteorological data. But the meeting also had long-term implications, for it is certain that Vikram had, if not before, then after the meeting, a larger game plan in mind. Ramanathan was an acknowledged expert on aeronomy and atmospheric physics and his expertise would form a significant component of the research project Vikram had in mind.

In 1943, Vikram undertook a trip to Kashmir to measure cosmic rays at a high altitude. High altitude studies in cosmic rays were considered useful because of the rapid increase of cosmic ray intensity with elevation and the possibility of investigating types of radiation that would not survive to reach sea level. Vikram was to point out in his PhD thesis that he would have preferred an altitude higher than 14,100 feet, which was the height at which studies had been conducted in a laboratory at St Evans in America. But finding no place at that height equipped with even basic amenities in India, he had settled for a lower altitude in Kashmir. Even that choice presented logistical problems which he describes in great detail in his PhD thesis. The description, however, also conveys a clear picture of the advantages of wealth and family that Vikram enjoyed and the support they provided for his research.[23]

The final choice of the site, Gangabal, he writes, for instance, was made on reaching Srinagar and after consultations with experienced trekkers including a Major Huddow, who had accompanied the last Nanga Parbat expedition. The governor of Kashmir not only provided guidance but also arranged the transport of forty pack ponies and fifty porters.

The party that left Srinagar on the morning of 3 September included Vikram, Mrinalini, his siblings Gira and Gautam, a laboratory assistant from Bangalore, a camp manager, a doctor of the Kashmir Medical Service, Dr Dayal Singh, the transport manager, Pandit Tikkalal, four personal servants, three helpers and a *khansamah* who came with the tents, furniture and provisions from a trekking agency and a guard provided by the state. The total number came to ninety and each individual had a riding pony.

The trek was extremely arduous with paths rising steeply and often disappearing altogether, necessitating a jump from one boulder to another. Vikram notes all these difficulties meticulously along with more pleasant observations such as the 'beautiful' ruins of an ancient stone temple at Nora Nag where they camped one night.

Trunkhal was the spot chosen for the first cosmic ray measurements. The expedition camped there for four days to perform the experiment. Gautam and Pandit Tikkalal meanwhile explored the entire neighbourhood of Gangabal Lake to choose a location for the next set of observations. They found a point at 13,900 feet on the spur of a slope overlooking Gangabal from the north. After returning to Srinagar, the party moved on to Gulmarg where they stayed, 'very comfortably', in Nedou's Hotel while Vikram took more observations there and later at Al Pathri, a four-hour horseback ride from Gulmarg.

Apart from an apparatus malfunction at Al Pathri, the expedition appears to have gone off smoothly, providing an early instance of Vikram's managerial abilities. From a scientific perspective the experiments were fruitful as well: a sizeable quantity of 8mm

Kodachrome cine film was utilized and Vikram concluded that the 'expedition has provided a great deal of experience in the performance of cosmic ray experiments at high altitudes'.[24]

But while Vikram was making progress with his scientific work, new complications arose at home. His marriage did not seem to have softened his parents' customary reserve. Though outwardly encouraging—Ambalal was supportive of his daughter-in-law and used to insist on attending her performances, even sitting with an umbrella through rehearsals at the Town Hall to protect himself from pigeon droppings—neither he nor Sarla seemed to act in a way that would make Mrinalini feel at home. Sarla, Mrinalini claims, had greeted her with the cutting assessment that she had always believed her son would remain a bachelor, a statement not calculated to alleviate her unease.[25] And Suhrid, despite being shifted to Bombay where more advanced medical facilities were available, was not improving.

Worse was to come. One day, Mrinalini and Vikram were standing in the street, watching a procession go by when a burning canister came flying through the air and hit her eye. It was a tense few days that followed. There was a danger of her losing sight in one eye. The treatment turned out to be long and anxiety ridden. Through it, Vikram, according to Mrinalini's biographer Harriet Ronken Lynton, 'never left her bedside'. Vinodini, to whose home in Kerala Mrinalini later went for Ayurvedic treatment, also recalls the telegrams that arrived daily to their remote village home followed by their sender, Vikram, in person. At some point, while Mrinalini was recuperating, Suhrid died.

Soon after, Vikram left the sombre atmosphere of The Retreat. His parents never quite got over the death of their eldest son. Erik Erikson found an air of melancholy about Ambalal when he came visiting almost twenty years later. Vikram returned to the IISc in Bangalore. The house on the hillock in Malleswaram was opened up again and made ready for habitation, its stone floors washed and the furniture dusted. The name Premalaya now seemed appropriate, for this time he had come to the 'abode of love' with his wife.

Their return caused a ripple of excitement in the sleepy garden city. Handsome, with twinkling eyes and a palpable charm, Vikram had always had charisma. Mrinalini's first impression of him, and one that was echoed by many others, was that he looked like a prince. Mrinalini herself, though not conventionally beautiful, more than made up with her attractive features, her lissome grace and exquisite taste. Together they seemed to have everything: good looks, wealth, success and the boldness to cross cultural and geographical distances for love. It was a fairy-tale romance. Schoolgirls in Bangalore stole trips to the quiet suburb to catch a glimpse of the glamorous couple driving past.

The reality, however, was not particularly glamorous. As soon as he returned, Vikram threw himself into work with feverish intensity. Between studying the time distribution of cosmic rays and embarking on his Kashmir trip, Vikram had developed, on the basis of a suggestion by Bhabha, 'a direct method' of measuring the intensity of the slow mesons with the Geiger counter.[26]

Slow mesons are particles created by the collision of primary radiation with atoms in the upper part of the earth's atmosphere and are found only near the place of their formation. In the course of his investigations into the slow meson, Vikram had noticed small variations in the intensity from day to day, and at different times of the day. This discovery had led him to digress from his original investigation and embark on a new study of time variations of cosmic rays.

He spent days, and often nights, within the drab walls of the laboratory. Mrinalini, tired of waiting for him at home, would sometimes come to see him and fall asleep on a folding cot, only to be woken up by Vikram in the early morning and sent home before Raman arrived. He was racing against the clock to complete the remaining work that would form the first part of his PhD thesis. That year he also produced a paper on 'The Method of Shower Anti-coincidences for Measuring the Meson Component of Cosmic Radiation'.[27]

Mrinalini, on the other hand, was not her former self. The accident and the near loss of an eye had left her weak and prone to despondency. Vikram encouraged her to resume dancing. At a time when women were not expected to work and dancing was frowned upon, Vikram's attitude towards his wife's career seems unusual. At his initiative, a floor was added to Premalaya to give her space for practice and he suggested getting a teacher to stay. He also involved himself in her performances, accompanying her on outstation shows, looking into all aspects of production and personally handling the stage lights.

The following year, with the war having ended, Vikram began to make preparations to return to Cambridge to work towards his doctorate. Aware of how upset Mrinalini had been about time lost due to her accident, he offered that she stay back to pursue her career. Reluctant to be separated from him, however, Mrinalini refused to stay back. And so, in 1945, after a tiring, bumpy Dakota ride, Mr and Mrs Vikram Sarabhai arrived in England.

They came to a country ravaged by war. Bombed-out buildings and low rations made for a gloomy welcome. Cambridge had lost many of its scientists to the war effort. Students whose doctoral research had been interrupted by the war were flocking back in droves but there was an absence of leadership, particularly in the once glorious nuclear physics department. Joan Freeman, an Australian-born scientist who fulfilled her life's dream by making it to the Cavendish in 1946, confessed to a feeling of acute disappointment.[28] After the initial shock, however, Freeman found many sources of consolation including the fifty-feet tall, high-voltage machines devised after Cockcroft and Walton's famous 1932 experiment, the exquisite singing of the choir boys in King's College Chapel and punting on the Cam.

Paul Adrian Maurice Dirac was there giving lectures on mathematics. George Lindsay, who was to become chief of the Operational Research Establishment of the Canadian Department of National Defence, Charlie Barnes, later senior professor at the California Institute of Technology, Godfrey Stafford, future director of the Rutherford Laboratory, and Allan Cormack who was to win the Nobel Prize for Medicine in 1979 were among the students at Cambridge in 1946. Freeman was part of a small group of what she calls 'colonials', a term for overseas students which included Canadians, South Africans and Australians but no Indians. She even mentions a Cambridge Interplanetary Society which was carrying out detailed theoretical investigations into ways and means of propelling rockets and other vehicles into interplanetary space, though at the time it appears that such enterprises were deemed 'impracticable' and were not taken too seriously.

One does not find any record in Vikram's papers of an association with any of the flourishing activities mentioned here. In Mrinalini's account of the time, Vikram was burning the candle at both ends. The introduction to his PhD thesis indicates that over the approximately thirteen-month period, he was working in two areas: one, the interpretation of the data on variations of cosmic ray intensity that he had collected in India, and two, experiments with high-energy gamma rays using a photofission cross-section.

The credits are understated giving the impression that much of the work was self-generated, a distinct possibility since the area Vikram was working on was fairly marginal to the reigning interests at Cambridge at the time. For the interpretation of data on variations of cosmic ray intensity he claims to have collaborated with a Dr P. Nicholson at the Cavendish but clarifies that 'I myself determined the subject matter and the scope of the investigations and designed the necessary apparatus'. The three investigations presented, he claims, 'are entirely original and were undertaken individually'.[29]

In the second part he gives credit to Dr W.E. Burcham for suggesting 'the accurate determination of the photofission cross section', for discussions on the technique and for giving 'valuable advice from time to time'. But again, he specifies that 'the entire experiment was performed individually and an original method of measuring the flux of X-rays has been suggested by me'. He thanks C.V. Raman 'for his constant encouragement and for supervising my work in India' and Bhabha 'for helpful discussions concerning cosmic rays'. He also confesses to being 'greatly indebted to E.S. Shire for supervising my research at Cambridge and for encouragement and advice' and is grateful for 'assistance and consideration received from various colleagues—in particular Dr W.E. Burcham and Mr D.R.L. Wilkinson and Mr E.B. Paul'.[30]

There is also a record of two papers prepared in collaboration with P. Nicholson on 'The Semi-diurnal Variation in Meson Intensity' in the Physical Society Cambridge Conference Report in 1947 and another on 'The Semi-diurnal Variation in Cosmic Ray Intensity' in the Proceedings of the Physical Society dated 1948.[31]

Long hours at the lab took their toll and Vikram went down with a mysterious illness that turned out to be malaria. He was laid up in bed. The couple were staying in a single room in a boarding house. Mrinalini, coping with the difficulties of the lack of fuel and food—the options were even more limited for vegetarians, most days they ate potatoes—and the limited foreign exchange disbursed by the Indian government, would have had a tough time but for the presence of Miss Williams, the governess who had worked with the Sarabhais and who came over to help. That winter was the worst Britain had experienced in a century. Transport was disrupted across the country. The movement of coal was affected and power restrictions had to be imposed.

Despite the gloom, it appears to have been a happy time for Vikram and Mrinalini, perhaps the happiest they were to know as a couple. Away from his forbidding family Mrinalini felt freer and the despondency that had assailed her since her accident seemed to lift. She helped Vikram with the proofs of his thesis. 'I would ask, "Is this English or science?" And we would laugh. We were very together [then].'

In March came the much-awaited thaw. The ice cracked, the snow melted, gushing down the streets of Cambridge in a gurgling flood. Freeman writes about the arrival of spring after that year's fierce winter announcing itself 'in a precipitate outburst of glory'. Snowdrops, aconites and crocuses 'transformed the dull earth with miraculous stretches of bright colour'.[32]

Vikram's dissertation was complete. For his oral examination Vikram travelled to Manchester to appear before P.M.S. Blackett, the distinguished scientist who would win the Nobel the following year for his investigations in nuclear physics and cosmic radiation. The examination went well; Blackett and a colleague recommended the award of a Cambridge PhD degree to Vikram. After the examination, Vikram and Mrinalini, who had accompanied him, lingered on to survey the physics laboratory. Blackett recalls vividly the 'splendid red' of Mrinalini's sari contrasting with the 'grey gloom' of the old Manchester laboratories.[33]

Vikram was awarded his degree. And Mrinalini discovered she was pregnant. They decided to go on a celebratory tour of Europe before heading home. At a shop in London, they picked up shoes for Vikram's little niece, Kalpana, his sister Leena's daughter. Leena had married Madanmohan Mangaldas, the scion of a leading textile family in Ahmedabad, at the age of twenty-two. The very next day ironically brought news of Kalpana's sudden and unexpected death. Vikram wrote feelingly to Leena: 'She was like one of those rare sunsets that fill the being with joy in one fleeting moment. I shall always cherish that joy.'[34]

But for the sadness brought about by the event, Vikram and Mrinalini had a fun-filled holiday. Vikram was set on building a theatre for Mrinalini's dance performances in Ahmedabad, so they spent some time exploring theatre houses in Europe. They ate in cafés, roamed the streets, met up with acquaintances. And when they finally returned in 1947, they were, as Mrinalini claims, 'full of exciting plans and hopes'.

On 15 August 1947, the long, tortuous struggle for independence ended. At the stroke of midnight, India became free. Like millions of other Indians, the Sarabhais turned on the radio for the first Indian Prime Minister Jawaharlal Nehru's speech: '[The future] is not one of ease or resting but of incessant striving so that we might fulfil the pledges we have so often taken and the one we shall take today. The service of India means the service of millions who suffer.'[35]

3

BUILDING AN INSTITUTION

As Gandhi's words had once stirred the people to revolt against the foreign ruler, so, in post-independence India, Nehru's call to service rained on a thirsting, eager land. The infant nation reeled under the bloody aftermath of Partition; a skirmish on the border with Pakistan had given an early intimation of the horrors ahead. Issues of unity, security, poverty, religion and language had to be tackled. But the spirit was more than willing. Chester Bowles, US ambassador to India during the 1950s, saw it in the eyes of the youth. '[In] their explosiveness and even their radicalism,' he wrote, 'is a sign of their eagerness to be summoned to a great democratic task of nation building.'[1]

Nehru was the rallying symbol. The Mahatma with his staff and loincloth had united the disparate millions and provided the movement with a conscience. But a newly freed people, making their space in an unequal world, felt the need for a more showy self-assertion. In every sphere—foreign policy, economics, federalism—Jawaharlal, with his aristocratic bearing, emphasized the need that was being expressed all over Asia for an indigenous path. Better still, he did it in the language and clipped accent of the country's erstwhile rulers. In his first meeting with the Indian prime minister, Bowles was deeply struck by both Nehru's devotion to Western concepts of democracy and by his firm determination to be Asian, 'to think and act independently'. The diplomat was to hear a similar sentiment expressed across the continent ('from Lebanon to Japan'), in the following months, but rarely, he claims, 'as eloquently'.[2]

Nehru symbolized India's pride. He also believed fervently in a participatory role for the people. 'I think that now in the new free India,' he said to Margaret Bourke-White, photographer for the American magazine *Life*, 'the time has come to ask ourselves the new question: what should we do?'[3] The sentiment found an echo across the country. An excited J.R.D. Tata, meeting Raj Thapar in London, asked her what 'a progressive industrialist should do at this juncture'. Thapar herself exulted: 'We were living in exciting times for truly this was a building time for India.'[4]

Nowhere was this mix of self-assertion and idealism more visible than in the world of science. In the pre-independence era it had been fashionable for Indian scientists to design their research projects in such a manner that some peculiarity or other of indigenous conditions would be highlighted. Vikram observed cosmic rays in tropical latitudes. Bhabha conducted experiments in the Kolar mineshaft, one of the longest in the world. Raman took advantage of India's abundant sunshine to study the scattering of light. 'Laboratory practice,' as social historian Itty Abraham points out, 'was being given tangible expression in political terms.'[5]

In other cases, personal difficulties proved a motivating force. Meghnad Saha, the Bengali scientist who developed the theory of thermal ionization, grew up walking ten kilometres to school every day, through a terrain prone to flooding. In his later life, he was understandably preoccupied with finding ways to harness the power of rivers. 'Vast powers are placed in the hands of man by successful research,' said Raman at the Asian Relations Conference (March–April 1947), 'which opens up a vista of possibilities for its beneficent application in the relief of the fundamental ills of humanity, namely hunger, poverty and disease.'[6]

Nehru, too, had immense faith in the abilities of science. Science, in fact, was one of the main spears of his proposed revolution. During his last term of imprisonment, clearly anticipating freedom, he had identified the three fundamental requirements for India's development: a heavy engineering and machine-making industry, scientific research institutions and electric power.

The significance he gave to science was evident from the fact that within ten days of assuming office, even while riots raged, he made time to attend a meeting of the Council of Scientific and Industrial Research (CSIR), the nodal body that had been set up by the government. Believing as he did that '[it is] through the method and spirit of science that we can ultimately solve our problems', he periodically enhanced the funds allotted to scientific research by the government and urged scientists not just to think of their 'individual search for truth' but in terms of 'a rapid bettering of' the forty crore people of India.[7]

The first of the five Indian Institutes of Technology was established in 1951 and a large number of national laboratories, specializing in different fields, were set up all over the country. 'If we had done nothing else during the last five years but the development of these laboratories,' Nehru wrote to his former cellmate Mahavir Tyagi in 1952, 'we would have some reason to take credit for our achievements.'[8]

Heavy industries received a push under the five-year plans, and programmes were launched against illiteracy and for health and land reforms. Of Nehru's priorities, the major issue still to be addressed was that of energy. And here too it was a scientist, his favourite scientist, in fact, who proposed a solution. The scientist was Vikram's friend from Bangalore, Homi Bhabha, who had decided to stay on in India after the war and establish an institute of fundamental research that the Tatas had agreed to finance. The sacrifice of a potentially glorious career abroad had established Bhabha's credentials as a patriot. But it was his proximity to Nehru that had made him the most powerful figure in Indian science at the time.

Bhabha's dizzy rise under Nehru's ready patronage has been a matter of great conjecture. It is believed that their shared perceptions of science and aesthetics may have had something to do with their unusual closeness. The prime minister was a lonely man surrounded by politicians who did not share his cultural predilections. Nehru's own indifferent educational qualifications might have led him to admire the intellect that Bhabha appeared to possess.[9] According to Nehru's biographer S. Gopal, Bhabha was one of the two people outside his family who addressed the prime minister as 'bhai', and he was able to sell to Nehru the idea of applying nuclear energy to power production at a time when the idea was perceived as a dim possibility even in the more developed West.

Ahmedabad, Gandhi's home and the stomping ground of Sardar Patel, deputy prime minister in the new government, could not have been unaffected by the mood that had seized the rest of the country following the departure of the British. Yet, there was the matter of its age-old obduracy. A city that had firmly retained its essential ethos through periods of extreme turbulence was unlikely to surrender to the winds of new change, at least not without tempering its response with something of its past, particularly since the city had a tradition of social consciousness.

This tradition was best typified by the mahajan and nagarsheth conventions. In Ahmedabad, the word 'mahajan' has many connotations. Literally it means the 'great one' and is loosely used to refer to a rich person or one of high social standing. It could also refer to the city's professional guilds. And then there is the abstract but widely understood implication in the word, of an old custom that made it obligatory for the rich to deploy some portion of their wealth and influence in the interests of the wider community. Hand in hand with this custom was the institution of the nagarsheth, invented in all probability by the Mughals to reward a certain individual for services to the court.

The nagarsheth was the face of the city. In 1725, when the Maratha army advanced upon Ahmedabad, the then nagarsheth is believed to have offered his own wealth to save the city from plunder. In gratitude, the city's guilds conferred on his family in perpetuity the right to collect a percentage on trade in the city. In return, the nagarsheth performed various public duties: adjudicating between guilds or interceding on their behalf with royal officials. If the monsoon was late, he would circumambulate the city walls pouring milk on the ground to appease the king of the gods, Indra.[10] The original nagarsheth family were Oswal Jains, but, according to business historian Dwijendra Tripathi, the position at some point developed into something more notional than real and came to be linked to social standing rather than inheritance, passing, for instance, from a trading to a textile family when the latter overtook the former in significance.

In Ahmedabad then, the existence of these traditions had long sanctified a version of benevolent feudalism. The rich had always considered the city's welfare their personal responsibility, extending protection at times of riots, for instance, or opening hospitals for the sick to tackle major epidemics. In these instances of largesse there was often a suggestion of personal advantage. In the 1930s, for example, the city's mill owners, displaying remarkable foresight, picked up four hundred acres of land in the wilderness across the river and set about establishing a series of educational institutions including a college for commerce, humanities, engineering, science and pharmacy with hostels and residential units for teachers.

The impulse was not altogether altruistic; the recognition that their pace of growth would soon generate a need for white-collar workers, secretaries, clerks, accountants and the like is said to have formed some part of the motivation. It was this combination of duty and pragmatism that brought about a rare unity among men who were competitors in business. As a group,. the sheths, it was said, were like a 'thick stick'—not easy to break.

In the late 1940s, in post-colonial India, the leading mahajan of Ahmedabad was a gentleman by the name of Kasturbhai Lalbhai. Kasturbhai came from a nagarsheth family but had had the misfortune of inheriting one of the most insignificant mills in town. To add to his disadvantages, he was coarse in appearance, buck-toothed and dhoti clad, blunt in speech and of a parsimonious mindset. Yet, in the early part of the century, this unlikely individual had emerged as a formidable leader both locally and nationally. He had taken on the mighty Tatas in the 1930s on a taxation dispute with nationalistic implications. And despite his relatively modest monetary standing he was invited to represent the industry on various boards and advisory committees set up by the government of free India. His exaggerated stature derived chiefly from his commitment to philanthropy and his extraordinarily strong principles.

His scrupulousness on financial matters was legendary. He once sent back to the ministry of commerce a single rupee that he had been paid in excess on account of the train fare to Delhi for appearance on a government committee. He even prosecuted a member of his own family for embezzlement. 'If you asked him to use expensive paper or a good-quality envelope to write a note to a friend, he would refuse, but he would gladly donate Rs 20 lakh to start a college,' comments advocate Nani Palkhivala who counted Kasturbhai among the small band of men who could be called 'builders of nations—not merely of business or industries'.[11]

Kasturbhai, as it happened, was a close friend of Ambalal's. Their friendship had been forged in 1918, at the time of the great textile strike, when Ambalal, recognizing his young colleague's negotiating skills, had co-opted him into the managing committee of the AMA, thus launching him into a successful public career.

Their relationship had deepened when the two became neighbours in Shahibaug. Only a compound wall separated their properties. And though business rivalry temporarily affected their relations, the families continued to be intimate. Kasturbhai had developed a particular fondness for Vikram that was to evolve into a strong mutual regard as the latter grew into adulthood.

It is intriguing that despite the presence of a formidable and much loved father, Vikram should have forged such a strong bond with Kasturbhai. It is equally intriguing that Kasturbhai, with sons and nephews of his own, should have been so drawn to Vikram. There is no doubt though that the bond was one of deep affection on both sides. Kasturbhai's biographer Dwijendra Tripathi recalls Kasturbhai being so moved once while introducing Vikram at a convention that he ended up making a longer speech than the main speaker. Mrinalini recounts a time from the early days of her marriage when she accompanied the two men to the Jain pilgrimage town of Mount Abu. Vikram and Kasturbhai became so engrossed in a philosophical discussion that they left her alone 'listening to bhajans in a temple'.

In many ways the earthy industrialist with his outspokenness and rectitude reflected the ideals Vikram had grown up with. And it was out of respect that he sought Kasturbhai's counsel on many occasions. But it was also a conscious feature of Vikram's strategy to enter into alliances for the furtherance of his goals. His approach was to treat every undertaking as a joint venture. He would seek alliances with central or state government agencies, funding institutions, universities, like-minded people and so on. Many of his joint ventures were with men older and more experienced than himself.

Padmanabh Joshi who wrote his PhD thesis 'Vikram Sarabhai: A Study on Innovative Leadership and Institution Building', from Gujarat University in 1986, believes that Vikram consciously tempered his own prominence to avail of the benefits of partnership. Each of his allies brought something crucial to the table: K.R. Ramanathan was an established authority in scientific circles, S.S. Bhatnagar, director-general, CSIR, and Dr K.S. Krishnan, director of the National Physical Laboratory (NPL), who were on the board of the Physical Research Laboratory (PRL) were influential men. And Kasturbhai, of course, had many useful attributes, not least of which was his proximity to Nehru.

Ashis Nandy observes that Vikram displayed a remarkable lack of insecurity about working with people 'brighter than himself'. In fact, these early collaborations were probably test cases for the theme of interdependence he was to harp on tirelessly at various fora some decades later. As experiments they were remarkably successful. Kasturbhai's earthy vigour was a foil to Vikram's urbanity. The former's canny entrepreneurial flair and the latter's imagination and industriousness were not only to result in the establishment of a string of influential institutions but would house them in architecturally innovative settings that would transform the drab landscape of Ahmedabad.

The Ahmedabad Textile Industry's Research Association (ATIRA) was one of the earliest of these ventures. In 1944, the colonial government in India had set up the Industrial Research Planning Committee under Sir R.K. Shanmugham Chetty to encourage industrial research. The committee had travelled to Ahmedabad to make the textile community aware of the government's interest. And the AMA had been positive in its response.

The idea was to build an institution modelled on the lines of research associations in Britain. It would be a pioneering effort in many ways. It would not only be the first enterprise to bring together the government and industry for the purposes of research, it would also be the first Indian industrial research and development unit to be run on cooperative lines. In time it would spawn a host of similar institutions for the textile industry in other parts of the country as well as for other industries.

The need for a project of this nature was overwhelming. Ahmedabad's sheths continued to be dependent on Manchester-based experts for technical guidance, an embarrassing reality for a flourishing industry (a 1950 report was to estimate the presence of eleven million spindles and 195,000 looms)[12] and a newly independent nation.

It was with Vikram's return from his second stint at Cambridge that the vague plan began to take shape. Kasturbhai asked Vikram to study the structures of industrial research institutions in the UK and Europe with a view to implementing them at home. It is easy to see why the mill owners should have leaned so heavily on Vikram in this matter. He was that rare entity: a trained scientist and one of their own, the son of one of the city's leading mill owners—the significance of the unlikely combination in a highly stratified business community cannot be overstated.

For Vikram's part, his involvement with ATIRA was a clear indication of his belief in applied science. He was to refer to it often in his public speeches. An undated quote from a brochure brought out by ATIRA on its silver anniversary, for instance, has him saying: 'The history of science is full of examples which alternate from being extremely practical to being extremely basic in their approach and it is through the interaction between the basic and the empirical and practical problems that we find the greatest and most fruitful developments of modern science and technology.'[13]

In 1966, at the Rockefeller University in New York he was to reiterate his belief, expressing concern over the tendency to place intellectual endeavour on a high social scale and putting research scientists and academics in ivory towers, because 'those who can pose basic questions are the ones who can best do applied work'.[14]

At another level, however, Vikram's pivotal role in starting ATIRA points to another striking feature of his personality which was connected with a certain pattern set by the family. Consciously or unconsciously, it was as if the women in the Sarabhai household always rebelled against feudalism and patriarchy while the men, however liberal and daring they may have been in social terms, did not disturb or even seek to address class inequality. Like her aunt Ansuya, Mridula, for instance, was sensitive to the reality of the working class, writing in her diary: 'The Ahmedabad mill owners cannot see the growing discontent among the workers or they do not wish to see it.'[15] Vikram, on the other hand, cast his lot firmly with the mill owners.

ATIRA was registered in December 1947. It was initially housed in the AMA building. A sprawling green seventy-five-acre plot had been earmarked in the campus of the Gujarat University for the new institute. Lockwood Green of New York were contracted to prepare a project report and laboratory plans. Achyut Kanvinde, principal architect for the CSIR, who had been involved with the planning and development of scientific research laboratories all over the country, and his associate Shankar Rai—a team Vikram was to rely on for many of his future projects—began to make plans.

While they waited for the main building and its ancillary structures to come up, the meagre staff of four—a mathematical statistician, a social psychologist, a high-polymer chemist and a physical chemist—began work in their new temporary premises in three rooms of the M.G. Science College. Vikram was the heart and sinews of the enterprise, but something else was evolving in another part of the premises that was also occupying a considerable share of his time and attention.

The emergence of top-notch scientists in the early part of the twentieth century, men like Raman, Saha and Jagadish Chandra

Bose, the last known for his pioneering work in millimetre waves, does not reveal the truth about the state of science facilities in India at the time. Independent patrons such as Dr Mahendra Lal Sircar, who set up the Indian Association for the Cultivation of Science in Calcutta where Raman did his Nobel-winning research, did their best to boost the study of science. But in the universities it was not a priority.

Calcutta University did not have a science department till 1914; and even then the college building had to be built with low-cost materials because of paucity of funds. When in the 1920s Meghnad Saha went as head of physics to Allahabad University, one of the country's five oldest universities, he found no apparatus for higher research and a workshop without electricity. When he requisitioned additional books for the library, he was asked to first finish reading the books that were already there.[16]

By 1945, Bhabha's Tata Institute for Fundamental Research (TIFR) had started functioning and some years later the national laboratories came into being. In a country of India's size, however, opportunities for higher research were few. It was not surprising under the circumstances that someone of Vikram's inclinations and means should have thought of setting up his own laboratory. Mrinalini believes the idea of PRL came to Vikram while he was travelling on a train in England when he was there as a student between 1937 and 1940, or so she recalls him telling her. On this journey, she says, he conceptualized the whole institute and its programme of research.

Given Raman's role in suggesting Vikram's field of research and the latter's discovery of time variations in Kashmir, which formed the basis for further research at PRL, this does not seem possible. It is more probable that Vikram could have been referring to his second phase at Cambridge, *after* he had interacted with Raman, Bhabha and Ramanathan and conducted his investigations into cosmic rays. In fact, this is very likely given the speed with which he moved into operation on his return in 1947.

His intentions at the start were modest. This was to be a fairly typical mode of operation for him. However expansive his vision, in practice Vikram displayed the cautious pragmatism of the Ahmedabadi businessman. He believed in starting small and building by stages. For PRL, small literally meant moving the workshop at The Retreat, where he had spent hours as a child operating lathes and drills, to the service quarters behind the main building of M.G. Science College. The college was a multi-storeyed building with a dome, set deep in the middle of a virtual jungle, a cricket pitch in front of it.

The Ahmedabad Education Society (AES) run by Kasturbhai Lalbhai contributed land for a new building; additional support came from the Sarabhais' own Karmakshetra Educational Foundation. The laboratory began functioning in November 1947. An asbestos sheet on two boxes formed a table for the staff; a few racks became the 'library'. Vikram's room was in a passage. K.R. Ramanathan, the grey-haired deputy director general of the Poona Observatory, had accepted Vikram's invitation to join the new laboratory after his retirement from the India Meteorological Department and in March 1948 he arrived to take on the posts of director and professor of atmospheric physics.

Word about the new laboratory spread. Most of the existing science institutes—and there were few to begin with—were still preoccupied with areas of classical physics such as heat and thermodynamics. Others, like Raman's institute in Bangalore and one in Benares, were focused on spectroscopy. For a young student keen on venturing into the exciting new areas of nuclear and cosmic ray physics, opportunities were rare. Gradually, students started to arrive. And on each one Vikram appeared to make an immediate impact.

Praful Bhavsar, for instance, the son of a businessman fallen on bad days, was not the typical research student. His keenness to study nuclear physics, however, had taken him on a futile search from Bombay to Poona till Dr L.A. Ramdas, the deputy director general of the India Meteorological Department, directed him to PRL and to Vikram. He turned up in August 1948 and found Vikram sitting in a small room wearing 'white khaddar trousers and a bright green shirt'. As Bhavsar recalls, Vikram was at the glass-blower's desk repairing a Geiger counter and paused to greet him with a warm smile. 'I was at once attracted to this very simple, unassuming person, who fitted in with the mental image in my mind of a young experimental physicist.'

In January, at the Indian Science Congress in Allahabad, R.G. Rastogi, a lecturer at Sagar University, had been urged by Sydney Chapman, a visiting expert in geophysics who had recently given a series of lectures on geomagnetism at the PRL, to look out for 'a young man with two or three students running after him', who had started 'an exciting new laboratory' in Ahmedabad. Rastogi did and was inevitably charmed into chucking up his job and joining PRL. E.V. Chitnis was an engineer with All India Radio, earning a decent wage for the times. He left it to join Vikram for a Rs 100 a month scholarship in 1951. U.R. Rao came with an MSc from Benares in 1953. Others like R.P. Kane, Satya Prakash and U.D. Desai joined in the intervening years while B.H.V. Raman Murthy and J.V. Dave also arrived to work with Dr Ramanathan. PRL had limited funds for scholarships, and many students, often at Vikram's suggestion, found work as demonstrators at local colleges, coming to PRL after work and cooking their meals on a hotplate alongside their electronic devices.

In February 1952, the foundation stone of the new laboratory building would be laid by C.V. Raman in the presence of luminaries such as CSIR's S.S. Bhatnagar, Homi Bhabha and Kasturbhai Lalbhai. The main building would be inaugurated in April 1954 by Vikram's family friend, Jawaharlal Nehru. But meanwhile work had begun.

Cosmic rays spend over 2.5 million years in interstellar space where continuous interaction with magnetic fields causes them to lose their original sense of direction. As a result, when they enter our solar system they are isotropic, that is, they have uniform density in all directions. However, encountering interplanetary magnetic fields within our solar system, they lose their isotropy. Vikram and other scientists working in this area realized that a careful measurement of the variations in the intensity of cosmic rays in time and space would further an understanding of the electromagnetic state of interplanetary space. Of course, all this was not as clearly mapped out in the 1940s. In fact, Vikram, like many others, initially believed that the variations in the intensity of cosmic rays were possibly due to a continuous emission of cosmic ray particles by the sun. It was only in the mid-1950s that he came to be convinced of the existence of electromagnetic fields in interplanetary space.

At the outset then, the effort was centred on studying the nature of the variations themselves. In his second phase at IISc, Vikram had designed an elaborate apparatus consisting of different arrangements of Geiger counters to take hourly recordings of four separate cosmic ray intensities. It was a tricky process since the fluctuations were not more than 1 per cent. And even to isolate these, the effects of meteorological conditions had to be cancelled out. Just before he left for Cambridge, Vikram had shifted the experiment to the Poona Observatory for a better understanding of the meteorological data. At PRL, the first step was to build on these preliminary investigations.

Following Vikram's instructions, his students made a series of Geiger counter telescopes using one-and-a-half-foot long cylinders and lead plates and set up a recording station to observe the variations. Simultaneously, K.R. Ramanathan, using his understanding of meteorological factors, prepared a format for measuring the atmospheric variables of the surface and upper atmosphere.

The project required a tremendous amount of patience and concentration, almost, as Vikram was fond of saying, like listening for music in a stormy sky. And at PRL, the obstructions were many and of a varied nature. One of Vikram's students, R.P. Kane, describes:

> Day in and day out recordings were made, first manually, later photographically, automatically. The rates did change during the course of the day, sometimes as much as 10–15 per cent, but these were all traced to loose wiring making uncertain connections which were frequently disturbed by the profusion of pigeons that inhabited the M.G. Science Institute and perched on the telescope, shaking it appreciably. The main power supply too was not much to boast about. The voltage varied widely and our established power supplies were no match. So the rates varied on all days except Sundays when the power load was less and the mains stability better.[17]

When the students pointed out the hazards, Vikram merely shrugged his shoulders and smiled. And the work continued. Over time, the instruments were improved. Geiger counter telescopes were lengthened to three feet. The pigeons and the erratic electric supply situation were tackled. Vikram went on to set up another station at a higher altitude in the hill station of Kodaikanal in 1949. And finally the data, the average of a few months' observations, revealed some sort of wavy, semi-diurnal structure of variations.

The same was proudly displayed to Bhabha when he came on a visit. He was not impressed. Like 'a curt sanitary inspector', Kane recounts, he asked for the error bars and remarked that he was not quite sure why a horizontal line should not be drawn through the points. Vikram, it seems, was undaunted and merely said, 'Yes, Homi, the errors are rather large. We will see what we can do about it.'

True to his word, Vikram set up super neutron monitors and large area scintillation telescopes at his recording stations to improve accuracy. In 1954, he also added a sea-level station at Trivandrum.

Despite his alleged curtness, Bhabha appears to have been sympathetic to his friend's efforts. By 1945 he had already set up the TIFR, which was to be the 'cradle' of India's atomic energy programme, and a year later the Atomic Energy Research Committee was formed under his chairmanship. In 1948, Nehru introduced the Atomic Energy Act before the Constituent Assembly and by 10 August 1948, a year after independence, the Atomic Energy Commission (AEC) was set up with a three-member committee. In 1954, Bhabha was made secretary of the newly formed DAE. As secretary of DAE he was to extend great support to Vikram.

While Vikram was occupied with setting up the first of his many institutions, Mrinalini had resumed dancing. After their return from England, at her husband's prodding, she had sent for dancers and musicians from Bangalore and formed a dance troupe. The notion of a Sarabhai daughter-in-law giving public dance performances raised eyebrows in conservative Ahmedabad but did not hinder her burgeoning career. In 1949, a local impresario watching her performance put in a word with the organizers of a festival in Paris; an invitation followed. Even though it was just for a day, Vikram persuaded her to go and accompanied her with baby Kartikeya and the nanny. The single performance turned into a tour and the press wrote delightedly about 'Les Bomb Atomique des Hindous'[18] and her husband, whom they called 'the Indian Joliot-Curie' a reference, of course, to Marie Curie's son-in-law, the co-discoverer of artificial radioactivity.

In Ahmedabad, the couple continued to live at The Retreat and were a part of the city's young, upper-class set which included Vikram's old friend Chinubhai Lalbhai and his pretty, sitar-playing wife, Prabha, Vikram's sister Leena and her husband, scions of local mill owners such as Navneet Shodhan, Harshvardhan Mangaldas and Baronet Udayan. There were dinner parties, treasure hunts and fancy dress events. There is a picture of Vikram at one of these dressed in a kabuki mask with gloves. Sometimes they would go to the Gymkhana Club. A few British families continued to live in the city and ensured that there were some evenings of ballroom dancing; Vikram and his friends excelled at the foxtrot and the waltz. At Makar Sankranti they would gather on the terraces of one of the sheth's houses in the pols and fly kites.

All this while, the fortunes of the Sarabhais had been multiplying rapidly. The year 1947 had been a great one for Calico Mills and Ambalal's winning streak showed no sign at all of abating. Since 1940 he had also been joined in the family business by Vikram's elder brother Gautam. Gautam had returned from Cambridge at the same time as Vikram with a tripos in philosophy and mathematics. One of the less loquacious of the Sarabhai siblings, Gautam was nevertheless full of innovative ideas which he applied to the business. He brought in a consultant from the famous London-based Tavistock Institute to suggest new management techniques and adopted Buckminster Fuller's design of a geodesic dome for the Calico Mills. Bharti, on her return from England, also began to take an interest in the family business.

Vikram, on the other hand, appeared to have been carving out his own independent path. Yet, there is reason to believe that his attention was not completely severed from the family's business interests. In Bangalore he had run into M.S. Sastry, a lecturer in chemistry at the Central College, at public events at the IISc. 'We got chatting,' Sastry recounts, 'and out of the blue he suggested I apply for a job with the Sarabhais in Ahmedabad. I followed his advice and got a job.'

If in his student days Vikram was keeping an eye open for talent to leverage the family business, then the possibility of his joining the family business was perhaps not as remote as it might have seemed. In 1950, he took the plunge by assuming chairmanship of the family's Baroda-based pharmaceutical concern, Sarabhai Chemicals. Indeed, the ease with which the mantle passed from Ambalal to Vikram and the purposefulness with which he was to expand the business and mesh it with his technological and nationalistic concerns suggest that some internal discussion in the family and in Vikram's own mind had preceded the decision.

His new assignment required Vikram to travel once a week to Baroda to visit the Sarabhai Chemicals plant. At the time there was no road link between Ahmedabad and Baroda and he would travel by train. On most trips he would ask one of his students from PRL to accompany him so that they could work on the way. On these trips, the students claim they came to know their supervisor better. For, between looking at the draft of a thesis or working on a paper, Vikram would talk freely. He would talk about 'his concern for the country and his strong desire to do something to change the pattern of our society'.[19] They also became familiar with his weakness for food, watching him battle with his temptation for boiled peanuts, *batata vadas* or whatever else the hawkers thrust through the iron grills.

On his way to the station from work he would make it a point to drop in on Mrinalini's cousin, Vinodini, who had moved to Baroda after her marriage. He would stop by 'every Thursday at four, probably because Mrinalini had told him not to leave Baroda without visiting us,' Vinodini recalls. Unused to keeping house, she was initially flustered by his visits (often with a group of companions) to her small flat. But Vikram, with his lack of self-consciousness and gregarious manner, she says, would soon 'put me at ease in my own house'.

❧

Till this point, it would seem as if Vikram was putting into place the blocks that would form the foundations of his life. He was married and had become father to two growing children. In PRL he had created a space that would be at the heart of all his endeavours. Though he was to come to be known far better for many of his other achievements, it was in scientific research, as he was to admit to anyone who asked, that he seemed to find his sustenance. In addition to PRL, he would travel every summer as visiting professor to the MIT in Boston.

Bruno Rossi's laboratory at MIT, at the cutting edge of X-ray astronomy and space plasma physics, was a magnet for physicists who had been drawn into defence work during the War and also for scientists from all over the world including France, Italy, China, Japan and Australia. Vikram and his students from PRL were frequent visitors and there was much reciprocity between the two institutions. 'I remember many springs [in Boston],' recalls Rossi's wife Nora, 'when with the blooming of the first flowers Vikram Sarabhai would arrive and brighten our days and evenings with his enthusiasm, vivacity and sex appeal.'[20]

Vikram's deep and unflagging loyalty to pure science did not, however, detract in the least from the seriousness with which he approached his other commitments. In fact, it seemed to enhance his ability to take up projects, work on them in a concentrated manner and leave them once they had reached a certain stage of maturity. The secret, according to him, was in establishing a firm foundation: 'The early beginnings of any institution are crucial, and the "culture" (or lack of it) brought by the first entrants plays a significant role in establishing norms, procedures, and practices.'[21]

Laying a firm foundation, however, was not an easy job. His experience with ATIRA showed him how hard it could be. In 1949, after being appointed honorary director of the proposed institution, Vikram set about hiring staff. He hired almost seventy people, most of them young like himself, with no experience of textile manufacturing. The decision to look for fresh, scientific minds rather than trained technologists was a conscious one though it is unlikely that he would have found people with exactly the right set of qualifications. The job skills required by an enterprise like ATIRA simply did not exist at the time and a certain degree of adaptation was called for. Someone with a basic degree in statistics, for example, became a spinning technologist; a physicist developed an expertise in textile manufacture and so on. M.M. Gharia, who joined ATIRA in the 1950s and went on to become its director, says, 'Vikrambhai caught them young and groomed them.'

By February 1952, a pilot mill had come up equipped with machinery and facilities for simulating the actual workings of a mill. Early studies threw up findings that suggested the possibility of solving problems seen as endemic till then by the industry. One study, for instance, confirmed that low productivity in spinning was due to inadequate maintenance of machinery and absence of process controls. Another proposed methods for reducing cotton wastage. Tamarind kernel powder, an agricultural waste product, was tested as a substitute for starch. Suggestions were made for improving ginning and weaving techniques, decreasing humidification costs, conserving energy and so on. An estimated Rs 20 crore, much of it foreign exchange, was to be saved by these innovations over the next two decades.

The pragmatic Ahmedabadi mill owners, cajoled by Kasturbhai into making an initial contribution of Rs 50 lakh, had reason to be pleased. But in actual fact they were upset.

At first glance their negative response seems inexplicable. The organization they had funded was promising them better returns and greater efficiency; what reason could they have had for complaining? The answer was simple. Ahmedabad's business community was used to functioning on instinct. What Vikram was urging them to do, as he explained at the association's first technological conference, was 'to adopt the scientific method as the basis of our operations...an approach which asks the questions "why and wherefore" at every stage...to understand the underlying rational basis for processes and operations rather than work on an empirical hit and miss basis'.[22]

For people used to operating on an empirical basis this was not good news. By seeking to understand and standardize practices, ATIRA was hitting out at tradition. And the sheths did not like it. In fact, as ATIRA's research workers began to assert their ideas, a trifle too aggressively, sections of the industry rose up in protest. The resentment surfaced at board meetings where Vikram's methods began to be openly attacked. It was probably unpleasant for Vikram to face the ire of his community elders and it probably helped that at this point he was too busy to let the experience weigh too heavily on him.

Most days, including Sundays, he was at PRL by seven in the morning. People living on his route claimed they could set their clocks by the progress of his small self-driven Standard down the street. On Mondays, in the late morning, he would meet with the senior staff at ATIRA. On other days, after checking on the ongoing construction activity for both the laboratory and the association, he would go to the white brick Calico building around noon. There, in his airy cabin with its coir matting, he would look into matters concerning Sarabhai Chemicals and meet visitors, most of whom were familiar with the multiple demands on his time and would come prepared for a long wait.

In the evening, Vikram would take a break to socialize or listen to music on the hi-fi equipment that he had himself made from parts picked up abroad. But soon after, he would return to PRL, often working late into the night. His students grew accustomed to hearing the sound of his chappals flapping or his low whistling as he raced up the stairs and to the sight of his lit window, a bright glow in the dark, cold night.

Mrinalini meanwhile was away much of the time performing in foreign countries, her troupe, Darpana, having made its mark

In 1950, the Government of India took Darpana to Egypt. In 1951, she was called to South America. Vikram travelled to Mexico City to be with her, taking along their son Kartikeya who was then four. The family stayed in a Spanish hacienda and spent time sightseeing. In 1954, Darpana toured thirty-eight cities in Europe. While she was gone, Vikram would sometimes invite himself to his friend Chinubhai's for lunch. 'Our house was close to Calico. Vikram would come over, stretch out on the floor and chat,' Chinubhai's wife Prabha recalls. 'He seemed lonely.'

Meanwhile, the impasse at ATIRA continued. Vikram remained undaunted as he continued to oversee operations and waited tactfully for the ruffled egos of his seniors to settle down. Kasturbhai Lalbhai's protective attitude helped boost his morale. But the going was not easy. After the owners, it was the turn of the technicians who worked in the mills and on whom ATIRA relied for information on working practices and procedures to turn hostile. Convinced that the association's staffers with their questionnaires were actually spies for the management, they refused to cooperate.

The resistance from various quarters must have been frustrating but it was not entirely unexpected. Vikram being familiar with the world of cotton mills had known to some extent what he would be up against and it was probably in anticipation that he had conceived of an industrial psychology division at ATIRA which would prove to be of enormous help in those early days. According to former director of ATIRA, P.C. Mehta, this division contributed greatly to the physical scientists' understanding of 'the human problems involved in introducing change'.[23]

One of the key figures in the industrial psychology division was a young woman called Kamla Chowdhry. Slim, dusky, with a hint of hardness in her attractive features, Kamla was a Punjabi khatri woman from a family of good standing in Lahore. In those days it was rare if not unheard of for an Indian woman to move alone to a strange city for work but Kamla's circumstances, to say the least, were unusual. She had been married to an ICS officer when, three months into the marriage, her husband, who was serving as a magistrate, was shot dead by a man on trial. A widow at twenty, Kamla had taken the unconventional decision to educate herself. Switching from mathematics, which she had studied at Calcutta University, to psychology, she had completed her master's and travelled to Michigan for a PhD.[24]

It was Kasturbhai Lalbhai, a family friend, who told her of a vacancy at the psychology department at ATIRA. Despite the admonition of her relatives, who felt she would never survive in a place like Ahmedabad, she applied and was selected to head the department. Almost immediately she was thrown into the unfamiliar world of textile workers and their problems. ATIRA's scientists were chafing at the bit and it was imperative that she try to procure the information that would help them conduct their studies as quickly as possible. She spent long hours talking to the millworkers, trying to allay their suspicions. Vikram often sent his driver and a flask of coffee for her safety and comfort.

Solicitude came naturally to Vikram. But in Kamla's case he had a greater responsibility for she was a good friend of Mrinalini's. Kamla and his wife had been students together at Santiniketan and had kept in touch. When Mrinalini and he were travelling back from a trip to the north, possibly the 1943 Kashmir expedition, Mrinalini had telephoned Kamla requesting her to meet them at Lahore station with milk and fruit. According to Kamla, Vikram, who was meeting her for the first time, had pulled her into the compartment on that occasion, locked the door and insisted that she accompany them up to Delhi. 'It was the kind of mad thing he would do,' Kamla recalls. 'We had to ask the stationmaster to send my driver home.'

Years later they were colleagues. And with their patient efforts and those of others at ATIRA, the barricades finally began to come down. The mill owners let go of their inhibitions and began to respond with more openness to the changes being suggested by the association. And the technicians slowly dropped their suspiciousness. Vikram's forbearance had paid off. From being a scapegoat for all parties, Vikram suddenly emerged as a binding force between the disparate parts: technicians, scientists, mill owners and the government. So appreciative were the technicians of his sensitivity towards their anxieties that in 1955 the Textile Technicians' Association asked him to be their president, the first time a mill owner had been given that honour.[25]

Significantly, his young team emerged from the experience with a fierce loyalty to the organization. Most people who started out with ATIRA were to stay till retirement, a pattern that was to be found in all of Vikram's enterprises. They also evinced a strong sense of belonging and pride in ATIRA, which probably flowed from Vikram's own attitude. Gharia remembers that when the new building came up—100,000 square feet divided into laboratories, offices, stores, precision workshops, an auditorium, a library, pilot mill and cafeteria, all centrally air-conditioned, a considerable novelty in those days—Vikram would not hesitate to rush up and 'physically yank away anyone careless enough to plant a foot on the freshly painted walls'.

But the loyalty was also inspired by Vikram's approach towards his staff. Just as he sought alliances with people more resourceful than himself, he was eager to share his ventures with his colleagues and co-workers. Time and again he would harp on the theme of 'mutuality' in all undertakings. Mutuality meant treating other human beings always as an end and never only as a means. Kamla, analysing his qualities as a manager, stresses his ability to communicate a sense of purpose and challenge; he encouraged the young to take risks while protecting them from others' destructiveness, an approach that resulted in strong teamwork and also inculcated 'a quality of integrity'[26] in those who worked with him.

Vikram's stress on hiring young people and creating an

appropriate working culture for them also had another aim. Padmanabh Joshi describes Vikram's 'three raised to the power of eighteen' theory which, in brief, works on the hypothesis that a piece of gossip narrated to three people and in turn repeated by each of them to three others and so on would in eighteen steps reach every Indian.[27] Joshi believes that he expected a similar process to occur in the institutions he set up: that a core group of motivated young individuals, constantly engaged in a process of regeneration, would try to enlarge the core group or generate more groups which would ultimately strengthen the core base of an institution and eventually, in Vikram's terminology, create a social impact the size of an 'avalanche'.

The ordeal of shepherding ATIRA in its early days had thrown Kamla and Vikram a great deal into each other's company. As a family friend she was often at the house, even helping with the children during Mrinalini's frequent absences. The growing familiarity coupled with the feverish excitement generated by the cranking up of a new enterprise had drawn them close. And soon it was clear to both that their relationship was becoming increasingly intimate.

In the absence of his own testimony it is hard to say what went through Vikram's mind at this point. From a conventional point of view it appeared that Mrinalini's focus on her career had left a void in their relationship which made him turn to Kamla. But the truth seems to be more complicated.

There is no doubt that Vikram had been captivated by Mrinalini in Bangalore. She believes, probably with reason, that it was her vivacity that helped him break out of the Sarabhai isolationist mould. As a newly married couple their relationship too had been intense. 'Do you remember,' Vikram wrote to her in an undated letter she quotes, 'for almost a year after we were married we could not sleep except in each other's arms?'[28]

As time went by, that carefree tenor seems to have slipped from the relationship. Under her lively exterior, Mrinalini revealed herself to be gripped by an inner loneliness that she traces back in interviews to her grief as a child at her father's death. The lifelong sense of desolation is described in a slim, rather melodramatic novel she scribbled when Vikram was working on his PhD at Cambridge. *This Alone Is True* is the story of a dancer who falls in love with a man but backs out of marriage when she realizes that his family will not allow her to dance. 'This was the solitariness from which there was no escaping, the unhappiness woven into each experience of joy, the echo of her childish terror.'[29]

Marriage, even to a man as encouraging and supportive as Vikram, did not seem to have lessened her fears. In her biography she refers to the eye injury she suffered soon after arriving in Ahmedabad as a 'decisive event' which, like her father's death, 'increased the sense of needing to depend on herself'. Her biographer Harriet Ronken Lynton is struck by the contradiction. 'She says things like this with evident earnestness, while at the same time declaring that Vikram was her rod and staff.'[30]

For his part, Vikram appears to have tried hard, too hard even, to make her happy. A detailed letter written to his parents in the mid-1940s about preparations for Mrinalini's performances suggests what could seem, to an objective reader, a stifling preoccupation with the minute details of arrangements for her shows.[31] Though she herself appeared to welcome rather than object to his interest, it is clear, from her biography, that he could not help lift her state of chronic despair.

In the circumstances it may seem then that Vikram was in need of companionship. At the same time it is interesting that he should have been drawn to Kamla. Those who knew Kamla well in those days describe her as being unpredictable. 'She could be excessively warm or cold, she could be extremely knowledgeable or diffident,' says Dwijendra Tripathi who was to be her colleague at the Indian Institute of Management, Ahmedabad (IIM-A). She had made her place in a man's world but, according to a friend, would insist on the privileges of femininity. She was moody as well, gay one day and despondent the next, a state many ascribed to her tragic past. An old woman, it was said, had predicted that she would always have 'a tear in her eyes'.[32]

Vikram, it seems, was drawn to intelligent women with a streak of morbidity. In an uncanny echo of Mrinalini's words, Kamla was to say of Vikram that 'his support made me strong' suggesting a need in him to adopt an attitude of benign guardianship in his personal relationships that was not dissimilar to his professional approach.

In all events, Vikram finally propositioned Kamla. According to her, it happened in a matter-of-fact way. He was going to Kashmir for a fortnight, he said, would she come with him? She claims she hesitated. A visiting professor from MIT was to accompany them. She talked it over with his wife and claims she was somehow convinced after the conversation that she should go. There had been little doubt as to her decision. 'It was not in my power not to do it [embark on the relationship],' she confesses.

4

TOWARDS A MODERN SENSIBILITY

On the evening of 1 May 1960 Ahmedabad wrapped itself in lights. People thronged public squares and government servants handed out sweets to children. They were celebrating the formation of the independent state of Gujarat. That morning, a colourful ceremony in Gandhi's former prayer ground in Ahmedabad had marked the region's formal break from the larger Bombay Presidency of which it had, till then, been a part. On the other side of the new dividing line, the Marathi-speaking population living in the remaining areas of the old Presidency was celebrating with equal gusto the birth of their own state, Maharashtra.

The creation of federal India had been under way through the 1950s. After independence, regional aspirations had come to the fore, of which language was probably the most powerful one. The break-up of the Bombay Presidency had been the culmination of a violent five-year struggle that had harped on and inflamed parochial, regional and linguistic sentiments in both regions. In fact, the largest cheers that day in Ahmedabad, capital of newly formed Gujarat, were for Ravi Shanker Maharaj.

The frail Sarvodaya leader had travelled to every village in the state during the course of the agitation, or so it was said. In his victory speech that summer morning he reiterated his message that Indians still felt like 'aliens' in their own country because English was the language of the courts, education and the state. The new state government, he hoped, would endeavour to introduce a true 'people's democracy' by adopting Gujarati as the language of state administration.[1]

The strains of this snowballing regional agitation did not appear to greatly affect the lives of Ahmedabad's elite. In fact, at a time when Gujarat's political leaders and activists were demanding a reassertion of ethnicity, the Ahmedabadi sheths, from behind their high walls, appeared to be reaching out to more distant influences. By then, many among the younger generation of mill owners, or 'managing agents' as they were called, were venturing out to acquire an education abroad, in England or more commonly in the United States. Their lifestyles reflected a mixed influence of the East and the West. Many of the professional technicians working in their companies came from outside the region where a specialization in engineering and mechanics was more easily available. And at conferences such as those organized by ATIRA—Vikram had voluntarily relinquished the directorship in 1956 but was still involved in the institution's public activities—the emphasis was on bringing visitors from outside to share their knowledge.

How genuine though was this opening up among the sheths? Two distinguished gentlemen who visited Ahmedabad in the late 1950s and early 1960s offer some clues. Prakash Tandon, who was later to become the first Indian to head the multinational Unilever's Indian operations, was a senior executive with the company and one of about a hundred guests to be invited from outside the city to ATIRA's annual conference in 1957, an experience he recounts vividly in his autobiography:

> The conference progressed like all conferences in India I have seen, except that this one tried all things. There were keynote speeches, votes of thanks, talks, group discussions on the stage,

> seminars in separate rooms, presentations by the seminar leaders, open discussions, a plenary session, a summing up; but in its rhythm it had a euphonic quality in which the views expressed were all in complete accord.... Speeches were made with unction on how the man, worker and manager should be understood and made to feel wanted, delegated, consulted and promoted. The unction was transparently sincere, but I could not help wondering how much of it was practised; for in such a highly structured and stratified society, democratic management could hardly have arrived except in theory...there had been talking for its own sake, an exercise in the statement of the desirable.[2]

In the evenings, after the deliberations, the visitors were invited to the homes of each of the elders in turn. In their beautiful homes, Tandon records, the guests were served spicy and sweet non-alcoholic drinks, soup in teacups, and Indian and Continental food on silver and Royal Doulton china. They were sent home promptly by nine. 'I was puzzled by all this hospitality,' Tandon confesses, 'showered on strangers with faultless impersonality, part of the pattern of self-imposed duty.'

A few years later, Erik Erikson visited Ahmedabad. He came first in 1962, to attend an ATIRA conference, and returned a year later to research a book on Gandhi's early political experiments focusing largely on the textile strike in 1918. On both trips he stayed with the Sarabhais. At one point during their stay, his wife Joan contracted dysentery, a crisis that caused a group consisting of half a dozen members of the host family, the medical school's chief of internal medicine, the head doctor of the mills and the chief secretary of the state of Gujarat to descend upon the house they had been put up in at The Retreat.

Erikson describes with a hint of baffled amusement how they proceeded to discuss the matter in Gujarati 'in an urgent and ominous way'. After perfunctorily seeking his consent to their decision to hospitalize the invalid, Sarla drove off with three servants to clean and prepare a hospital room with flowers and fresh bed sheets. After a while, he writes, Sarla reappeared in her limousine 'to pack Joan off'.[3]

Both accounts provide a perceptive and uncommon insight, uncommon both in terms of access and the objectivity of perspective, into the closed world of the Ahmedabadi elite, the environment that had nourished and sustained Vikram till that point. What both visitors—Prakash Tandon with his robust Punjabi–corporate perspective and Erik Erikson with his sharply honed analytical faculties—seemed to have sensed is a certain turgidity of atmosphere. The Ahmedabadi elite was hospitable, in fact overly so. As Tandon points out, hospitality was extended freely, with no expectation of anything in return, and Erikson's experience was one of extreme solicitude. And yet this was just half the story.

Vikram's experience at ATIRA had already shown that the Ahmedabadi entrepreneur, though quick to make the gesture, was suspicious and had to be persuaded to change. The experiences of Tandon and Erikson, however, bring to the fore more forcefully another feature, namely, the unconsciously patronizing attitude of the rich mill owners. It invited the outsider in and yet made him feel ill at ease.

In the case of the Sarabhais this sensation was probably sharpened by the stated loftiness of their aims. Ambalal and Sarla, remarkable individuals both, had created an island in their pursuit of perfection. Erikson, for instance, notes how, despite the exquisite simplicity of their dress (he in the finest raw silk, she in khadi) and the deference shown to them by high officials at public functions, they seemed 'somewhat isolated from their peers'. The impression he receives is of a 'stubborn and somewhat self-righteous people made tolerant however by what they themselves have suffered from the orthodoxies of their respective castes and their social milieus'.[4]

There are many reasons to believe that Vikram was not free of these particular family traits. There is a trace of unction, for example, in the ease with which at the tender age of twenty-three, following his Kashmir expedition, he urged scientists and government scientific departments to cooperate in setting up a permanent high-altitude laboratory in the Himalayas.[5]

Apart from his staggering self-assurance, there was his early maturity, his youthful preoccupation with philosophy and his need to convert his ideas into institutions. There was also his compulsive need to record in detail his non-scientific experiments and make theories of the same. This last could be said to flow from his training as a scientist. But, when considered with other factors, it seems to suggest that he was very clearly persuaded of an almost paternal role for himself with regard not just to his family but all the people he interacted with, the nation and then humanity as a whole.

The characteristic was extremely evident in his approach to Mrinalini's career, for instance. At one level he could be seen as an extremely supportive husband to a working woman. But at another level he had managed to take over the activity itself, making it part of a larger project, carrying responsibilities and a social function that she had never envisaged. This much is clear from the rather weighty answer he gave to the BBC in response to a question on the formation of Darpana. 'In all of north India and western India there has been a rather mixed influence on our cultural life through many different invasions....' he explained. 'I think south Indian music and dance has, to people like me, a purity which is quite remarkable. It is also pursued with a seriousness which is very appealing.... I thought...if indeed one could get an outstanding group of dancers and musicians with the south Indian traditions [to] come and be transplanted in the soil of Gujarat and that if one did this seriously enough and long enough, in fact, over a generation or so, a whole group of young girls and, hopefully, boys would grow up with this tradition and then become serious performing artistes themselves, then one had perhaps contributed something to this enrichment of the artistic and cultural life of north India.'[6]

Vikram's attentiveness to Mrinalini's career, in the early days at least, smacked of excess and brings to mind an aspect of Ambalal's personality seen, for instance, in his exaggeratedly serious view of the promise he had made to Vikram in his childhood about purchasing a toy in England. But, however prone Vikram may have been to this sort of behaviour, he seemed, from his latter-day personality, to have succeeded in weaning himself away from it. All those who knew him in later life testify that he was the least pompous, least self-righteous and least ponderous of men. And in part he may have helped bring about this transition by doing something fairly dramatic in 1953, something that indicated a repudiation to some extent of the attitudes that had seemed natural to his family. He moved out of The Retreat.

There were, of course, many practical reasons for the move. Mrinalini had never felt entirely at ease there and it was possible that Vikram too was feeling constricted by its rules. Prabha Lalbhai, for instance, recalls Vikram having to open up various storeroom locks just to provide a late-night coffee for his friends. At the same time, it is significant that Vikram did not build himself an independent house in the neighbourhood or even on the estate itself as many of his siblings did. In fact, of the eight, he would be the only one, except for Leena who married and moved into a home of similar if not greater affluence than her own, to set up an independent home in Ahmedabad outside the walls of The Retreat.

The fact that Vikram not only moved out of his family mansion but chose to put a considerable geographical distance between his old life and his new one lends itself to another interpretation. It is possible to read his move as a deliberate exit from the cloistered world of Ahmedabad's privileged, a determined shrugging off of the oppressive vestiges of feudalistic attitudes. For it was across the Sabarmati, far away from the sprawling, palatial mansions of Shahibaug and the close-set pols of the fortified city that he was to plant his flag. It was here, amidst the broad avenues and as yet unbuilt spaces, that he was to scatter his vast dreams in the shape of immense building blocks that would in time come to represent the modern face of the city.

If indeed this was so, it was still not a case of outright rebellion. For, Vikram did not ally himself with any opposing group of people, especially not the political movement that was building up for the creation of an ethnically distinct Gujarat, for instance. In fact, the inveterate reconciler of contradictions that he was, Vikram was attempting to forge a new class entirely. It was a professionally trained, salaried class, a kind of social segment that did not take root easily in the entrepreneurial, feudal Ahmedabadi soil.

The creation of this new class was tied in (as everything Vikram did invariably would be) with a social and national purpose. He had already made a beginning using science and technology as a vehicle; now he was on the verge of giving shape to another one of his pet interests: management.

According to the former director of IIM-A, Jahar Saha, Vikram fervently believed that management techniques could be used for the betterment of society. A former colleague, M.R. Kurup, confirms this view: '[Vikram] felt [it was] the lack of able managers that had brought about the failure of public enterprises.'[7]

In India, however, the concept of professional management was little known, not just in public enterprises but even in industry. Most Indian businesses were family owned and passed on from father to sons. Though the scions of business families were beginning to travel abroad in quest of a management degree, the concept of formal management education was not a familiar one in the country.

Vikram decided to bring about a change. In 1956, acting again in tandem with Kasturbhai Lalbhai, he started the Ahmedabad Management Association (AMA) to conduct research and provide training to employees of companies. From a small room in a bank building, the AMA was to grow into a full-fledged institution. It was also to be the precursor for the ambitious IIM-A.

In the 1950s though, the IIM-A was little more than a vague proposal. The Ford Foundation, set up as an 'independent, non-profit, non-governmental organization' (a description questioned by some who believed the organization acted as a cultural arm of the US government) by Henry Ford in 1936, had mooted the idea of setting up two management institutes in the country. Vikram, apparently unruffled by Ford's ambiguous credentials and spotting a perfect opportunity to put his belief in the possibilities of professional management into practice, spoke to his firm ally, Kasturbhai Lalbhai, and Jivraj Mehta, soon to be the first chief minister of independent Gujarat. With their support he began to campaign avidly for bringing one of the management institutes to Ahmedabad.

The characteristics of the entity that Vikram was pushing were modern, professional and cosmopolitan. He had already made some progress in this direction by insisting on a merit-based selection criteria for employment at PRL and ATIRA. Thanks to this, and much to the dismay of chauvinistic elements in the state, the two institutions were drawing people from all over the country. But Vikram was not content with bringing the country to Ahmedabad; he seemed to be intent on opening up the world to his peers.

S. Ramaseshan, referring to the unusually strong inclination both Homi Bhabha and Vikram displayed for setting up public institutions, speculated that the fact that they had been born with a silver spoon perhaps engendered the urge to 'try and bring others to their level'. Bhabha at the time had persuaded top-class scientists, such as the maverick Paul Dirac, to visit India.

Vikram, like Bhabha, was also well connected with the international scientific community. He was secretary of the

International Institute Subcommittee on Cosmic Ray Intensity Variations and a member of the Cosmic Ray Commission of the International Union of Pure and Applied Physics. Apart from Bruno Rossi, he was friends with several scientists like James Van Allen, soon to go down in history as the discoverer of the 'Van Allen belts', the two belts of radiation girdling the earth, Bertrand Goldschmidt who was to help found France's Atomic Energy Commission, Sydney Chapman, P.M.S. Blackett and Victor Neher. Distinguished scientists such as Philip Morrison, Alexander J. Dessler, Donald A. Glaser, Linus Pauling, Y. Sekido, and Maurice M. Shapiro visited PRL. In 1951 or 1952, the Joliot–Curie couple had also come to PRL and were guests at The Retreat.

Over the years, Vikram was to display a strong faith in international collaboration. He would encourage students and colleagues in his various institutions, often making the arrangements himself, to acquire training or attend seminars abroad and represent their country at global meets. These actions bore fruit as is evident from the testimonies of various PRL alumni including Harjit S. Ahluwalia who writes of an extremely significant model he developed in collaboration with Dessler.[8] In the late 1950s, however, an opportunity close to Vikram's persuasion presented itself of its own accord: the announcement of the International Geophysical Year (IGY).

The IGY, starting July 1957, was one of the most eagerly anticipated events in the scientific calendar of the time. The event had come up in response to the growing worldwide interest in the possibility of using satellites for scientific exploration. The idea was to initiate an internationally concerted study of the earth's atmosphere and oceans to prepare for a time, not so far away, when man could actually probe space. The objective—unusual, given the secrecy and chauvinism sparked off by the war and the competition soon to emerge over space between the US and the USSR—was the shared search for knowledge. The kind of goodwill and cooperation it sparked off in the international scientific community would be unparalleled for years to come.

Given its scientific focus and Vikram's views on international collaboration, it was to be expected that PRL would have been an eager participant in the IGY. In fact, PRL's director, Dr K.R. Ramanathan, an active member of the national committee of the International Union of Scientific Committees, was picked by the Indian National Science Academy to head the Indian National Committee for the IGY.

The preparations had started a few years before. Two of Vikram's students, N.W. Nerurkar and Bhavsar had begun to develop a cubical meson telescope. Professor Victor Neher of CALTECH, California, came as visiting professor for a year and with PRL's Satya Prakash worked on components for a neutron monitor. Upendra Desai built the east–west telescopes which U.R. Rao would operate during the IGY.

George Clark, a member of Bruno Rossi's team, came to India in 1955-56 to observe the behaviour of cosmic showers near the equator. Vikram took George to the southern hill station of Kodaikanal where one of his most senior students, E.V. Chitnis, had collected a vast amount of data. Chitnis's findings were so large they would not fit even in the powerful Russian computer at the Indian Statistical Institute (ISI) in Calcutta. Vikram helped him take the data to MIT where they had the latest IBM, a tube version which occupied an entire basement. 'It was not much better,' Chitnis recalls wryly. 'It broke down all the time.'

As part of the IGY, PRL joined hands with MIT and a Japanese scientific contingent to set up a giant meson monitor at a high-altitude laboratory in Chacaltaya, Bolivia. By then the data that PRL had collected from its chain of cosmic stations in India had become part of the global network. And Vikram's proposal for a worldwide study of cosmic ray variations with standardized equipment was included in the programme of the IGY. It was a heady time for the Ahmedabad-based research centre. And at a symposium on cosmic rays held at the TIFR on 23 February 1958, Vikram proudly reported on the contribution made by his laboratory to the Cosmic Ray Programme of the IGY.

Vikram's own research programme on cosmic ray variations and the experiments set up by his students at PRL as part of it, meanwhile, continued their course. A new development around the mid to late 1950s was the idea, proposed by Eugen N. Parker and others, of the presence of a solar wind in interplanetary space.

Parker was a professor at the University of Chicago. As a frequent visitor to the university—Vikram went to Chicago often to meet C.V. Raman's nephew, the brilliant astrophysicist, Subramanyan Chandrasekhar, and to keep himself abreast of cosmic ray studies being conducted there—Vikram had probably come into contact with Parker. He saw merit in the latter's hypothesis—his handwritten notes between 1965 and 1971 at the Vikram Sarabhai Archives in Ahmedabad make repeated references to Parker, solar wind and his theory—and set up experiments to pursue this new line of thought.

In a tribute to Vikram and his 'significant contribution' to the study of cosmic ray intensity variations, P.M.S. Blackett was to refer specifically, among other things, to his 'early appreciation of the importance of the off-eliptic properties of the solar wind and interplanetary magnetic field for the 11 years solar modulation process and of the role of gradients in the cosmic ray density perpendicular to the elliptic plane in the interpretation of the solar daily variation.'[9]

Between setting up experiments and attending international conferences on cosmic rays, Vikram was by now thoroughly involved in the running of the company that had been allotted to him from the family kitty. Sarabhai Chemicals, a relatively new concern for the Sarabhai Group started up in the mid-1940s, had come about because the then ruler of Baroda, in a bid to push industrial activity in his town, had offered industrialists large swathes of barren land at concessional rates. Ambalal, who was one of those approached, had acquired fifty acres with the notion of setting up a manufacturing unit for health care products.

The pharmaceutical industry in India was not very well developed at the time. The country did not have the requisite technological expertise and some form of collaboration with an international manufacturer was unavoidable. Kasturbhai Lalbhai who entered the business around the same time had formed a joint venture with the American Lederle Laboratories. The Sarabhais had opted for a technical collaboration with the New York-based E.R. Squibb & Sons. At the time Vikram took over as chairman, Sarabhai Chemicals was a small-sized concern with just a few simple formulations and some bulk pharmaceutical chemicals on its list.

Ambalal in his time had been a pioneering businessman, introducing new technologies and work styles to business. Calico, for instance, according to V. Gangadhar, an Ahmedabad-based journalist who had worked in its shares and purchase department for a while, was the best professionally administered mill with 'hardly any interference from the family'. But though many of Ambalal's initiatives were praised for their progressiveness, the textile magnate maintained a certain divide between his business and his social concerns. Despite his admiration for Gandhi and the involvement of the women in his household with the freedom movement, he was likely to be less equivocal about his sympathies where business was concerned.

Vikram had achieved a far greater integration of potentially contradictory impulses. It was a fact commented upon by his family members in different ways. Mrinalini observed that unlike most people 'who have two faces, private and public', Vikram 'had only one'. Kartikeya maintains that Vikram's motives, in whatever he did, were the 'same'. A look at Vikram's jottings in the late 1960s provides further proof of this attribute. The points on paper are the same as those made in his speeches. There are no asides, no private reflections, and minimal cancellations or doodles, revealing an unusually clear and focused mind.

There was no doubt that Vikram had inherited his ancestors' sense of enterprise and the financial canniness for which his community was fabled, leading Ashis Nandy to describe him as a 'bania'. His practical mind was to become evident time and again, in the detailed cost–benefit calculations he would make or the forthright way he would lay out the money angle to job interviewees.

But just as he carried pragmatism to institutions of research, technology and education, he brought to business a spirit of innovation and patriotism. In short, Vikram's approach to business was no different from his approach to his other activities.

M.S. Sastry, Vikram's acquaintance from Bangalore who had moved from Calico Mills, remembers Vikram's first day at work at Sarabhai Chemicals. 'He was walking around touching things as he went by, checking for cleanliness. "It is a pharma unit, we must have cleanliness," he said. Then we had a meeting and he left.' But, with a preparedness that was to become all too familiar, Vikram, it became clear, had already mapped out a blueprint for his new charge. In 1951, K.J. Divatia, a US-trained chemist, interviewed with the young chairman for a job at Sarabhai Chemicals. 'He told me, "I want to set up a basic industry from scratch."'

The new home Vikram and Mrinalini moved to was on the outskirts of Ahmedabad where the city met the rural hinterland.

In those days Usmanpura was little more than a village with a cluster of hutments, the faint occasional tinkle of a cow bell and smoke rising from dung fires. The plot they found, high on the banks of the Sabarmati, was dirty and ridden with garbage. But there was something about it—the breeze fanning up from the river perhaps, or the gentle, sleepy air of the surroundings—that reminded them of Premalaya, the house they had occupied in Malleswaram, and they settled upon it.

Vikram asked his youngest sister, Gira, who had just returned after an apprenticeship with the American architect Frank Lloyd Wright, to design the new house. The name they had picked for it was Chidambaram, so called after one of Shiva's five dance halls. There was nothing traditional about it though. The house Gira designed had a contemporary feel to it with large windows on either side giving a view of the lawns and the river. The interiors were furnished in an eclectic manner with low Scandinavian-style chairs and bookshelves, large, white floor cushions, and an American-style dining section. 'Raw silk curtains, abstract paintings, modern European ceramics and glassware, Japanese drawings of lobsters and horses, Indian rural pottery and woodwork, a sitar next to a hi-fi. Bach, Bismillah Khan and *West Side Story*,' was how one visitor described it.[10]

In the meantime, Vikram continued making his weekly trips to the plant in Baroda. At some point, a motorable road had come up between the two cities, an event that cheered him considerably. Vinodini Mayor remembers her doorbell ringing early one morning and Vikram charging in excitedly, shouting, 'I came by car! I came by car!'

He brought the same enthusiasm to bear upon his work. At Sarabhai Chemicals, his claim of wanting to build an industry from scratch had caught the imagination of its young professionals. Despite the fact that subsidiaries of multinational pharmaceutical giants were considered good for little more than packaging and marketing the imported products, men like Divatia and M.S. Sastry had no difficulty believing Vikram. 'He was so clear-headed about it from day one,' Divatia explains.

Not everybody was so easily swayed, however. The elders in the company were miffed with the change of guard from Ambalal to an untried thirty-one-year-old and their resistance threatened to pose a major stumbling block to Vikram's ambitious blueprint. There were other areas of potential conflict as well, for example, relationships with foreign collaborators and the government, which was a minefield of restrictions and red tape. Vikram had already proven his ability to handle conflict with ATIRA. But a research institution run with public funds was not the same thing as a self-owned business enterprise. And given Vikram's keen interest in management as an academic discipline, it is interesting to see how he approached the challenges in his own company.

In the first few years his focus was on managing people. In those days the pharmaceutical business comprised family-managed companies such as Ranbaxy, Cadila and Cipla, and foreign-controlled multinationals like Glaxo and Pfizer. Against this backdrop, Vikram, no doubt with Ambalal's approval, decided to turn Sarabhai Chemicals into a professionally managed company. He converted the operating and service activities into independent profit centres and put them under various chief executives. The CEOs were to report to Vikram as chairman but he also appointed a supervisory board consisting of the company's senior personnel. By giving the board the authority to direct and coordinate the company's affairs, Vikram successfully dissipated resentment from his elders.

With his collaborators he was charming. So charming that he was greeted with flowers on his frequent trips to New York (J.R. Geigy, a Swiss company he was to sign an agreement with later, even offered him two top-of-the-line Mercedes Benzes which he had to turn down because of Indian governmental restrictions). It helped perhaps that Squibb shared some of his preoccupations, such as a near manic obsession with hygiene.

The story goes that Dr Squibb personally signed each bottle that left the company gates. Vikram was apparently prone to quibbling over some of Squibb's regulations ('why two days for housekeeping, why not a day and a half?'[11]) but gave the experts sent by the company his full backing.

In 1956, Vikram entered into a collaboration with J.R. Geigy for making pharmaceuticals and dyes. Geigy were also the makers of the whitening agent Tinopol, which proved to be a huge hit, blazing a trail through India on the back of a memorably shrill jingle. Two years later, Sarabhai Chemicals also put up a joint venture with E. Merck of Darmstadt, Germany, for the manufacture of Vitamin C. These two deals made the Sarabhais pioneers in the local manufacture of bulk drugs and started the process of backward integration that Vikram had committed himself to.

Even though the company was expanding rapidly, Vikram spent no more than a day a week in Baroda, occasionally calling his executives over to Ahmedabad. In a speech some years later on the 'Control and Management of Public Sector Enterprises'[12] he was to emphasize the distinction between 'abdication of authority' and 'delegation' and bemoan the lack of self-discipline in this regard on the part of those in a position of authority.

Vikram's preferred source of control was information. According to his former colleagues, he read every page of the voluminous reports sent to him by the company CEOs and put whole days aside for board meetings. Nothing escaped his eye. M.R. Raman, former production director of Sarabhai Chemicals, recalls travelling to Bombay with a colleague to confabulate over a serious problem. Vikram who was with them on the overnight train started up some idle chit-chat about brands of toothpaste and the electric toothbrush that had just been introduced in the United States. 'His light-heartedness did not throw me off-guard,' writes Raman. 'As expected, the very next moment he turned into a one-man court-martial which continued for hours in Bombay.'[13]

Intimidating though his attentiveness could be, Vikram's staff welcomed it. 'It was important,' Sastry claims, 'for us to get Vikrambhai's reactions.'

One of the reasons why Vikram was to be successful in all his enterprises despite their variety and the geographical distances separating them was his ability to connect with people. Words like 'trust', 'mutuality' and 'collaboration' have often been used to describe Vikram's attitude towards professional relationships. The high-sounding phrases do not adequately convey the very human warmth he was capable of demonstrating. Those who came in contact with him over the years were to have varying assessments of his abilities in various spheres. But there was no doubt about the potency of his charm.

'He would just embrace you!' is how a fellow scientist described it.[14] Dwijendra Tripathi who was to join the IIM-A claimed, 'I did not rate him highly as an administrator. But he really knew how to build people. He had the unparalleled ability to make you feel at home in his company.' Kamla observed that one came away from a meeting with him feeling 'somewhat more whole, somewhat more responsible, and somewhat more charitable to others'.[15]

Those who had professional dealings with Ambalal describe him as an affable man who would not be above eating lunch at the Calico café and offering unsolicited advice to his subordinates about calorie content. Vikram's charm, however, was of a far more intense quality. There are stories of former staffers putting his picture in their lockers or, as Sastry did when he retired after decades of service, taking a portrait of Vikram home to put up in his drawing room. Vikram's affection also extended to a seemingly limitless number of people.

He would greet everybody, it was said, from the sweeper to the most senior executive with extreme friendliness. Even his students at PRL noted that he would visit the workers in the workshop before going up to his office. He would display a touching concern for people's personal difficulties. He once had an employee's quarters repainted to alleviate his spouse's allergy and repeatedly offered to help a senior colleague procure a foreign posting to avail of medical treatment for his ailing child. Such large-hearted gestures were frequent and came naturally to him but there was a kindness and sensitivity evident even in his mundane, day-to-day dealings with people.

He would come when invited by his staffers to their children's birthday parties or their amateur musical recitals. Even in summoning his subordinates to his office, the latter claim, there would be a request and a courtesy. 'People who are higher up in the hierarchy tend to assume their needs are greater than those of others. He really did not see it that way. For him intrinsically people were people and that really governed the way he dealt with organizations,' says his son, Kartikeya.

He was to spell out his views in a talk some years later: 'One wants permissive individuals who do not have a compelling need to reassure themselves that they are leaders through issuing instructions to others; rather, they set an example through their own creativity, love of nature and dedication to what one may call the "scientific method".'[16]

Vikram's affectionate humility can be attributed to the values ingrained in childhood and his extraordinarily compassionate nature. But it is likely that he was also strongly influenced in this regard by his understanding of science. Science at a theoretical level had taught him about the interdependence of all organisms; at the practical level he would have learnt it was critical. As Werner Von Braun was to say in an interview in the *New York Times* in October 1957, 'So many things in modern science have become so wide in scope, so intricate that more and more it takes groups of experts to do the work.'

Vikram seemed to have grasped early in life that he would always need the support and cooperation of large numbers of people, all kinds of people, including the lowly craftsmen who helped make the instruments used by him and his colleagues for their scientific experiments. In fact, in those days when instruments were made mostly by hand, good craftsmen were a precious asset: Khimjibhai Mistry, the carpenter who had helped Vikram build a steam engine as a child, found a job at PRL. Another craftsman, a glass-blower from Ahmedabad, was sent to Manchester for training and proved so good that the laboratory wanted to keep him back.

'Indians tend to be individualistic. [Vikram] was unusual in the sense that he built teams,' claims former Prime Minister I.K. Gujral, who interacted with Vikram in the late 1960s. Vikram's approach was no doubt rare and hence shrouded in an aura of nobility; it could be argued, however, that like a good vania he was selecting the most practical course open to him in the achievement of his ambitious and multiple goals.

Apart from nurturing people at all levels, Vikram had also learnt from two men whose management styles he admired—Ambalal and Bhabha—that parts of an institution could be built around certain talented individuals. Ambalal, for instance, while interviewing Prabhash Kumar Mukherjee, a bright postgraduate from Calcutta's famed Presidency College, told him that he aimed to hire 'gems'. Bhabha was known to start a whole new department at TIFR if a brilliant scientist with a particular specialization approached him for a position. When D.V.N. Sarma, a chain-smoking statistician at ATIRA, came to Vikram some time in the late 1950s and said he was bored with his job, the latter came up with an innovative solution: the Operations Research Group (ORG), the country's first market research agency.

Bearing the hallmarks of Vikram's penchant for modest beginnings, the fledgling company started by feeding data on salaries and turnover of the Sarabhai enterprises into its only asset, an IBM. Inspired by the store audits he had seen abroad, Vikram then suggested that ORG start studying consumer trends for the company's products. He allocated an initial budget of Rs 1500 for six months and suggested that salesmen from Swastik, the Sarabhais' Bombay-based oil mill (which he had taken over in 1957 and where he had launched pioneering processes for extracting oil from oilseeds and manufacturing synthetic detergents), do the rounds of stores tracking sales. Once the experiment proved successful it would be extended all over the country, he said.

ORG was to flourish. But not everything Vikram attempted was successful. In fact, one of the initiatives closest to his heart proved a bit of a let-down. The initiative was a slimming food supplement called Limical based on the American Metacal. Fervent food faddist that he was, Vikram was certain it would fly off the shelves and was extremely disappointed when it failed to meet his expectations. He did not give up trying to sell it though. Friends and relatives amusedly recall him imbibing spoonfuls of it every morning and making vain efforts to persuade others at the breakfast table to try it.

Vikram was obsessive about watching his weight. He rose daily, at the crack of dawn. He performed twelve suryanamaskars in the early light and swam as often as he could. At home, despite the varied fare that graced the Sarabhai table—appams, dal, soups—he stuck to a sparse diet of a single roti with papad, yoghurt, mango pickle and salads which he liked to toss himself. Family members, however, remember him constantly nibbling. 'He would pick up morsels from my plate saying, "not my plate, not my calorie",' laughs his daughter Mallika.

Pictures of Vikram around 1956 show a gradual physical transformation. His figure has filled out and though there is no trace of the flabbiness he was so vigilant about, the waif-like figure has given way to a manly frame. There is a distinctly mature and vigorous air about him as he approaches his forties. And deep and plentiful laughter lines around his eyes. 'He was always optimistic, always willing to entertain any dream. Even if a child said he wanted to swim some river, Vikram would immediately start figuring out ways in which it could be done,' says Mrinalini.

Friends remember him as a cheerful person given to suddenly breaking into song. The K.L. Saigal hit from *Street Singer*, 'Babul mora', was one of his favourites as was a nonsensical Bengali ditty. He was an inveterate whistler. One of Mallika's childhood memories is of marching up and down the carpet with her father behind her whistling the tune from *The Bridge on the River Kwai.*

By this time he was more or less a full-time single parent. Mrinalini was away continuously. There were trips to Ceylon and South-east Asia, partly arranged by the Indian government. From her biography it appears that much of this travelling involved bad accommodation and shoestring budgets. There were complaints from the troupe. And Mrinalini was not in the best of health. Regardless, Darpana went on an extended trip to Europe.

Vikram wrote regularly, letters of encouragement that also filled her in with details about Mallika's tonsillitis and Kartikeya's studies. 'The lawn is sprouting—with a light shade of green—like Kartik's beard before he shaved. Lots of love and xxx—Viki,' said one.[17] In September 1959, he wrote about the children jumping all over him and insisting on sleeping in his bed at night. Parenting was clearly a full-time responsibility, for two months later he exclaimed in another letter: 'Vikram Sarabhai went shopping with the children at 4 p.m. on a working day.'[18] Another went: 'We are really missing you but in a nice way, but not pining way, so please try to be relaxed and peaceful and a prima donna.... I go on wishing so much, almost praying in my way, that this tour should be satisfying to you.'[19]

Chidambaram was now alive with the sounds of activity. There were two, sometimes three, cars in the driveway, a white Sunbeam Talbot with red upholstery, a green Bantam and a Dodge. Playing hide and seek between them were Vikram's faithful shadow, a hairy dog called Sparku, and a litter of Siamese cats Vikram had brought back with him from Baroda for Mallika. Kartikeya and his friends ran amuck on the lawns; Navroz Contractor recalls breaking a glass pane while playing 'golf' in the garden. 'Vikrambhai came in just then and saw it but he never said a word.'

The year 1959 was an eventful one for Ahmedabad. Distinguished people came calling. The Duke of Edinburgh, Prince Philip, came at the invitation of the Ahmedabad Management Association. Mrinalini rose to the occasion by organizing a wedding-style feast for the visiting royal. The Rockefellers, Blanchette and John Rockefeller III, also came by around this time. Mrinalini it appears was anxious that Chidambaram would seem too modest for their wealthy American friends and suggested putting them up at The Retreat till Vikram said firmly: 'Mrinal, they are coming to see us and will accept us as we are.'[20]

It was a picture of perfect domestic felicity and yet a shadow hovered over it, the shadow of the other woman.

Disproving her family's predictions that she would not last in Ahmedabad, Kamla had not gone anywhere. If anything she had made herself even more at home in the once alien city. She had built herself a house by the river and called it Avantika, the name of the capital of the ancient warrior king Vikramaditya. The relationship between Vikram and Kamla had continued and had even been strengthened by Vikram's growing interest in professional management, Kamla's area of specialization.

'Vikram and Kamla fitted perfectly like the tenons and mortises of a dovetail,' writes Prakash Tandon of their relationship. 'He spoke freely and was projective; she was slow and had to carefully define her thoughts before she expressed them and then only hesitatingly, withdrawing from each answer. He could think on his feet while her voice dropped when faced with an audience of more than two. He was always advancing while she was withdrawing. She had to feel wholly at ease, almost at a level of intimacy, before she would project; he was at home anywhere. I saw Vikram and Kamla together at conferences and there appeared always a perfect rapport between them professionally, an aura of deep relationship…. Their conversation was always around human relations and management, seldom on current affairs or people, except about their colleagues and men in their fields.'[21]

Neither she nor Vikram made any attempt to hide their relationship. He would come and go freely between the two houses. 'Everybody knew, but nobody would talk about it,' says an old Ahmedabadi.

One of the reasons the affair raised few eyebrows was probably because of the Sarabhais' reputation for eccentricity and permissiveness. Vikram's aunt Ansuya had had a close relationship with her colleague, labour leader Shankerlal Banker, while Vikram's brother Gautam and his partner Kamlini Khatau were known to hold unconventional views on marriage.[22] Within the Sarabhai fold the family motto of doing 'whatever seemed right' according to one's heart prevailed. 'Everything was allowed,' claims a family member. 'There was an incredible amount of broad-mindedness. But there was also an element of indifference in the openness.'

The unspoken acceptance created a strange ambience for the relationship between Vikram and Kamla and that between the two and Mrinalini. Vikram was not given to conventional views of morality. 'Absolute right and wrong,' he often used to say, 'do not exist in the values of those who have understood the Upanishads or those who have followed the concept of relativity.'[23] Yet, there was in this case, in the early days at least, a curious lack of dilemma such a situation would have ordinarily produced.

According to those in a position to observe the situation from close quarters, Vikram continued to admire, even adore, his wife. At the same time, his very open relationship with Kamla did not provoke the sort of reaction that would have been expected from a wife, particularly one as bold and outspoken as Mrinalini. There was, in fact, an air of high jinks about the triangular relationship, with the three continuing to socialize together with friendly exuberance. But the light-heartedness was not to last. And Vikram's inability to anticipate his wife's deep sense of hurt was to betray a startling naivety in a man capable of immensely complex reasoning.

While his personal life was taking a new and ominous shape, Vikram's dream of starting a world-class management institute in Ahmedabad, with the assistance of the Ford Foundation, had run into rough weather. A team of researchers sent from the US to survey Indian conditions had reported back in shock that poverty-ridden India was more in need of primary schools than management education.

Disappointed but not disheartened, Vikram met representatives of the Ford Foundation again and made the request for a second team of researchers to be sent. The second opinion proved more favourable. Armed with it, Vikram went to Harvard University to seek its involvement in the project. Kamla, with her qualifications, was naturally involved from the very start; in fact, the IIM-A was very much a joint dream for the two of them. They also roped in Prakash Tandon who had become a friend after his visit for the ATIRA conference and who, with his Harvard experience, was able to add value to their efforts.

But even as Vikram was battling to bring Harvard to Ahmedabad, his home town was moving surely in another direction. Following the establishment of an independent Gujarat, local politicians had kept parochial sentiments, particularly those regarding language, alive. The reigning debate was over the introduction of English in schools. If an alien language had to be taught, the politicians insisted, it should be at a later rather than an early stage.

As head of PRL, Vikram was part of Gujarat University's decision-making apparatus; Umashanker Joshi, former vice chancellor of Gujarat University, recalls him being a 'lone voice' for the cause of modernizing higher education in the region.[24] Given his anti-parochial views, Vikram was expectedly horrified by the virulence with which local leaders were opposing the early teaching of English in schools. Fearing it would make Gujaratis less qualified for availing of employment opportunities outside their state, Vikram took an unprecedented decision. The elections for vice chancellor were around the corner and he decided to throw his hat in the ring.

It was a tough fight. Vikram was a well-regarded figure. He came from a prominent family and his contribution to the city, in terms of its institutions, was well known. But he was pitted against a formidable opposition. And he had no experience at all of the rough and tumble of politics. Looking back, it seems extraordinary that Vikram should have catapulted himself into a situation where he would be so much out of his depth. Umashanker Joshi maintains that 'he [Vikram] expected much from the university and was a little frustrated'.[25] It is possible that Vikram was of the opinion that even failure would succeed in focusing attention on his viewpoint. Or he grossly underestimated his opposition.

For, the academic world in Gujarat had become heavily politicized. Caste played a significant role. The university was firmly in the grip of the Congress clique of upper-caste Brahmins such as Thakorebhai Desai, Maganbhai Desai and Chimanbhai Patel. Their leader was Morarji Desai, then known as the uncrowned king of the state. For them the election became a prestige issue.

Vikram, even with the support of his influential ally Kasturbhai Lalbhai, was no match for the seasoned politicians who labelled him an 'establishment man' and a 'representative of the mill owners'.[26] They bullied senate members and issued a three-line whip to their party men. Vikram eventually lost to a nondescript, retired school inspector called Lalbhai Desai.

V. Gangadhar, who covered the colourful election as a reporter, recalls that Vikram did not appear to be overly bothered by his defeat. Given his philosophical bent of mind (Kane remembers him once quoting from the Gita: '*karmanye vadhikaraste*—keep aloof enough, so that you can judge every issue objectively'),[27] it is likely he took the failure in his stride.

Kartikeya, however, is curious about the lessons his father drew from the experience. 'I think he might have concluded that he did not have to be in a certain position to do the things he wanted to do.' If that was indeed the message Vikram took home from the incident, he had reason to be encouraged in his belief. Harvard acceded to Vikram's proposal. The IIM-A came into being in 1962.

At the turn of the decade, Vikram's executives at Sarabhai Chemicals were a perplexed lot. Over the years they had got used to their chairman's eccentric managerial style. They were used to his periodic flashes of inspiration, like the time when oil was discovered in Ankleshwar and he had picked up 250 acres of land predicting that the region would develop into a petrochemical-based chemicals, dyes and pharmaceuticals centre. They had realized that though he was seldom present to look after the day-to-day affairs of the company, negligence would invite his immediate attention. One of their colleagues, for instance, had been forced to cancel his vacation when a piece of glass was discovered in a vial. They knew also that persisting with an unfavourable proposal would just be met with a grin and a wry 'still bowling aren't you?'[28] They had become accustomed to all his ways and yet he had succeeded in befuddling them, once again.

The issue was ORG's annual audit. The small-scale experiment had succeeded beyond all expectations and the senior staff at Sarabhai Chemicals were understandably exultant. But the chairman, instead of rejoicing at the edge it would give them over their competitors in the pharmaceutical business, was pushing the strange notion that ORG should be a separate profit centre and sell in the open market. 'Competition was important to Vikrambhai,' explains K.J. Divatia. 'His view was: "if you fight you have to give your competitor the same weapons." That meant even we had to buy it.'

The same was the case with the Sarabhai Research Centre that came up in 1960 and Sarabhai Glass set up in 1961 to make bottles and injection vials that were sold in the open market. As these developments indicated, Vikram was on his way to achieving the rather implausible dream he had started out with of establishing 'a basic industry from scratch'. And he was laying down similar terms for all his companies. 'I didn't agree with him then,' Divatia admits. In fact, it took some time for him and his colleagues to come around. By then they were in the middle of another ambitious undertaking: the production of antibiotics.

For a while Vikram had been convinced of the necessity of producing bulk drugs such as penicillin and streptomycin within the country and had asked his US counterpart, Squibb, for the know-how. The Indian government, however, was keen on retaining a monopoly over the area and licences were hard to come by. Vikram had thought of a way to work around the restrictions: he had sold one of his existing units and bought a failed company called Standard Pharmaceuticals in Calcutta that already had a licence for producing penicillin. And he had applied to the government for the foreign exchange that would be required to buy machinery. It was to be the beginning of a long struggle.

While Vikram had been expanding the business in Baroda, the IIM had been taking shape in Ahmedabad. Kasturbhai Lalbhai, who was managing the project, had agreed, at Vikram's suggestion, to invite the renowned international architect Louis Kahn to design the building. Vikram sat with Kahn for hours across the dining table at Chidambaram, discussing ideas and concepts. Though he had no formal training in building design, Vikram had a keen interest in the subject. This was evident in his friendship with local architects such as Balkrishna Doshi and the attention he paid to the architecture of all the institutions he had developed till then, including the semicircular amphitheatre he had asked his favourite team of Kanvinde and Rai to build for Darpana next door to Chidambaram.

Till the structure was ready, the IIM-A was housed temporarily in a Shahibaug bungalow. Kamla, the institute's first senior professor, had been dispatched to Harvard to attend its advanced management programme.

In choosing Harvard Business School, Vikram was not just choosing an established partner but also an educational philosophy. Much would be made of Harvard's famous 'case study method' and its application at IIM-A, but the method was merely a vehicle. What was more important, as Ravi Mathai, Vikram's successor at IIM-A, was to point out, was the idea that 'a substantial element of reality was brought into the classroom in written form based on the actual experience of people who made and implemented decisions in industry'.[29] This was to permeate every area of the institute's functioning. It would translate into an emphasis, for instance, on the functional areas of management education such as production, marketing, finance, accounting and so on. It would influence the recruitment policy, which was to hire both academicians and practitioners. It would lead to the setting up of a committee system which in turn would lead to a bond being formed between members of the diverse faculty around specific administrative activities. It would also spread to various sectors of national activity such as banking, agriculture, government systems and education. In fact between them, Kamla and Vikram, according to Ravi Mathai, 'devised and implemented many structures and processes aimed at ensuring the institute's organizational viability'.[30]

One such process was training. To generate cohesiveness among the faculty and give each member an opportunity to understand the educational philosophy, Kamla and Vikram decided to send the newly recruited faculty members to the Harvard Business School's teachers' training programme. Dwijendra Tripathi, who had been hired as an assistant professor, was among them.

'Vikram, when he was in Boston, would come and have lunch with us at the faculty club. I told him I needed money to prepare a crash programme with Indian case studies. He passed the proposal immediately and then he made some light-hearted comment about businessmen being "boors",' Tripathi recalls. One evening, Vikram even invited the eight-odd IIM-A staff recruits over for a vegetarian meal he had cooked himself. 'He noticed that no one was touching the booze,' Tripathi relates, 'so he had a little wine to start the ball rolling and then, of course, the ice cracked.'

Though Vikram was the honorary director, he did not, according to Tripathi, spend more than 10 per cent of his time at the IIM-A. The rest was disbursed, in his customary fashion, over a host of other involvements, the number of which were growing by the day. In late 1962, he was fetching the Eriksons from Delhi airport to convey them to Kashmir, where they were to visit the cosmic ray laboratory PRL had set up high in the mountains, before proceeding to Ahmedabad. On the flight, Erikson writes, the two men conversed about the American Academy's conference on 'Alternatives to Armed Conflict' to which Erik had gone and the International Pugwash Conference from which Vikram had just returned.[31] Presumably, this was the London conference of the Bertrand Russell–Albert Einstein-inspired Pugwash Movement that had brought together scientists from all over the world to discuss the dangers of atomic power. This is the first hint of Vikram's interest in the moral debate over atomic power and a significant one, given the controversy that was to crop up regarding his stand on the subject.

Giving a rare insight into Vikram's state of mind regarding a current event, Erikson mentions that their hearts were 'heavy' because 'up there along the snow-capped horizon of our flight view the Chinese were streaming through the passes'.[32] The reference, of course, was to the attack by Chinese forces and their successful dislodging of Indian troops from the Thagla Ridge in September 1962.

At the time the Eriksons were in Kashmir, however, it is clear that nobody was anticipating a war. There were merely rumours of a 'border incident'. Prime Minister Nehru, instead of pressing the alarm button, went ahead with his travel plans: London for a conference; then Colombo. In Srinagar, too, the Eriksons and Vikram witnessed a colourful pageant in honour of a visit by the Indian vice president Zakir Husain. They were met there by Gautam Sarabhai, 'bearded and princely', and the next morning they visited the cosmic ray laboratory at a height of 9000 feet.

But the Chinese threat was indeed ominous. By mid-October, the Chinese army had overrun Indian posts in the east and captured posts in the western sector. The country trembled as rumours spread of the eastern state of Assam being overrun. Nehru sent urgent requests for help to the US and Britain. But then, just as suddenly as they had come, the Chinese withdrew. They left behind a hurt, vulnerable and betrayed nation. Nehru's health declined and two years later he was to die, a broken-hearted man.

In Ahmedabad, however, the years 1961-62 witnessed yet

another Sarabhai-led institution put down roots: the National Institute of Design (NID). This project had been initiated by an energetic cultural doyenne, Pupul Jayakar, a close friend (one of the few to be in a position to honestly make that claim) of Nehru's daughter, Indira. Jayakar had liaised with the government and the influential American industrial designer and design philosopher Charles Eames to chart out the proposal for an Indian design school. Gautam and Gira Sarabhai were enthusiastic about the project and pushed for it to be located in Ahmedabad.

Vikram, though not as keenly interested in design as his two siblings, did have an appreciation for aesthetics. Alaknanda, wife of the economist I.G. Patel—both friends of the Sarabhais—recalls long discussions with Vikram about the finer points of pottery and textiles. It was perhaps this interest that led him to give Gautam a helping hand with NID. He tapped local industrialists, including his old ally Kasturbhai, for finances; he also put together a 'brains trust' to discuss fundamental issues involved in the institutionalizing of what was a new discipline in India. Kamla, Kamal Mangaldas, Balkrishna Doshi and consultants from London debated questions such as 'What is design?', 'Can it be taught?' The trust met for about six months from middle to late 1962 and, according to Professor H. Kumar Vyas, one of the oldest faculty members, Vikram was a vital part of all these meetings. 'This tradition of operating from the basics was very much Vikram Sarabhai's contribution.'

Given all his hectic parlaying and travelling—by now Vikram's itinerary read something like this: Boston, Berkeley, Paris, Baroda, New Delhi, Srinagar, Gulmarg, Bombay and Ahmedabad—it would seem as if he had little time for anything else, least of all the painstaking, time-consuming process of scientific research.

Nothing could be further from the truth. Vikram's handwritten notes to himself, dated 5 February 1965, Anand, and other undated notes on the stationery of the Curtis Hotel in Minneapolis, the Pan Am Hotel in New York and the Ashoka

Hotel in New Delhi, refer to 'interplanetary space', 'magnetic fields', 'red Sun corona', 'earth as the great spectrometer'; they list references, slides, equations, so on and so forth, suggesting clearly that wherever Vikram was in the world, and at whatever height, physics was never far from his mind.

In fact, Vikram was about to embark on the most breathtaking adventure of his life, one that would offer the potential for fulfilling not one but the two passions closest to his heart: scientific research and development.

5

LAUNCHING INTO SPACE

In 1865, Jules Verne in *De la Terre à la Lune* had written about three men travelling around the moon in an artillery shell. H.G. Wells's *The War of the Worlds* had a more disturbing impact in 1898 with its account of an invasion of earth by Martians while Konstantin E. Tsiolkovsky, a physics teacher in a Russian village, had envisaged spaceships and rockets fuelled by liquid hydrogen. One can assume with some certainty that Vikram could not have been unaware or unmoved by the fanciful flights of these dreamers. In the first half of the twentieth century though developments in rocketry had made the possibility of physical space probes increasingly real. And then, on 4 October 1957, the Russians launched an 83.6-kg satellite, Sputnik 1, into the heavens. And all hell broke loose in the US.

While the US immediately deployed its immense wealth and manpower (some of it from overseas such as Werner Von Braun, who had been absorbed in the American effort) in a desperate bid to beat its communist rival, Vikram seems to have been setting the ground for a plan that had possibly been brewing in his mind for some time.

When exactly Vikram came up with the notion of a space programme for India is not known. R.G. Rastogi, his former student, claims to have heard him talk prophetically of setting up a rocket-launching programme 'by 1963' as far back as in the 1950s. Praful Bhavsar, who had taken a leave of absence from PRL to do post-doctorate work at the University of Minnesota, recalls Vikram telling him something similar in 1959 and adding that he would like him to return to India to help.

Bhavsar even recalls repeating the conversation to Professor Jacques E. Blamont of the University of Paris who was visiting Minnesota around the time. Blamont had just initiated the French Space Research Program and his interest was reportedly piqued by what Bhavsar told him of Vikram's plans. In 1958, the International Council of Scientific Unions had established the Committee for Space Research (COSPAR), and Blamont, like Vikram, was scheduled to attend the committee's first space science symposium in Nice in January 1960. He told Bhavsar that he would use the occasion to meet his Indian colleague. 'They did meet and became friends,' Bhavsar relates. In fact, Blamont came to India in November 1963, and Vikram's notes of 6–14 January 1965 also refer to a seminar in Kodaikanal at which Blamont and others such as Sydney A. Bowhill, an American professor of electrical engineering and a prime mover of middle atmosphere research, and Ramanathan were present and had spoken.

It is, of course, obvious, given his area of interest and his international exposure, that the possibility of using rockets for space experiments must have been an intensely desirable one for Vikram. Yet the truth was that at the time, let alone a programme of artificial satellites and rocket launchers—which Vikram was to unfold over time—even a modest rocket programme seemed a fairly audacious idea.

According to Rastogi, even Vikram's co-director at PRL, K.R. Ramanathan, was openly sceptical. 'He is too young, he has no idea how the government functions. He will not get the money nor will the establishment scientists allow it to happen.' This, according to Rastogi, was the senior man's view. But

Ramanathan had not counted on the chief weapon in Vikram's formidable arsenal of contacts: Homi J. Bhabha.

It is tempting to speculate that Vikram and Bhabha, the two princes of Indian science, used their youthful days in Bangalore to spin dreams for the future. It is tempting to imagine them sharing their precocious hopes in the rambling wild landscape of the IISc or sealing a blood pact under the bright lights of the West End. It is tempting because of the uncanny sureness with which they set about their plans and the suggestion of complicity in so many of their actions.

In August 1961, for instance, more than a year before the Chinese invasion and at a time when Nehru was still very much at the helm of the country's affairs, the union government, urged by Bhabha, identified an area known as 'space research and the peaceful uses of outer space' and placed it within the jurisdiction of the DAE. As part of the move, PRL was recognized as the 'appropriate centre' for research and development in space sciences. And Vikram was co-opted into the board of the AEC. More interestingly, in February 1962, the DAE created the Indian National Committee for Space Research (INCOSPAR) under Vikram's chairmanship to oversee all aspects of space research in the country. Vikram had overcome the first seemingly impossible hurdle.

The next step apparently was to find a suitable location to establish a sounding rocket programme. A sounding rocket was a bit like a large firecracker that pushed upwards till its motor was exhausted and gravity pulled it down again. The motors were generally, but not exclusively, made of a solid propellant and there was a telemetry system to enable the flight to be tracked from the ground. Scientists used sounding rockets to test their experiments at higher altitudes. Sophisticated sounding rockets could transmit data during the flight itself and some even had sensors to point the experimental payload in the correct direction.

Sounding rockets were of use not just to scientists. The technology in the sounding rocket was the same, in an embryonic form, as that required to send an orbiting satellite into space (to give some idea of the difference: sounding rockets require a velocity of about 2000 m/s while a velocity of 28,000 m/s is required to send anything into orbit round earth). As such they were a useful tool for space technologists to cut their teeth on.

A site for a sounding rocket programme would need to be isolated, in view of the danger of falling debris. For reasons that will soon be clear, it also had to be as close to the magnetic equator as possible. One of Vikram's oldest students, E.V. Chitnis, was deputed to find a suitable site.

The successful release of Sputnik 1 and the subsequent space race had resulted in an unexpected windfall for PRL. Despite Vikram's unorthodox workspaces—trains, the corners of crowded airport lounges—by the end of the 1950s many of his students had completed their doctoral studies. American laboratories opened their arms to these bright young men. Praful Bhavsar went to the University of Minnesota, Chitnis to MIT, U.R. Rao worked with the Japanese scientist and pioneer in x-ray astronomy Minoru Oda.

In July 1962, Chitnis, who had become member–secretary, INCOSPAR, took off on the first of his many trips across the southern coast of the country. He was to make almost 200 sorties, buffeted by the monsoon clouds in a Dakota, before shortlisting three options. In November, Bhabha and Vikram went over to have a look.

There is a photograph of the two men taken while they were on this mission that allows us to visualize the moment. There is Bhabha, a trifle portly with thick-framed glasses in a short-sleeved safari suit pointing into the distance. Vikram, in a shirt with sleeves rolled up and light trousers, follows Bhabha's pointed finger. Behind them the tall, proud palm trees rise into a clear sky.

The plane they travelled in seemed to almost brush the tops of the emerald fronds massed over the coastline between Trivandrum and Alleppey. Chitnis had requested the pilot to let Bhabha occupy the co-pilot's seat but had been denied permission. The next best thing he could ask for was that the pilot fly as low as possible. A fleet of fifteen big American-built cars waited at Trivandrum airport to take them to the shortlisted sites. For two days they scoured the humid landscape. Vellana Thuruthu ('white elephant island'), twenty-five kilometres outside the town of Quilon, was easily cancelled out. 'We steered clear of it for fear of it becoming a national joke,' Vikram is reported to have said.[1]

On the second night they accepted V.V. Giri's (then governor of Kerala) invitation to dinner. At Raj Bhavan, Chitnis recalls how, while Bhabha was making polite conversation with the governor and his guests, a Switzerland-based Indian couple, he heard a 'psst' behind him. It was Vikram asking for a comb. A few minutes later, a dapper Vikram, hair neatly in place, sashayed out and mingled with an easy familiarity. 'I was waiting to introduce him to the governor's guests,' Chitnis explains, 'but it was unnecessary. He always knew everybody!'

All parties eventually settled in favour of a picturesque fishing village called Thumba on the outskirts of Trivandrum. The site had several advantages, among them its proximity to the airport and its low population. There was another unforeseen but extremely beneficial factor: the presence of two remarkable individuals of local influence—the bishop, the Right Reverend Dr Peter Bernard Pereira, and a dynamic young collector, Madhavan Nair. Both were to persuade the few resident fishermen to move out of their thatched huts to the brick and mortar sites built nearby, ensuring an unusually peaceful displacement programme.

The DAE was looking to develop both a rocket-launching site as well as a research and development centre. So the area that was eventually selected included not just the long stretch of beach but the stub of a hill behind it. According to R.D. John, executive engineer with the Central Public Works Department (CPWD) whose services had been recruited for the project, Vikram clearly erred on the side of caution by not picking up more land when it was available. As far as the main building was concerned, he had planned for it to accommodate only 200 people. But Bhabha, with his grander sweep, was, in this case, more realistic in the advice he proffered. 'No Vikram,' he apparently said, 'plan for 400.'[2] And then, observing the humidity, he announced that it would have to be air-conditioned as well.[3]

Vikram, meanwhile, pressed ahead. Preparations had been under way since the beginning of the year to put together a team for the upcoming programme. An advertisement put out in an Indian embassy publication in Washington DC had enticed several Indians from NASA and American universities, including many of Vikram's former students from PRL. Some were drawn from the atomic energy programme. In addition, Vikram's peers and friends were also on the lookout for possible recruits. The most promising find to have come to Vikram's attention this way was a shy, reedy Muslim boy from a small pilgrim town in Tamil Nadu. M.G.K. Menon of TIFR had come across him at the Aeronautical Development Establishment, a defence laboratory in Bangalore, and called him to Bombay to meet Vikram for an interview.

A.P.J. Abdul Kalam was to go on to head the country's missile development programme and become President of India. In his autobiography *Wings of Fire*, he describes his first encounter with Vikram:

> I was almost immediately struck by Dr. Sarabhai's warmth. There was none of the arrogance or the patronising attitudes which interviewers usually display when talking to a young and vulnerable candidate. Dr. Sarabhai's questions did not probe my existing knowledge or skills; rather they were an exploration of the possibilities I was filled with. He was looking at me as if

> in reference to a larger whole. The entire encounter seemed to me a total moment of truth, in which my dream was enveloped by the larger dream of a bigger person...[4]

Dr K. Kasturirangan, who would be chairman of the Space Commission and Secretary, Department of Space, Government of India, between 1994 and 2003, applied to PRL in July 1963. He, too, was struck by the first encounter:

> Dr Sarabhai started by telling me that my pay would only be Rs 200, and perhaps it was better for me to work in a bank. I realized he was probing my mind. But I was adamant and only when he was convinced of my determination to pursue science did he tell me about his agenda for space. It took only a crisp fifteen minutes. He was humane, seized of ground realities and had a vision.

From among the several bright young men who had come together for the space programme, Vikram put together a small group to send to NASA, to the Goddard Space Flight Center and the Wallops Island facility for training. Given that the programme's first mission was in keeping with the spirit of global cooperation that had emerged with the IGY, American assistance was readily forthcoming.

Both the United Nation's Committee on the Peaceful Uses of Outer Space and COSPAR had identified the need for a sounding rocket launch station on the magnetic equator to fill gaps in the knowledge about the 'equatorial electrojet', a stream of electric current flowing in a narrow band on either side of the equator. Praful Bhavsar recalls Blamont rhapsodizing: 'Build a range at the equator so that the whole world will see the beautiful trail.' The international scientific community, therefore, had reason to be pleased with the Indian initiative and was ready to pitch in. The French space agency, the Centre National d'Etudes Spatiales (CNES), supplied a radar, the Russians a computer, the Minsk. The Americans promised training and much else.

On 21 November 1963, India was ready to stage its very first blast-off. Many weighty names in science and technology had gathered for the occasion. Blamont was there as were his assistants Mary Lise Channin and Michel Autier from France and observers from Brazil and Argentina. Arnold Frutkin, Robert Duffy, Ed Bissel and others were there from NASA. The Indian contingent included Bhabha and eminent scientists Dr A.P. Mitra, then with the NPL, and Dr P.R. Pisharoty, founder director of the Indian Institute of Tropical Meteorology, Poona. The governor of Kerala was there along with the district collector and the bishop.

The world was watching. The setting was one of stark beauty. The gentle waves sparkled under the sun while the trees reached darkly into a breathtakingly azure sky. And yet, for the Indians massed about the bronze sands, the moment was shot through with tension.

For so much had already gone wrong. The Nike–Apache rocket supplied by NASA had been flown to Delhi by US military air transport, but the truck that was bringing it down to Cochin had broken down along the way, leaving its precious cargo stranded in the middle of nowhere. Once that wrinkle had been ironed out, it was discovered that the French payload, which was to be released in the atmosphere, could not be fitted into the American rocket. Ratilal Panchal, PRL's expert mechanic, had to be flown down from Ahmedabad. Praful Bhavsar and Kalam supervised him as he scraped it by hand. Camera assistants had been trained to photograph the cloud that would be released by the rocket from four vantage points in Kanyakumari, Palayamkottai, Kodaikanal and Kottayam. But there was the possibility that the phone lines would fail, making communication impossible. And the sky could turn dark and make the images fuzzy.

In the circumstances it was not surprising that when the moment arrived, when the rocket rolled out on a truck to the launch pad, the sultry air was thick with tension. And almost immediately things went awry. As the rocket was being hoisted onto the launcher, the hydraulic system of the crane developed a leak. Technicians moved in to shift the rocket manually. The rocket was in position. But then the remote system to raise the launcher to the correct angle malfunctioned. The team conferred and sent a man to operate the controls on the launcher itself. That having been done, everything seemed, at last, in order. An alarm sounded to clear the area around the launch pad. Vikram's team members prayed and held their breath. Just then, Pramod Kale, at the time a new student at PRL, noticed a worker still fiddling with the launcher controls. With a shout he dashed out and dragged him away.

At 6.25 p.m. the rocket streaked away into the gathering dusk. Minutes later, a sodium vapour cloud emerged high above, tinged orange by the setting sun.

R.D. John recalls the moment. 'We were all there in the oval canteen. We were jumping with joy. Bhabha too.'[5] Vikram sent home a telegram: 'Gee whiz wonderful rocket shot.'[6]

Historically, rockets had been used for military purposes. The Chinese used them in the thirteenth century. Tipu Sultan used them against the British in the eighteenth century. The next hundred years saw the Russians, the Americans and the Germans enter the arena but the impulse continued to be aggressive. Even the scientific experimentations and studies carried out on rockets—and a great deal was in the 1940s and the 1950s—were linked to military applications. Studies were conducted, for instance, on the effects of the atmosphere on radio communications or on the possibility of using the sun's light in guidance systems for missiles. And it was the Cold War that gave a fillip to the US space effort, leading to studies on the design and use of artificial satellites and missile technology.

The Indian space programme broke the mould.

From the very beginning the thrust of the Indian space programme was peaceful. Sounding rockets were a useful tool for space science as they could go higher than balloons to provide information about wind velocities, shears and regions of turbulence in the atmospheric band between 80 and 180 kilometres. For a country as backward as India, even a modest sounding rocket programme was an ambitious undertaking. But it was soon clear that Vikram's agenda was far more colossal in scale. And he was in a hurry to implement it. According to Kalam, Vikram chose the very next day following the launch of the Nike–Apache rocket to talk to his team about his dream of an Indian satellite launch vehicle.[7]

If there were questions as to what satellites in India would be used for, a space science seminar organized by PRL in January 1963 offered a hint. Held in Ahmedabad, the seminar was inaugurated by Bhabha. Just before he was to go on, Bhabha asked Vikram what he should say. Chitnis, who was present, reports that Vikram said, 'Say we are doing satellites for communications.' It was a fairly cocky assertion to make. In 1962, the Soviets had just about launched the world's first early bird or synchronous satellite, and even in 1964, when the International Telecommunications Satellite Consortium was formed in Washington, it seemed as if only rich nations would ever be able to maintain and use satellites.

Yet, in papers and public addresses throughout the late 1960s, Vikram was to unveil an even more ambitious range of expectations from space technology. It was a programme that, according to eminent Japanese space scientist Hideo Itokawa, 'caused a big sensation internationally among the scholars of space science'.[8] Vikram's focus, however, was primarily national. His explanation of long-range weather forecasting, an application of the greatest immediate significance for India, for example, provides some idea of the depth and breadth of his vision:

> The sun provides the driving force for almost everything that happens on earth—weather, rivers, vegetation, fossil fuels and, of course, life itself. But in contrast to the apparent constancy of the sun and the complete dependability of sunrise and sunset, we experience a capriciously variable environment, the fury of hurricanes and lashing ocean waves, droughts and floods, starvation one year and bumper crops another, and uncertain radio communications. The natural scientist looking for the subtle links through which the sun affects the earth and our lives has at last acquired in the exploration of space a dramatic new capability for study.[9]

By 1970, his list had expanded to include applications in agriculture, forestry, oceanography, geology, mineral prospecting and cartography. But apart from these applications, Vikram believed that many benefits would accrue from the very existence of the space programme itself. In a paper on 'Space Activity for Developing Countries' published in the science and technology series of the American Astronautical Society of California in 1966, he talked about its potential to stimulate growth in advanced fields such as electronics, chemicals, cybernetics and in materials engineering, the possibility of collaborative relationships with organizations, scientists and technologists in foreign lands and, crucially, the nucleus of a new culture where 'people in diverse activities learn to work together for the purpose of a single objective'.[10]

This was Vikram's dream: linking technology with development, serving the needs of the masses while nurturing a highly sophisticated work culture and scientific abilities. One of his favourite phrases was 'leapfrogging'. It referred to his great faith, along with Bhabha and Nehru, in the ability of technology to enable developing countries to circumvent the long, arduous processes followed by the Western world. As he put it:

> There are those who preach that developing nations must proceed step-by-step following the same process by which the

> advanced nations themselves progressed. One is often told that such and such a thing is too sophisticated to be applied. This approach disregards what should perhaps be obvious—that when a problem is great, one requires the most effective means available to deal with it.[11]

At the same time, while extolling the need to learn from the strides of the developed world, he was not above taking a dig at its occasional stupidity. In one of his much-quoted passages from 'Sources of Man's Knowledge', a national programme of talks broadcast in 1966, he made it clear that 'in India the immediate goals of our space research are modest. We do not expect to send a man to the moon or put elephants white, pink or black into orbit around the earth.'[12]

The jibe was clearly aimed at the two superpowers who by then were vying like eager schoolchildren to outdo each other in the race for space. In January 1961, the US had sent a chimpanzee called Ham into space atop a Redstone rocket; in April, the Soviet Union pronounced Yuri Gagarin the first man in space. But Vikram was not being facetious while talking about pink elephants. His comments mirrored an extremely serious concern about the possibility of the space programme being hijacked from his desired social aims. 'There is a real danger,' he pointed out,'[that] developing nations may adopt a space programme largely for this glamour, devoting resources not through a recognition of the values of which we are talking about here, but from a desire to create a sham image nationally and internationally.'[13]

So Vikram's aim was clear. It was to establish, step-by-step, a space programme that would advance scientific research as well as offer applications of great social and economic relevance. In retrospect, and given the original impulses of space programmes the world over, it is astonishing that Vikram was able to maintain a strict focus on peaceful ends. It is even more astonishing in the light of the ambiguity long maintained over the dual purpose—

energy and security—of the DAE under which the space programme was born.

It was not as if Vikram was unaware of the military potential of the technology he was developing. 'He would have been a fool to not understand Intercontinental Ballistic Missile (ICBM) applications,' laughs Vasant Gowarikar who joined the programme in the late 1960s. 'Vikram knew about defence applications like the back of his hand.' Nor was Vikram unconcerned about the threat to the country's security. This much is clear from an incident mentioned by journalist Raj Chengappa.

The incident took place in November 1962 at a meeting of the Electronics Committee headed by Bhabha. At the meeting where the recent Chinese invasion was still on every mind, a radar expert, Group Captain V.S. Narayanan, was asked why it was not possible to create a radar system to pick up both ballistic missiles and aircraft. Narayanan apparently responded brusquely, saying the cost was too high and that there was no point in detecting missiles unless there was a counter. 'We need our own ballistic missiles to punch our enemy back with. We need to have a deterrent. Are we ready for it?' Silence greeted his remark. Then, the person who had asked the question clapped him on the back. It was Vikram. He did not appear offended in the least but invited Narayanan to breakfast instead to talk more on the subject.[14]

Vikram's concerns about security did not, however, at any stage, bring about a shift in his priorities for the space programme. Missiles, when they were eventually manufactured, were made by the Defence Research and Development Organisation (DRDO). And though the military programme was in no way connected with the space programme, the lines of communication between the two were far from closed. Says Kale, 'We were very clear that space was for peaceful purposes but we had the capability that could help and if the government wanted it, it was there. Defence people would come to see us and vice versa. For us it was very open.'

The launch of the sounding rocket programme, though time consuming, did not cause any break in Vikram's scientific pursuits. K.G. McCracken from MIT and U.R. Rao continued to work painstakingly on finding a method for taking into account the effect of geomagnetic bending upon the directions of arrival of cosmic ray particles on earth. Other students set up experiments to obtain data on the configuration of the magnetic field and on the plasma parameters in interplanetary space.

Experiments were also sent up in balloons or on rockets, sometimes with little success. Kasturirangan remembers Vikram asking him, after a particularly disastrous series of attempts, if the 'Spanish armada' had returned. 'He was always joking but he would also show you how to learn from failure by setting up review systems. He encouraged us to take risks. It helped us do the same when we came to occupy positions of responsibility.'

Though many of its students were spending more and more time in Thumba, PRL buzzed with activity. Vikram had initiated a practice common in many Western universities—that of the faculty getting together informally over tea in the mornings. He made it a point to drop in to exchange some light-hearted banter or discuss the cricket score coming over the four tracking radios in the laboratory.

It is quite extraordinary that while as a scientist Vikram was laying the foundations for a hugely ambitious state-owned programme, in his other avatar as a businessman he had been engaged in a tedious battle with the government. As an entrepreneur his was not an unusual plight. Almost every Indian businessman in the early years of independent India would have voiced complaints of discouragement and a seemingly insurmountable amount of red tape. Prakash Tandon describes the frustration vividly in his book:

> A trip to Delhi always began with a sick feeling deep inside me. The single daily Viscount left at dawn, after a restless night when I thought of the early morning alarm and what new problems were in store during the day—some surprise, a setback. Would one be down again to the bottom of the snake, and slowly start moving again in the hope of striking the lucky bottom of a ladder?[15]

Through the late 1950s, the Sarabhais had been involved in a stand-off with the central government over permission to manufacture antibiotics. 'The meetings were very frustrating,' recalls K.J. Divatia. 'There were quarrels and hot discussions with people like the then minister for industries, Manubhai Shah. Vikrambhai was very adamant about what he wanted to do but he rarely lost his temper. He would say let us not be non-cooperative with the government.'

His patience is evident in his letters to the government which are shot through with phrases such as 'grateful' and 'I trust you will forgive' (even when asking about a two-year-old licence application) and signed with a scrawl 'Vikram A. Sarabhai'. G.D. Zalani, who was appointed liaison man for the Sarabhais in the capital, claims Vikram usually left the business of meeting bureaucrats to his CEOs unless the significance of the matter warranted a personal meeting. There was enough cause for him to be in Delhi frequently though and Zalani, whom Vikram often laughingly complimented on his good looks, had the unenviable task of seeing to his eclectic needs. 'He was always putting me in odd situations like telling me to hold the fort with a group of top scientists. Or he would suddenly want idli for breakfast and I would have to hunt for it. Invariably, I would end up eating his expensive breakfast while he had some cheap idli.'

While in Delhi Vikram always stayed at the Ashoka Hotel. Though not as posh as the privately run Oberoi, the government-owned hotel was centrally located and the Sarabhais were faithful clients. Room number 30, a suite with a sitting room and bedroom, was permanently booked for him at a special concessional rate (Rs 50 full board). He was driven around in the city by the company driver Babulal, who Ambalal had instructed to drive at a maximum of 40kmph though Vikram, invariably behind schedule, was always urging him to 'go faster'. 'He would give me high blood pressure by turning up late for flights, leaving me to wait with a boarding card at the airport,' says Zalani.

Zalani was not the only one to feel the pressure of Vikram's energetic pace and impossible schedules. All his executives had stories: of being left waiting for a cab while he raced ahead on foot to his next appointment, or of the time he fixed two lunch engagements, one in New York and the other in New Brunswick, or when he misplaced his air ticket in New York and the president of Squibb had to phone the vice-president of the airline to issue another one, and of course, of the countless times they had to come up with an assortment of personal items such as cufflinks, a cake of soap or a pair of trouser buckles because Vikram had, invariably, forgotten his own.

He was casual about his appearance. The colourful shirts he had worn in his youth had given way to light coarse cotton shirts and trousers, and suits for formal occasions, often made of khadi. According to his nephew, Kamal Mangaldas, a spur in one foot due to a bone problem meant he could not wear shoes, and observing his suit-and-Kolhapuri-chappals ensemble the extremely natty industrialist J.R.D. Tata once remarked in exasperation: 'Oh you Sarabhais, how you dress!' Vikram did not, however, look kindly on casualness from his executives in matters of appearance. Any lack of form or propriety in dress would evoke a strict reproach. He was equally intolerant of line managers who evinced no interest in new developments that affected their areas of work, expecting them to have at least a nodding acquaintance with such matters.

Yet, his colleagues enjoyed his company. He was 'an incurable optimist' displaying a 'puckish sense of humour' even when things went wrong, wrote M.R. Raman in the in-house company magazine.[16] His eccentricity also made for a fairly entertaining experience. Writing in the same magazine, N.R. Nadkarni, a former director of the Sarabhai Group of companies in Baroda, described his 'capacity to switch suddenly from one subject to another and deal with several different matters all at one time'.[17] When Nadkarni complimented him on his 'multi-channel brain' while expressing concern about fatigue, Vikram apparently told him that dwelling on one subject too long was boring; it was more relaxing to switch to other subjects.

Another device Vikram found relaxing was a short nap after lunch. Nadkarni talks about the time he, Vikram and an executive from Squibb were travelling from New Brunswick to New York. They were going at sixty miles an hour and chatting when Nadkarni suddenly noticed that Vikram had gone completely silent. 'I realized he had fallen asleep. After three, four minutes he woke up completely refreshed and resumed the conversation.'[18]

As far as the run-in with the government was concerned, Vikram eventually had to throw in the towel. When the government refused to give him foreign exchange for machinery to produce penicillin, he entered into another collaboration with Squibb. It was not the situation he had hoped for, but it was better than nothing.

'Did he think he was infallible?' Kartikeya remembers T.N. Seshan, India's colourful former election commissioner, who worked closely with Vikram, putting this question to him some time after his father's death. It was a relevant query.

Most people who interacted closely with Vikram found him a loving and sensitive human being, one who, as Kamal Mangaldas puts it, 'had a way of making people want to give him their best'. At the same time, most would have admitted that he set a punishing pace. He rose in the early hours of dawn and worked furiously till late into the night. He travelled feverishly in the days when air travel, within India at least, was restricted to the government carrier and subject to sudden strikes and delays. He spoke of time as a rubber band that could be stretched, and would argue with his children when they complained about his frequent absences till, to prove their point, they showed him a calendar with coloured squares to mark the days he was home. There were often times in his childhood, Kartikeya recalls, when Vikram would break a promise to take him swimming, for instance, and rush off to work instead.

The frantic pace of Vikram's life, the distances he covered, the vast sprawl of his involvements, the burden of his responsibilities would have felled a multi-limbed, many-headed deity. Others often found it hard to keep up. Seshan, too, exhausted by the long hours, once found himself unable to stir when Vikram arrived to fetch him for an early-morning flight and ended up missing it. On another occasion, Vikram's personal assistant, N.V.G. Warrier, almost fainted at an airport. Put together, these instances seem to indicate that Vikram tended to have a somewhat unrealistic perception of ordinary human capacities.

Nowhere was this more evident than in his relationships with his women. Most people can handle just about one occupation well in a lifetime. Vikram could apparently manage several, simultaneously and successfully. But from his behaviour it appeared that he was trying to extend the same principle to his personal life. He had a wife and a mistress. Two lives, two homes. And he did not appear to believe he had to make a choice. Kamla claims that the question of divorce never came up, nor would she have 'liked it'. Mrinalini maintains that she loved her husband too much to contemplate leaving him. The way she describes it, however, gives some idea of what Vikram had in mind: 'He wanted me to make her [Kamla] feel a part of our family which somehow I was perhaps not generous enough to do, though God knows I really tried.'[19]

Ever the reconciler, Vikram seemed to be attempting to find a solution that would hurt neither woman. In doing so, however, he appeared to have little idea as to the impracticality or the unrealistic nature of his expectations. In fact, he seems to have been taken aback on finding that Mrinalini, after the initial bout of spiritedness, was visibly distressed. 'It devastated Amma,' says Mallika feelingly. She herself was so affected by her mother's unhappiness that she mutinied against her father, refusing to talk to him, sit at a table with him, or even stay in the same room when he entered.

Mrinalini's pain both astonished and agonized Vikram. In a letter, he tried to persuade her of his continued affections:

> Do you really believe that I do not love you, wish to look after you and, what is more important, wish to be loved by you as I am with all my faults?.... I need so much your tenderness—as you need my shoulder to rest your head on.... Please, Mrinalini, don't doubt me. I love you dearly—not only as the mother, but as a woman. And I shall never stop feeling this way for anyone else's sake.[20]

The tone of the letter conveys an acute yearning for sincerity. Some years later, Vikram was to tell his daughter that the dilemma was heart-wrenching because he loved both women. At the time, though, Vikram, as it happened, was hurting both. In different ways. If Mrinalini was suffering a delayed reaction to his betrayal, Kamla had reason to be unhappy with him for professional reasons.

The problem with Kamla stemmed from the controversy over Vikram's likely successor as director at IIM-A. In the twelve months following its establishment, Vikram had put into place a non-hierarchical system of administration and introduced a culture that, in the words of Dwijendra Tripathi, 'would have been very difficult to change'. But by the end of the year, Vikram was chafing at the bit and keen to move on.

Kamla, the institute's most senior professor and de facto director, was the obvious choice to succeed him. But the authorities at Harvard had nixed her elevation perceiving her to be not firm enough. Prakash Tandon, who was then chairman of IIM-A, claims that Vikram was upset by the board's decision but 'dutifully' looked for an alternative. Rumours, however, alleged that he was dragging his feet on her account. Discouraged by the talk, Vikram distanced himself from the proceedings. 'He felt unbelieved and therefore unwanted,' claims Tandon. 'He also felt he had let Kamla down when he did not resign from the board.'[21]

It was in a state of anguish that Vikram wrote to Mrinalini: 'It is impossible to consciously trample on anyone—but this is what I am doing all the time with those who I love. So much so that no-one is really convinced or is confident of my love.... Who am I to blame but myself?'[22]

In this hour of darkness Vikram had nobody to turn to. The lack was not so much of friends but of a total and utter inability to confide. The Sarabhai code of self-reliance, of 'churning the depths', did not allow an ordinary dependence on others. 'He was brought up to be the strong one, the responsible one,' says Mallika. 'He believed he could not let people down even if it was just to express a doubt or a quandary. Not being self-reliant was considered a weakness, a flaw in character.' As a result 'he could not talk to anyone, he had no levels of intimacy'.

His chosen solution was the Gandhian one of self-punishment. 'When the world outside and all our relationships get tangled up like this,' he wrote to Mrinalini, 'what else can one do but withdraw into oneself—not stop long but pay the price.'[23] His nephew, Kamal, built him an outhouse on the river bank, at the bottom of the slope from Chidambaram. Ghoghu, the glass-fronted hut filled with his papers and his enormous record collection, became Vikram's retreat.

Work was his other refuge. In the early 1960s he oversaw the installation of a satellite telemetry station and a computer centre in Ahmedabad. The frequency of his trips to Baroda had increased as he, along with his old neighbour from Shahibaug, Arvind Lalbhai, who had become chairman and managing director of the Ahmedabad-based Arvind Mills Ltd, joined the board of Gujarat Fertilizers, an important project for the new state. Meetings of the high-powered Electronics Committee that had been set up under Bhabha, on the other hand, frequently took him to Bombay.

Outwardly, Vikram showed no signs of turmoil. In fact, colleagues and acquaintances saw him laughing and making merry at all times. Navroz Contractor who had joined the College of Fine Arts in Baroda (with some help from Vikram) often got a call from him when he was in the city. 'He would bring me jazz records from abroad.' Pallavi Mayor, Vikram's niece, recalls being on a flight with him and the governor of the Reserve Bank and noticing the sleeve of Vikram's silk shirt fall off. 'It just dropped off,' she recalls. 'I felt so sorry for him thinking maybe he had nobody to look after him. But he made a big joke out of it. He was always making everything fun. Always living!'

Pramod Kale recalls Vikram taking him for dinner to his eldest sister's house in New Delhi. Mridula at the time was fighting a high-voltage campaign for the release of the jailed Kashmiri leader Sheikh Abdullah, a campaign that was to make her persona non grata with her old friend Nehru. Vikram, Kale remembers, cautioned him against 'breathing a word on Kashmir'. 'He seemed amused by everything that was going on,' he recalls.

The sheer ebullience and productivity with which Vikram filled his waking hours seemed to surround him with an air of invincibility. But he was very human. Not infallible. And there was at least one clear sign by the mid-1960s that he was winding down. M.S. Sastry describes the incident:

> He had gone to Rossi's lab at Harvard as he did every year. I was in Baroda. He called me, told me to fly down and meet

> him on a particular day at Boston airport. He had something important to discuss. I landed up as required. He arrived at the airport in a Hertz rental. A student was carrying his luggage. He had a [scientific] model in his hand which he asked me to hold. He looked extremely tired, almost asleep.
>
> He came to suddenly and asked for lime juice. I went to the counter and got him a 7 Up. He immediately asked for a second one. Then he said, 'I will talk to you on the way to New York.' But he was not able to talk. We reached New York. His wife was at the airport. Vikram finally said to me, 'I am too tired. I can't talk to you.' So I came back to India with no clue about what he wanted.

It is an unsettling narration. The symptoms clearly point to a state of exhaustion. The inability to talk, the physical dependence, the unquenchable thirst, and the vulnerability are in every way so uncharacteristic of Vikram that they evoke sadness. What is even more disturbing about the incident is the unsettling certainty that the desperately needed break would not be forthcoming. Rest was not one of Vikram's manifold blessings.

In fact, dark clouds were on the horizon. In 1964, Ambalal, who had suffered a series of small strokes, fell seriously ill. A year later, Mridula was served with a detention order by the government for her activities regarding Kashmir. She was asked to proceed to Ahmedabad to be put under house arrest at The Retreat. Concerned about the effects on her father's health she refused until the police agreed to stand out of sight at the gate. Gita, meanwhile, lost her young son in a tragic accident. Vikram, she says, wrote a 'beautiful letter' of condolence using imagery from Kalidasa's poetry.

In August 1965, India complained of massive infiltration into Kashmir by disguised military personnel from the Pakistani side of the ceasefire line. On 1 September, Pakistani troops attacked the Chamb sector in the border region between Kashmir and Jammu, threatening to cut off India's only road connection with Kashmir. India responded by invading the Pakistani part of the Punjab.

A full-fledged though undeclared war broke out between the two neighbouring countries. Both the Soviets and the US showed an interest in halting the conflict. The UN was able to persuade the combatants to accept a ceasefire on 23 September. It was an uneasy truce and a meeting was scheduled at the beginning of 1966 in Tashkent. The incident, however, had made one thing clear, at least to South Asia expert Gunnar Myrdal: 'Neither India nor Pakistan can develop in peace, much less wage war, without large-scale foreign aid.'[24]

6

ASSUMING BHABHA'S MANTLE

Vasant Gowarikar was studying to be a chemical engineer in the UK when the Nike–Apache rocket streaked across the southern Indian sky. He remembers reading about the event in the local papers and it may have been at the back of his mind, he says, when a couple of years later he mentioned in passing to the Indian High Commissioner in the UK that he was thinking of returning to India. The High Commissioner, Jivraj Mehta, former chief minister of Gujarat, said he would keep an eye on a suitable opening. Gowarikar thought no more of it and continued with his work on tactical missiles at the Summerfield Research Station.

Then one day in the latter half of 1966 he received a letter from the man he knew had been responsible for the Nike–Apache launch. Vikram Sarabhai was in Geneva and expected to be in London shortly. Could they meet?

'We met in a hotel,' Gowarikar relates. 'He told me about the space programme. He had planned it all: the various rockets, all the stages. He asked me to come and work for him, to take charge of propellants. I said I didn't know anything about propellants. He said, "So what? I know nothing about space technology and I am the director!" He left me to think about it for a couple of months. And then we met again.'

His eyes brighten with the memory. 'That night I will never

forget. Vikram talked to me as if we had known each other for years. He talked about his vision. He talked about technology and about "leapfrogging". He fascinated me. He hypnotized me.' A friend who met Gowarikar after the meeting testified that he had stars in his eyes.[1] Vikram had apparently offered him two options. One, the AEC because Gowarikar's family was in Bombay—'It will all be laid out for you,' he had said. 'But if you want a challenge, come to Trivandrum.'

Vasant Gowarikar went to Trivandrum. And the challenge exceeded even his wildest expectations. He found a town with scarce accommodation and few restaurants. The pioneers of the space programme, he learnt, were transported to Thumba in battered public buses and had made their office inside a church building that did not have even a roof to keep the pigeons out. 'All those facilities which Sarabhai had talked of,' wrote R. Aravamudan, who had moved from the Atomic Energy Establishment in Trombay, 'were still very much a dream.'[2]

Gowarikar was installed in a cowshed that Vikram promptly named 'Gowarikar Nagar'. 'There was a gap between the door and the floor through which reptiles would creep in every day,' Gowarikar recalls. 'I was working with high explosives but apart from depositing our matchboxes at the entrance there were no precautions.' There was a slapdash energy to the whole enterprise. A black and white photograph by Henri Cartier Bresson of two men in vests on their haunches bent over a payload evocatively captures the atmosphere.

Following the successful launch of the Nike–Apache rocket in 1963, the French company Sud Aviation had offered a contract to produce their Centaure sounding rockets and a small team had travelled to France to train in solid propulsion and hardware fabrication. Meanwhile, the Indian government had given Vikram the go-ahead for a Space Science and Technology Centre (SSTC) to manufacture a series of indigenous sounding rockets.

The series was named Rohini. A later series would be called

Menaka. The idea of naming rockets after apsaras was Mrinalini's. Vikram, who believed strongly in the power of terminology, liked the political resonance inherent in the suggestion, given the American penchant for naming rockets after Greek gods.

These early rockets were fairly elementary, rigged out of ready-made seamless aluminium tubes with fins and a nozzle, the last tied with a rope to be retrieved in case of an explosion. The space boys would shoot them off the sands and run for shelter behind coconut trees. It was dangerous but, they claim cheerfully, 'we were young and didn't know any better'.[3] The rockets were fired with cordite blocks procured from a factory in the neighbouring state of Tamil Nadu and transported with reckless abandon in a jeep over Thumba's uneven roads. Gowarikar's job was to create a fuel more suitable for rocket propulsion.

There was only one problem. Gowarikar knew nothing about polymers, the material he was supposed to work with. His was not an unusual predicament. Kalam, nicknamed 'busybee' by his colleagues, was given the task of finding a substitute for expensive American fibreglass nose-cones with no domestic precedents. Someone else was involved in making payloads. Everyone at the SSTC was involved in developing the technology part by part from virtually nothing.

Vikram provided help wherever he could. A team was sent to study the Japanese facilities. ('We are Asians, let us study our own instead of going to the West.')[4] He brought his old friend S. Ramaseshan, who by then had joined the National Aeronautical Laboratory, from Bangalore to Thumba for his input on the nose-cone problem. 'Whenever he found anyone of us going over his head and attempting a task for which he did not have the capability or skill, Professor Sarabhai would reassign the activity in such a way so as to lower pressure and permit better quality work to be performed,' claims Kalam. At other times, 'he would bring someone from the developed world for a technical collaboration. That was his subtle way of challenging each one of us to stretch our capabilities.'[5]

Vikram's methods were not always pleasant, however. One of his tactics was to throw the same challenge at two or more people, encouraging a fierce competitiveness. Gowarikar, for instance, was pitted against A.E. Muthunayagam, who was developing a solid propellant based on a natural rubber resin. The race was frenzied; Gowarikar called his product 'Mrinal'—in an effort to curry favour with the boss, his colleagues alleged[6]—and both were to claim vociferously, for years, that theirs was the propellant that fired the first fully indigenous sounding rocket. 'We were in the air all the time, thinking big,' Gowarikar exults. 'The insistence on indigenization all the time was a great motivation.'

In fact, the morale was consistently high, urged by Vikram's exhortation to push with the 'thin edge of the wedge'.[7] Structurally though the programme was in a state of perpetual flux. Satish Dhawan, when he came to the space programme after Vikram's death, found a rapidly swelling organization of over 3000 people with no formal systems of administration.[8] The five-member committee Vikram had appointed to oversee operations apparently bickered bitterly in his absence but was united in its keenness to show him results. 'It was chaotic,' admits Gopal Raj, 'but it was the only way an innovative technological programme could have taken off.'

Vikram with his experience of long-distance management kept the strings firmly in his hands. He would arrive in Thumba every fortnight for a couple of days. He would move around the site all day, studying the progress made by various teams, and host after-dinner discussions at the Mascot, a hotel in Trivandrum, or in his room at a guest house in Kovalam. More often than not, the discussions would stretch late into the night. More than his physical presence, it was the atmosphere of trust and security he created that appeared to encourage each member of his growing

The Sarabhais with Rabindranath Tagore, 1920 (Courtesy Dr Vikram Sarabhai Archives, Nehru Foundation for Development, Ahmedabad)

Uttarayan
Santiniketan, Bengal
November 1, 1935.

It is with great pleasure that I recommend the application for admission of Mr. Vikram Sarabhai to the authorities of the Cambridge University. He is a young man with keen interest in Science and I am sure, a course of study at Cambridge will be of immense value to him. I know him personally and his people. He comes of a wealthy and cultured family in the Bombay Presidency and he has a brother and a sister studying at Oxford at the moment. In my judgment, he is a fit and proper person for admission to the University.

Rabindranath Tagore

Tagore's letter recommending Vikram's application for admission to Cambridge (Courtesy Dr Vikram Sarabhai Archives, Nehru Foundation for Development, Ahmedabad)

Child Vikram (Courtesy Dr Vikram Sarabhai Archives, Nehru Foundation for Development, Ahmedabad)

A suggestion of easy compliance in his readiness to pose (Courtesy Dr Vikram Sarabhai Archives, Nehru Foundation for Development, Ahmedabad)

Ambalal and Sarla with Vikram and Gita (Courtesy
Dr Vikram Sarabhai Archives, Nehru Foundation for Development, Ahmedabad)

Vikram with the toy engine he made (Courtesy
Dr Vikram Sarabhai Archives, Nehru Foundation for Development, Ahmedabad)

At Cambridge before the Second World War: Vikram was glued to his scientific studies (Courtesy Dr Vikram Sarabhai Archives, Nehru Foundation for Development, Ahmedabad)

At the Indian Institute of Science, early 1940s:
'A baby's skin with the appearance of milk flowing through it' (Courtesy Dr Vikram Sarabhai Archives, Nehru Foundation for Development, Ahmedabad)

With his Mrinalini, 1942: both had sworn never to marry
(Courtesy Dr Vikram Sarabhai Archives, Nehru Foundation for Development, Ahmedabad)

The Sarabhai Clan, 1963: Seated in the front row are Vikram (third from the right) and Mrinalini (second from the right); Seated in the middle row, from left to right, are Mridula, Anṣuya, Ambalal and Sarla; Kartikeya is standing in the last row, fifth from the right (Courtesy Dr Vikram Sarabhai Archives, Nehru Foundation for Development, Ahmedabad)

Vikram and Mrinalini with the children (Courtesy Hemendra A. Shah)

Vikram with his children: In Mrinalini's absence he was an attentive single parent (Courtesy Dr Vikram Sarabhai Archives, Nehru Foundation for Development, Ahmedabad)

With Jawaharlal Nehru and his aunt Indumati Chamanlal, 1954:
The Nehrus had affectionate ties with the Sarabhais (Courtesy Physical Research Laboratory, Ahmedabad)

With Jawaharlal Nehru (Courtesy Physical Research Laboratory, Ahmedabad)

With mentors and friends: from left to right, S.S. Bhatnagar, Homi Bhabha and C.V. Raman (Courtesy Physical Research Laboratory, Ahmedabad)

A strong faith in international collaboration: Vikram with P.M.S. Blackett (front row, right), C.F. Powell (second row, left) and Homi Bhabha (Courtesy Atomic Research Centre, Mumbai)

Vikram and Bhabha scouting locations for the sounding rocket programme, 1962 (Courtesy Indian Space Research Organisation, Bangalore)

Scientists and delegates at the Professor Sydney Chapman lecture series at PRL, late 1947: Vikram is seated third from right, K.R. Ramanathan is seated third from left (Courtesy Physical Research Laboratory, Ahmedabad)

With Indira Gandhi at the Pugwash Conference, Udaipur, 1964
(Courtesy Atomic Research Centre, Mumbai)

Addressing the first press conference after taking over as chairman of the Atomic Energy Commission of India, 1966 (Courtesy Bhabha Atomic Research Centre, Mumbai)

Vikram wanted to use television as a medium of development: here he is seen with Prime Minister Indira Gandhi at the *Krishi Darshan* Programme, New Delhi, 1967 (Courtesy Bhabha Atomic Research Centre, Mumbai)

With Prime Minister Indira Gandhi at CIRUS, 1967 (Courtesy Bhabha Atomic Research Centre, Mumbai)

Examining a rocket at TERLS (Courtesy Indian Space Research Organisation, Bangalore)

At the rocket launcher site TERLS (Courtesy Indian Space Research Organisation, Bangalore)

Vikram and Sarla with C.V. Raman: laying the foundation stone for the Community Science Centre, Ahmedabad, 1968 (Courtesy Dr Vikram Sarabhai Archives, Nehru Foundation for Development, Ahmedabad)

The rocket boys: from left, Dr S.C. Gupta, Madhavan Nair, A.P.J. Abdul Kalam, Vikram and H.G.S. Murthy (Courtesy Indian Space Research Organisation, Bangalore)

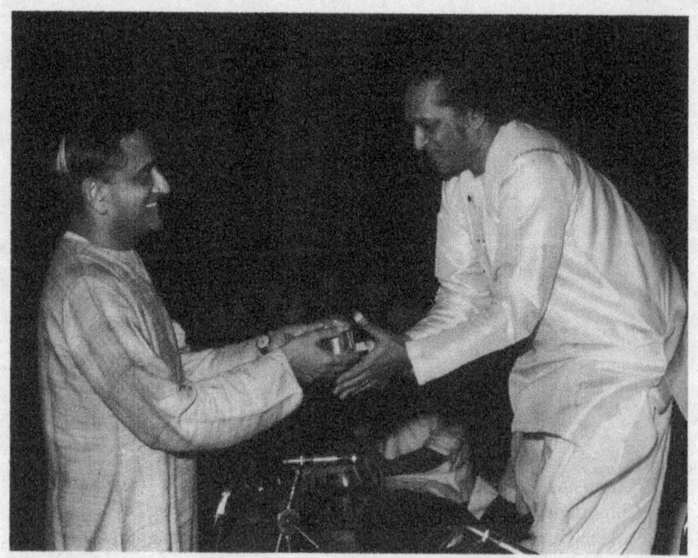

'First the education of the senses': Vikram with Pandit Ravi Shankar (Courtesy Dr Vikram Sarabhai Archives, Nehru Foundation for Development, Ahmedabad)

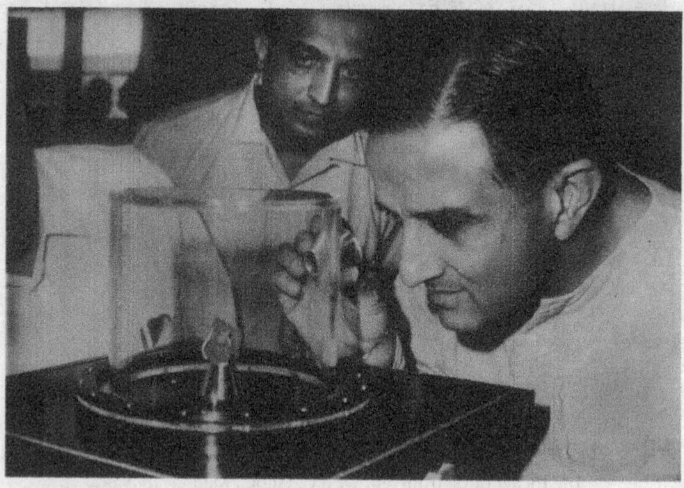

Vikram and Praful Bhavsar examining a sample of a moon rock (Courtesy Physical Research Laboratory, Ahmedabad)

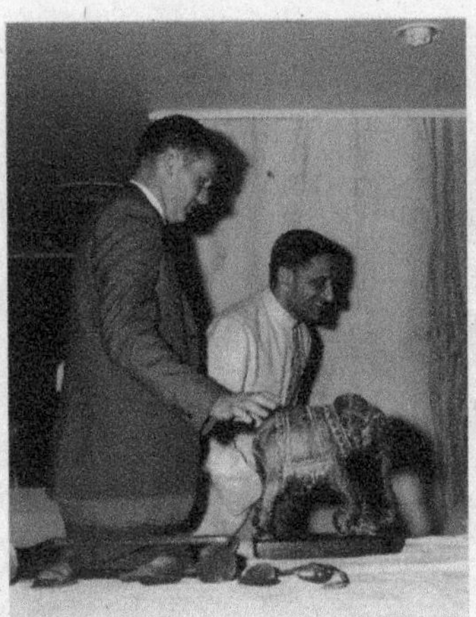

With American astronaut Neil Armstrong at the Tata Institute of Fundamental Research, Mumbai (Courtesy Physical Research Laboratory, Ahmedabad)

Vikram with Dr Kurt Waldheim, President of the first United Nations Conference on the Exploration and Peaceful Uses of Outer Space (1968) and later Secretary General of the United Nations, and his wife (Courtesy Dr Vikram Sarabhai Archives, Nehru Foundation for Development, Ahmedabad)

As President, International Atomic Energy Agency Conference, Vienna, 1970 (Courtesy Dr Vikram Sarabhai Archives, Nehru Foundation for Development, Ahmedabad)

team to strive harder. And in a country where the heavy hand of bureaucracy was so palpable the significance of these cannot be underestimated.

For example, R.G. Rastogi recalls how Vikram's name alone was able to get him, overnight, a passport, a ticket and scarce foreign exchange to attend an important conference in Belgrade. Or how when he got into an argument with government electricians while rigging up some equipment in Thumba, Vikram protectively moved in saying he should be arrested first as head of the institution before they touched his scientists. But Vikram seemed to do more than merely support his men. He made them feel they were part of a larger enterprise. He gave them a dream.

R.D. John, the civil engineer who had been drafted in from the CPWD for what he thought would be a six-month project, initially wondered: 'Why are we wasting money on this rocket firing?' It took him very little time to become a zealous convert to the lofty aims of the programme ('without space no one can live').[9] He was to stay on for three decades, to become the chief engineer of the Department of Space, and evolve, for the first time, specifications for the unprecedented requirements that were thrown up such as computer flooring or special type of painting in the propellant and plane deflection plants.

In fact, most of the early recruits would go on to assume positions of prominence and responsibility in the programme. Praful Bhavsar, for instance, would be programme director for Remote Sensing Applications (1978–86) and chairman, Remote Sensing Area (1976–86). E.V. Chitnis would assume charge of the Satellite Instructional Television Experiment (SITE) in 1975-76 as project manager and become director of the Space Applications Centre (1981–85). Vasant Gowarikar would become director of the Vikram Sarabhai Space Centre (VSSC) in Trivandrum in 1979, and U.R. Rao would assume the chairmanship of ISRO for the years 1984 to 1994.

'I have always been struck by the dedication of the ISRO staff and its identification with the goals of the space programme,' Gopal Raj observes. As he points out, despite the rough conditions in the early days, few people quit. Quite simply they would not have had the time to even think about other options given the constantly mounting challenges Vikram threw at them.

In February 1968, Prime Minister Indira Gandhi was invited to the site of the Nike–Apache launch to dedicate the officially designated Thumba Equatorial Rocket Launch Station (TERLS) to the UN. It was a simple ceremony with invitees seated in three rows on the beach. There were speeches and flowers. After the ceremony, Vikram met with his senior colleagues and told them it was time for a full-fledged feasibility study on developing a satellite launch vehicle.

To anyone unused to Vikram's style, this would have seemed a preposterous suggestion. The various aspects of the technology—propellants, hardware and so on—were still at an early stage of evolution. The space programmers had not even managed to send up a two-stage rocket. And already Vikram was talking about a launch vehicle that would not only have to shoot upwards in a number of stages, but also release a satellite at the right height and angle.

There was, of course, no doubting his seriousness. A team went to work on sourcing suitable models, while Chitnis, the man who had located Thumba, and Pramod Kale embarked on a search for a launch site on the east coast where the earth's rotation would provide a greater push to the launch vehicle. For Kalam, meanwhile, Vikram had found yet another test.

In his autobiography, Kalam describes how, in early 1968, Vikram summoned him to Delhi.[10] The meeting was at the Ashoka, at the ungodly hour of 3.30 a.m. Used to Vikram's eccentricities, Kalam followed his instructions unquestioningly and found himself being ushered in with another man who turned out to be Group Captain V.S. Narayanan from Air Headquarters, the same man who had brusquely told Vikram about the need for an Indian missile defence strategy.

Vikram, according to Kalam, ordered coffee for both and proceeded to unfold a plan to develop a rocket-assisted take-off (RATO) system for military aircraft which would be particularly useful on the short runways in the Himalayas. An hour later, they were on the Tilpat range, on the outskirts of Delhi, looking at a Russian RATO with Vikram asking them if they could pull off something similar. Both said they could.

Soon after that dawn encounter, Kalam and Narayanan were both drafted into the newly formed missile panel in the defence ministry. Ostensibly Vikram had nothing to do with the panel but from Kalam's account it is clear that he kept himself informed about its deliberations. It was his 'usual practice', he claims, to brief Vikram after every meeting of the missile panel.[11]

In all the excitement of the evolving space programme, Vikram had, as usual, found time to spin off a couple of small-scale pet projects in the mid-1960s—the Nehru Foundation and the Community Science Centre.

Since the early 1960s, Vikram had begun to note down ideas for a foundation that would bring together people to explore concepts of development, a sort of think tank for which, associates claimed variously, he had got the idea from Professor C.A. Doxiadis, the Greek architect, planner and founder of ekistics, the science of human settlement, or from Princeton, which sheltered the likes of Einstein during the Second World War. Vikram proposed to start the Foundation, which he named after Nehru, on a piece of land he owned at Thaltej, just outside Ahmedabad, using the proceeds of the S.S. Bhatnagar Award for Science he had been given in 1962.

One of the early projects undertaken by the fledgling Foundation was the setting up of a Group for the Improvement of Science Education (GISE). Science education was and had been a matter of extreme concern for Vikram for many years. Raja Ramanna, a fellow physicist, was on a panel with him to discuss science curricula and recalls his passionate involvement in the subject.[12] The GISE came up with the conclusion that 'if the understanding of science by students or by adults is to be promoted, what is needed is a facility where those who wish to teach and those who wish to learn can come together and conduct basic experiments and be exposed through audio-visual and other means to the latest developments of science, science teaching and technology'.[13]

In 1965, Arnold Frutkin, assistant director of the NASA programme, introduced Vikram to Axel Horn, a designer of education programmes and materials. Vikram met Horn for breakfast at the Plaza in New York and, with his 'powerful' and 'stimulating' talent, charted out a basic plan of action. By September next year, Mr and Mrs Horn were in Ahmedabad with a brief for the former to conceptualize a programme that would provide 'interested science teachers and students with equipment and access to working scientists not available in the public school system'.[14] This programme was the basis for the Community Science Centre, which was housed in a building designed and constructed by one of the graduating students at the local school of architecture. Vikram's mother Sarla donated the funds.

Though he was not directly involved in the running of either of these two institutions, Vikram's pace was getting ever more frenzied. Kamla complained that keeping up with him was like walking on a treadwheel, 'one goes on but gets nowhere'.[15] And instead of slowing down, his life had got even more complicated as a result of certain unexpected developments.

In January 1966, Lal Bahadur Shastri, the mild-mannered Congressman who had taken over after Nehru as prime minister, died of a heart attack in Tashkent where he had gone to sign peace terms with his Pakistani counterpart President Ayub Khan. On the day his successor, Nehru's daughter Indira Gandhi, was being sworn in, news came of Homi Bhabha having died in an air crash. The coming together of these disparate occurrences was to decisively alter the course of Vikram's life.

The mid-1960s were a traumatic time for India. Two wars in quick succession had ravaged the economy. Rebellions had broken out in Punjab and the North East, and various parts of the country were reeling under famine. At a time such as this, an untried, inexperienced and hesitant politician might not have seemed like the best choice for prime minister. Yet, it was the only kind of leader that had been acceptable to the various contentious factions of the Congress.

Indira Gandhi was painfully aware of her vulnerability. A gawky, awkward woman, she had had a meagre political career till then in the shadow of her father's colossal stature. She had been Congress president and then a minister for information and broadcasting in the Shastri cabinet. Years of playing hostess for her father had given her a shrewd understanding of the cut-throat world of politics. She knew that her inherited problems were immense and that she was surrounded by enemies.

She was, moreover, not possessed of a warmth that would enable her to reach out for help. Her childhood had been insecure and lonely, shadowed by her mother's frail health and her father's intermittent imprisonment. She herself had suffered from tuberculosis that entailed long periods of convalescence in distant sanatoria. An impetuous marriage that might have offered some relief from her enforced state of solitude had long fallen apart. Mistrustful, with a shyness that was often mistaken for hauteur, Indira, on the day of her formal ascension, might well have felt she was stepping on to a bed of burning coals. The news that Bhabha, her father's friend and a potentially strong ally, was no more must have been a considerable blow.[16]

It also left the controversial atomic energy programme headless.

Indira's advisers first recommended S. Chandrasekhar, Vikram's friend and physicist at the University of Chicago, as the right person to replace Bhabha. In a conversation with his biographer Kameshwar C. Wali, Chandrasekhar gives the impression of a fairly haphazard appointment process. The person who called him from the PM's Office with the offer, he claims, seemed taken aback when he pointed out that he was an American citizen and there would be security considerations following from that. 'These people were totally unprepared,' Chandrasekhar maintains.[17] In any case, he declined.

Another round of discussions ensued, from which Vikram emerged as the most acceptable candidate. There were murmurs that Indira's choice had political undertones; her arch rival in the Congress was Morarji Desai, the man who had opposed Vikram's bid for vice chancellorship of Gujarat University. There are not many takers for this theory, however. Ramanna, who could be said to have been leery of many of Vikram's ideas, claims in his autobiography that his choice as chief of the AEC was 'unanimous'.[18] Experts on the subject also widely agree that the concern then appeared to be to find a person of stature sufficient to maintain the clout of the programme both domestically and internationally. In any event, the decision was taken. Indira asked Vikram if he would take Bhabha's place.

Looking back, it is easy to see the portentousness of the offer. Like a bet set down before a gambler in the dying hours of the night, it sat on the table, pleading for a response. People close to Vikram immediately read the ominous signs. 'I was not happy about it,' Mrinalini says categorically. 'He was already working so hard and this was a public job.' Others, including his mother, dissuaded him, warning that he would end up sacrificing his scientific interest, his personal life; that he would get 'caught up'.[19]

No one perhaps was more aware of the pitfalls than Vikram himself. It has been suggested by some that he was inclined to accept the offer partly because it would have been hard for him to turn Indira down and partly because of the immense clout that came with the job. Neither appears to be true. He had already refused reported offers of public office. Besides, he was a wealthy and influential man who had shown himself to be dismissive of the petty perks of power. His cabin at PRL was not air-conditioned because he did not want, as he said, to avail of a facility he could not provide for his colleagues. As chairman of the AEC he was to become even fussier, insisting on, among other things, carrying his own briefcase. 'He was very conscious of how easy it was to fall into what he called "feudal habits",' says Ashok Parthasarthi who was on the Interdisciplinary Policy Planning and Management Services Unit of the AEC.

It seems more likely, given his family history and the kind of explanations emerging from people who knew him best, that he was attracted by the possibilities that the position could open up for him. Kartikeya understood it as a 'natural progression' in his career: 'He really saw ambition as ambition for India. The post was probably an opportunity to do things on a scale that would have made a difference.' Gita, too, recalls him saying that it was 'enlarging' whatever it was 'he was trying to do'.

It is likely that Vikram looked upon it as a chance that might never come again. The chance to see his ideas and aspirations to their natural culmination. It is likely that he sensed the price he might have to pay. How much he hesitated will never be known, but eventually he decided to pick up the gauntlet.

Zalani had lunch with him at the Ashoka the day he apprised the prime minister of his decision. 'Well, Zalani, I have done it,' is all he said. His letter of acceptance was more forthcoming. 'I am attracted by the opportunity for taking over the work which was started by Dr Bhabha,' he wrote. 'The task of pushing ahead with the application of science and technology for the needs of the nation under your leadership is an inspiring one, which I am happy to shoulder...'[20] The letter also clarified that his associations with PRL, the space programme and MIT would continue.

Some sacrifices, however, would have to be made. Government regulations did not permit an involvement in private enterprise. Vikram had to resign all his positions in the family business. Sarabhai Chemicals gave him an emotional farewell. By the mid-1960s, the humble enterprise that Vikram had inherited was well on its way to becoming one of the country's leading pharmaceutical concerns. At the ceremony, Vikram had tears in his eyes as he talked about leaving 'the garden I have nurtured'.[21]

The Sarabhai family was thrown into a tumult by the event. Vikram's brother, Gautam, had to shoulder the additional responsibilities of business overnight. 'I wonder how he felt about it,' Gita says, recalling the event with clear disapproval. What apparently made it worse, according to her, was the feeling that Vikram's decision was unilateral. 'If it had been discussed, it might have been better but to leave it like this!'

Vikram did not stay to face the recriminations of his siblings. While the authorities in Delhi ran a back check into his extensive holdings for security purposes, he was on his way to deliver a pre-scheduled talk on 'Implementing Change through Science and Technology' at the International Symposium on Science and Society in South Asia at New York's Rockefeller University. From there he travelled to Britain.

'We were surprised to see him turning up in a government-loaned car,' recalls S.M. Chitre, who was studying with Vikram's nephews, Anand and Suhrid, and the astrophysicist Jayant Narlikar, in Cambridge at the time. 'He did not tell us about his new job or that he had come to meet Sir John Cockcroft.' Cockcroft was the distinguished scientist who had set up the British atomic power programme.

In London, Vikram had lunch with Raja Ramanna, head of physics at the Indian AEC. 'It was indeed a pleasant surprise to me,' Ramanna later noted, 'to notice that he had already made all the necessary preparations to enter into the field of nuclear technology in all its aspects.'[22]

On 1 June 1966, Vikram entered the crowded room at the AEC. Flashbulbs went off and reporters jostled to get a better view of the man who had taken the place of the formidable Homi

Bhabha. Vikram Sarabhai was a name they were already familiar with. But now, there was just one question they all wished to ask him: 'Dr Sarabhai, what about the atom bomb?'[23]

Homi Bhabha and Vikram Sarabhai. There are so many parallels between the two men that several decades after their unexpectedly early deaths, they have come to occupy a somewhat interchangeable place in the public mind. So much so, hagiographical accounts of their lives even tell the same anecdotes about both, such as the story of the discarded withered tree stump which each one is supposed to have rescued with a feeling reprimand to the gardener about respecting old age.[24]

In reality, however, both men had vastly dissimilar personalities. The differences were strikingly evident in the varying styles of the programmes they set up.

The space programme started out with a modest budget and a low profile. The atomic energy programme, in contrast, had burst on the scene with the flamboyant assertion, 'no power is costlier than no power'[25] and the frills to match: autonomy, secrecy—greater even than for the defence-related programmes of the UK and the US—and abundant funds (nobody in the Indian government, despite concerns about economy, had ever denied an 'urgent demand of the department', Nehru confirmed in a statement to the Lok Sabha).[26]

The space programme was located in a stretch of wilderness on the southernmost tip of the peninsula with few modern facilities and a makeshift office in a church building. The atomic energy programme's research establishment sprawled over several lush, landscaped acres in an eastern suburb of the country's commercial capital, Bombay, with an office complex designed by Italian architects to Bhabha's exacting standards (specifications covered even the alignment of funnels, and the 'maharaja of

Trombay', as Bhabha was jocularly called, is said to have supervised the layout of the flower beds by helicopter).[27]

When Vikram wanted to create an approach road of 100 feet rather than the 60 foot one at Thumba, the Kerala state government, according to R.D. John, 'was not enthusiastic'.[28] On the other hand, the Tamil Nadu chief minister, K. Kamaraj, deputed his minister for industries and senior officers to assist Bhabha when the latter evinced interest in setting up a reactor in the state.

Satish Dhawan, Vikram's successor at the space programme, confessed to having been surprised by the warmth of his reception, due largely to the high identification of the space technologists with the goals of the programme.[29] At the AEC, on the other hand, Vikram found himself entering a hornet's nest after Bhabha's demise, the effects of a more individualistic culture that was a direct effect of Bhabha's personality.

Homi J. Bhabha, whose likeness was to grace every lobby and corridor of the AEC's various units, was a complex individual. Itty Abraham who referred to letters and views of Bhabha's seniors and colleagues in his early years abroad for his book, *The Making of the Indian Atomic Bomb*, suggests that contrary to his colossal reputation in India, Bhabha had a very different image in the Western mind. In the West, Bhabha's much-touted scientific achievements, his artistic pretensions and love of Western music, far from impressing people, had caused confusion. Used to more clear demarcations between 'blacks' and whites, his colleagues had responded to him with exaggerated superciliousness, turning him into a Caliban-like figure, 'almost speaking physics but not quite, physically present but betraying his unscientific origins, a child of the world who had yet to come to full maturity'.[30]

The perception must have hurt; it appeared to have played a significant role in shaping Bhabha's psyche. His manner towards subordinates was often described as scoffingly disdainful and he took a particular delight in behaving imperiously with Westerners.

'He liked to make the white man wait,' is how a senior American academician put it.[31]

The atomic energy programme was thus founded on a shaky self-esteem with the need for demonstration apparent in its every aspect: its size, its prominence and the tall, rather vague claims on which it was based. People at TIFR and DAE 'passionately believed that developing atomic energy would greatly benefit India', maintains former AEC chairman M.R. Srinivasan, 'although we were not very clear in what precise manner'.[32]

By the time Bhabha died, the atomic energy establishment at Trombay had expanded into the country's largest scientific institution with 8500 employees. In the intervening years, three research reactors had come up and considerable progress made in the areas of training, prospecting for atomic minerals and the fabrication of fuel elements and electronic instruments. Yet, a fundamental shift of direction had taken place. From describing itself as the provider of unlimited, cheap energy, the AEC had slipped seamlessly into the equally monumental mission of safeguarding India's security concerns.

Admittedly, this was not an entirely new role. A dual purpose had been written into the atomic energy programme from its very inception. By cosseting it, shrouding it in secrecy and approving, among other things, a plutonium extraction plant, it seems clear that the Indian government had always been supportive of a technological effort in that direction. The support, however, appears to have been clearly for a covert operation. It is believed that in November 1962, when Bhabha penned a note to Nehru on China's imminent nuclear explosion and asked him for permission to conduct a test, Nehru had thrown him out.[33]

Maintaining the ambiguity was considered essential, the key, in fact, to the government's diplomatic strategy. Nehru sold India's 'restraint' as a bargaining point at international fora; it allowed India to occupy the moral high ground, to criticize the hypocrisy of the West in seeking to roll back programmes in the developing world while maintaining their own arsenals. It allowed India to push for total disarmament while retaining its own option on the bomb. As George Perkovich, author of a book on India's nuclear programme, points out, India was, and would continue to be, 'fiercely jealous of its sovereignty, resistant to any inequalities and inequities, wary of any semblance of colonialism, and righteous in its demands for disarmament'.[34] The strategy also ensured continued cooperation from the developed world in technological and economic areas.

On 24 October 1964, months after Nehru's death and a week after China exploded its first nuclear device, Bhabha, however, made what has come to be known as a legendary broadcast on All India Radio where he talked of the atomic bomb. It was a deterrent, he said, and it was cheap (Rs 17.5 lakh for a ten-kiloton explosion, Rs 30 lakh for a two-megaton one, and Rs 10–15 crore for a stockpile). A few days previously he had said India could explode the bomb within 'eighteen months' of a decision being taken to do so.

His claim was glaringly erroneous on at least one count—it failed to include the high cost of setting up and maintaining reactors, reprocessing facilities and other infrastructure required to produce the raw material and design and make weapons.[35] Prime Minister Lal Bahadur Shastri clarified a month later that contrary to Bhabha's assessment, the cost of a single atom bomb was of the order of Rs 40–50 crore.

But the ball had been set in motion. Over the next few months the subject was avidly discussed. Both the US and the USSR were talking of nuclear explosions for developmental purposes and the US had even suggested the possibility of exporting know-how under what it called the Ploughshare scheme for making peaceful nuclear explosives which could be used for massive engineering projects. Later reports released by the Americans indicate that Bhabha may have approached them in February 1965 for help to design a Ploughshare device with a view to taking India's nuclear explosives quest forward.[36] The growing anti-proliferation lobby persuaded the Americans to refuse Bhabha's appeal.

Meanwhile, a skirmish occurred on the country's north-western flank in the marshy land known as the Rann of Kutch, which would later turn into a war between India and Pakistan. In April, Shastri, possibly to counter ongoing political pressure or in response to Pakistan's aggression, gave Bhabha the go-ahead for theoretical work on a peaceful nuclear explosion with the proviso that no experimental work was to be done without his clearance. Apparently, Bhabha summoned Ramanna to his office at the Yacht Club and gleefully waved the permission. 'It meant we were finally on our way,' Ramanna observed.[37] He was to be chairman of the group for the Study of Nuclear Explosions for Peaceful Purposes (SNEPP).

Bhabha's keenness on the subject is both puzzling and revelatory of the attitude that was driving the atomic energy programme. Judged on his own target of producing 1000 MW by 1965, the programme had been unsuccessful. Also, as the agreements signed with the Americans and Canadians for building reactors in Maharashtra and Rajasthan showed, the promised indigenization was still a long way away. It is likely that on both counts he could have been forgiven, given the scale and technological sophistication of the programme. Itty Abraham suggests, however, that when the time came, in the 1960s, for the programme to fulfil its primary and mundane responsibility of providing electricity, it was perceived as a comedown for the participants who began casting around for a more glamorous raison d'être.[38]

The shift may not have been as deliberate as it appears with hindsight but there is little doubt that around the mid-1960s the expectation of power from the atomic energy programme had been superseded by an assumption of its capability to develop weapons for the country's defence. Bhabha's rhetoric had kicked up immense public interest and debate. But none could have been more excited than the people at the AEC itself. In one way or another—plugging natural uranium-heavy water reactors that would make India less dependent on foreign resources and produce plutonium, for instance—the technologists at AEC had always been pushing for weaponization.

Assertions by various senior-level former AEC staffers indicate an astonishingly uniform belief in their role with regard to India's security and no evidence of any moral qualms about atomic warfare. The chief driving force appears to have been a combination of the need to achieve technological prowess and the need to show the same to the world. Raja Ramanna, a prominent proponent of this view, admitted that there was no discussion ever between him and his colleagues on the subject of 'whether we shouldn't make the bomb'. What was more important was '*how*' it was to be done: 'For us it was a matter of prestige that would justify our ancient past. The question of a deterrent came much later. Also, as Indian scientists we were keen to show our Western counterparts, who thought little of us those days, that we too could do it.'[39]

And then in came Vikram and burst the bubble.

Vikram's association with the atomic energy programme predates Bhabha's death. Bhabha had inducted him into the board the previous year. Vikram's position as head of the emerging space programme was probably sufficient reason for his induction. But there is an entry dated 29 January 1966 in his handwritten jottings to himself—listing points, possibly, of discussion under the headings 'Jha' ('Indo-US meeting, Planning'), 'Dharma Vir' ('AEC, Indo-US meeting, disarmament'), 'PM' ('Visit AEC, Problems PC that space. Commission, Committee Culture') and 'JRD' [underlined]/'Dharma Vir' ('Space research, rocket development, Indo-US Meeting, Disarmament')—which indicates that he was not only on familiar terms with all the heavyweights of the programme but also hobnobbing with them on subjects beyond the specific aims of the programme.

In fact, for many years before his induction into the board of the AEC and quite apart from his later role as its chairman, he had been a keen participant in the intellectual and scientific debate over nuclear power and its applications. He had been to the London Pugwash Conference in 1962. He was a member of the Continuing Committee of the Pugwash Movement, of the Institute of Peace and Conflict Research in Sweden and was to set up the Indian Pugwash Society in 1967 to 'promote discussion and knowledge and to stimulate general interest in and to diffuse knowledge in regard to problems relating to science and to world affairs'.[40]

R.R. Revelle, a professor of science and public policy at the University of California, who met Vikram at many related conferences, in places as varied as Addis Ababa, Venice and London, maintains, 'With his profoundly complex mind, Vikram was fascinated by the intricate chess game of nuclear arms control.'[41]

Some insight into his thinking can be found on a plain sheet of paper on which he has scribbled on 5 February 1965 the following phrases: 'What is Pugwash?', 'Great imbalance', 'Balance of terror', 'Army tanks, missiles, alliances', 'Non aligned—self interest', 'Atom bomb Chinese What should we do?', 'Economic realities for India'.

Some of this mulling over found its way to the talk Vikram gave in December–January 1965-66 on 'Security of Developing Countries' at the Pugwash Conference in Addis Ababa, Ethiopia.[42] The speech gives an indication of the thinking he was to bring to his new assignment.

He started his speech by introducing the idea that the triangular polarization of the world in the 1950s had brought about a reciprocal neutrality between the East–West blocs on the one hand and the non-aligned countries on the other, thereby encouraging a situation where 'developing nations could resort to the use of force in settling their mutual disputes'.

Nuclear arms in the long run being cheaper than conventional weapons, he explained, the reigning situation was 'most conducive for the proliferation of nuclear weapons'. At the same time, he maintained, the effects of an arms race in retarding the growth of living standards in developing countries would eventually endanger 'the stability and security of the big powers as well as the developing countries'.

Under the circumstances, he argued, big powers had a responsibility not only to disarm (nuclear and conventional weapons) but also to set up 'a system of safeguards and collective security which can come into effect speedily and without political overtones whenever the territory of one nation is threatened by another'. In short, he was urging the West to play both saint and policeman. 'As a citizen of a developing country,' he concluded, 'I feel that the solution rests as much on an understanding on our part of the facts of life as it does on the attitude of the big nations towards the problem.'

It was definitely not a world view calculated to make him popular with his prospective teammates at the AEC. But in at least one case he had reason to expect hostility regardless of his thoughts and opinions.

Homi N. Sethna was a chemical engineer educated at the University of Michigan. He had put in a stint at the Imperial Chemical Industries in London before returning to India in 1949 to work for the AEC where he was put in charge of constructing plants for various purposes such as the extraction of rare earths from monazite and for producing pure thorium nitrate. The stocky Parsi engineer quickly built up a reputation for efficiency and reliability and was one of the five members comprising the second-rung leadership under Bhabha. The other members were Brahm Prakash, head of the metallurgy division; R. Ramanna, head of physics; A.R. Gopal-Ayengar, director of life sciences; and A.S. Rao, head of electronics.

On Bhabha's death, Sethna, convinced that he was the rightful successor to the late chairman, jockeyed arduously for the position. Some even claim he produced a letter showing that he was entitled to be in a supervisory position in Bhabha's absence.[43] Failing in his efforts he turned his disappointment into a battle against the new chairman. He was to adopt a bitterly adversarial position throughout Vikram's tenure and was to be responsible for nudging many chroniclers of the atomic energy programme towards a view of his perceived rival as a woolly-headed Utopian, an idealist weaned on Gandhian and Jain ideas of non-violence, lost and baffled in the manly thicket of the nuclear power-driven real world.[44]

There is no doubt, particularly judging by the list of his technology-driven successors, that Vikram, with his philosophical inclinations and moral ambivalences, was an unusual choice to head the atomic energy programme. It is equally true that he abhorred the notion of nuclear warfare ('[it] is one of the biggest threats to the survival of human beings. If atomic warfare were to break out on a global scale this would be a terrible catastrophe for the world....').[45] His ideas may well have been unpopular—they certainly failed to influence the direction the programme would eventually take.

But it would have been uncharacteristic, to say the least, for Vikram to have been guilty of the kind of blundering romanticism he was accused of. He was an admirer of Gandhi who believed in never starting 'what you have not clearly circumscribed in your own mind or what you are not ready to suffer for to the very end'.[46] Vikram himself had told M.G.K. Menon that in his view processes had to be started 'like a prophet—infallibly accurate as to what the consequences will be'.[47] And in this case he was not unaware of what he was to be up against. Before accepting the AEC assignment he is believed to have told the then cabinet secretary, Dharam Vira, 'It is not going to be easy to succeed Bhabha. It is not only taking over a job, it is also taking over a thinking.'[48]

The other suggestion that Vikram's Jain heritage was somehow emasculating was again off the mark for two reasons. In the first place, the Sarabhais were not dogmatic followers of religion. Ambalal had made it clear that his religious and philosophical beliefs were to be tempered with pragmatism even if it meant the taking of life. In his approach to certain matters, such as non-vegetarianism ('If someone were ill and it were prescribed I see no objection'),[49] Vikram was to show a similar attitude.

The suggestion also misinterprets the meaning of non-violence in Jainism. Given the philosophical inclinations of both father and son it is a necessary clarification to make. Lawrence Babb seeks to correct the mistaken impression that the religion's emphasis on non-violence is an argument for meekness or docility. In fact, Babb claims:

> Martial values, albeit in transmuted form, are crucial to Jainism's message and to its understanding of itself. The Jina is a conqueror. He is also one who might have been—had he so chosen to be—a worldly king and a conqueror of the world. But instead the Jina becomes a spiritual king and transposes the venue of war from the outer field of battle to an inner one. The metaphor of transmuted martial valour is basic to the outlook's tradition and integration.[50]

This passage, in fact, provides a key to Vikram's state of mind when he took up the challenge of the AEC job. He was aware of the stakes. Possibly he had made space for a potential defeat. But perhaps like Gandhi, who, Erikson maintained, would never 'play' unless he was in a position of such moral dominance that he could convince himself and others that the force of his mediatorship was 'for their own good', Vikram had made up his mind that he had a moral imperative to 'play'.[51]

From the very outset it was clear that Vikram had a plan. And it was a departure from what had gone before. 'Sarabhai's rhetorical understanding of atomic energy—whether for development or defence—was far more carefully calibrated than Bhabha's,' writes Itty Abraham.[52] Perkovich observes: 'Sarabhai saw matters differently [from the AEC technologists]. Rather than asking what it [nuclear explosive capability] would mean to his standing to lead India into the nuclear explosive club, he asked what material good it would do for India.'[53] This argument—coldly logical—may not however have been quite what an audience primed with the red-hot rhetoric of technological prowess would have wanted to hear. Virtually every question at the momentous press conference in June 1966 dealt, in one way or another, with the bomb. 'What about the bomb?' 'How long will it take us to make it?' 'What is our capability for a prototype?'

Vikram's response was lengthy but simple. A prototype, he said to a stunned press corps, was a 'paper tiger' and 'paper tigers do not provide security'. 'If you want to rely on the atom bomb for safeguarding your security,' he continued, 'this is not achieved by exploding a bomb. It means a total defence system, a means of delivery...long-range missiles...radars, a high state of electronics, a high state of metallurgical and industrial base.... I would like to emphasize that security can be endangered not only from outside but also from within. If you do not maintain the rate of progress of the economic development of the nation...we should think of an internal as well as an external threat.... So the real problem in this whole question relates to the utilization of national resources for productive (*sic*) and social welfare against the burden of defence expenditure which a country can bear at any particular time.'[54]

It was a clear blow to the mood for a demonstration that Bhabha and his team had been enthusiastically building towards. But it was not, as many read it, a farewell to arms. As Itty Abraham points out: 'Contrary to the pacifist position he is often thought to have held, Sarabhai did not reject atomic weapons outright as a means to national security. What he was adamantly opposed to was the appearance of an aggressive military posture without the necessary infrastructure and means to back this position up.'[55]

And India, in Vikram's opinion, did not have the necessary infrastructure. In response to a question on developing a missile system he pointed to the pessimistic findings of the electronics committee. 'We can only go step-by-step. It is not the question of having to or wanting to,' he said. 'In developing our grassroots economy, we have to first of all develop a metallurgical base and an electronics base, and all this cannot be done without a good agricultural base. I do not see how you can be for all these things unless the country makes more gross national product.'[56]

With this answer Vikram was making it clear that he was in favour of consolidating the country's 'internal security' first. What he meant by 'internal security' he had already spelt out. But privately it is likely that he had other concerns in mind. Social concerns for instance. In his jottings in an undated entry that seems to have been made in 1966, he writes: 'Problem more important than Atomic Energy. Of the young—Protests world over. Cynicism of the older generation. Great discrepancy between what they preach and what they do.'

The economic argument, the guns versus butter dilemma, however, is what he chose to highlight in his June press conference. And by itself, it had to be admitted, the dilemma was hardly novel. Others had reached a similar conclusion before, most notably the political commentator Romesh Thapar, who wrote in the *Economic Weekly* (31 October1964) that a bomb in the hands of a beggar 'does not make him king',[57] particularly when there were others who had bombs and the ability to deliver them.

Amidst the ongoing controversy though it was not a view expected from within the AEC. And critics could well argue that it left Vikram's intentions regarding nuclear weapons still unclear. There were possibly several good reasons why he could have chosen to keep it so. One of them was his seeming determination to restore to the programme its original focus: the production of cheap, plentiful energy.

In his book on the atomic energy programme, *India's Nuclear Estate*, Dhirendra Sharma describes the Bhabha phase as 'Personalized' and the Vikram phase as 'Regulatory'. Vikram kicked off the 'Regulatory' period by donning a hard hat and visiting the uranium mine in Bihar's Singhbhum district. His handwritten jottings of the time demonstrate a preoccupation with hardware. Phrases such as 'FBR', 'Material Testing', 'Fuel Testing', 'Coolant Technology', 'Control System', 'Safeguard and Supplies', 'Filter Production Unit', 'TAPP fuel' and 'RAPP I' are scrawled all over a notepad with the letterhead of the Chairman, AEC. He had taken some pains to acquaint himself with his new teammates as well, for among the jottings is a page with names of senior personnel and against each, the duration of service and type of work performed.

Almost immediately on assuming charge, Vikram made arrangements for many of them, senior scientists and engineers of the AEC, to visit the US, the USSR and France to acquaint themselves with the latest trends in reactors, high-energy physics, applications of radioisotopes and radiation biology. In September 1966, he himself set off with a team comprising Sethna, Brahm Prakash and others on a study tour to observe breeders and other forms of advanced reactor technology in the US.

Vikram appeared to be using every means to shift the priorities of the atomic energy programme back to energy, including invoking the Bhabha mystique. For instance, on 12 January 1967, at a ceremony held to rename the atomic energy establishment at Trombay the Bhabha Atomic Research Centre (BARC) after its late founder, Vikram heaped praise on his predecessor, calling him a 'creative administrator', a 'dynamic leader', a 'tireless worker' and, significantly, 'a pioneer in promoting international cooperation in the peaceful uses of the atom'. Bhabha's stand, he said, had often been misunderstood abroad by those 'who had not recognised that he was the principal advisor to Nehru who decided on the basis of a national choice that India would develop her programme only for peaceful purposes'.[58] It was not bombs but 'islands of self-confidence', Vikram concluded stirringly, that 'keeps our heads high'.

But what Vikram had also done with his responses at the press conference was to move the decision of whether India should or should not make nuclear weapons, out of the scientific and technological arena where it had strayed and into the sphere of politics. It was not merely a technological decision, he was saying, but a political one.

It is fairly certain that in those early days he had the full backing of the prime minister. Indira, callow politician that she was at the time, was beset with numerous difficulties. Severe famine had necessitated the import of wheat shipments from the US and Indira had been arm-twisted into devaluing the rupee to procure the same. She continued to be vulnerable as well to the political machinations of the powerful 'syndicate' of party leaders that had propped her up. Withdrawn and defensive, there were few people she could trust and she seemed to look upon Vikram as one of them.

Their relationship appears to have been tinged with friendliness. Indira was just a year older than Vikram. They had been married the same year, 1942. She had once discussed with her friend and biographer, Pupul Jayakar, the need 'for a flexible mind that could hold the strength and beauty of heritage yet would participate in the technological revolution'.[59] Vikram and his dancer wife Mrinalini were as close an answer to her prayers as she was likely to find.

Indira went so far as to display flashes of informality in her relationship with Vikram. She called him by his first name and once, at a science-related meeting in Kodaikanal, those present noticed the prime minister scribbling on a piece of paper, folding it several times and passing it on to Vikram. It said: 'Can't Mrinalini do something about these dreadful curtains?'[60]

Vikram, for his part, appears to have treated her with due deference. A stickler for discipline—he was uneasy about Kartikeya bunking school to watch a cricket match once even when, as his son amusedly points out, 'the principal was his own sister'—it is unlikely he would have ever crossed the line of acceptable familiarity. There was, however, a hint of gallantry in his dealings with the relatively young, attractive prime minister. His private secretary, K.R. Ramnath, maintains that it was his job, when Indira came to town, to pick up a bucketful of the most beautiful red roses he could find. On one visit, he recalls, Vikram selected a single bud to present to her at the airport and came back to the car blushing like a schoolboy because she had accepted it in preference to all the other floral tributes on offer.[61]

In the months that followed Vikram's assumption of office, he received support from varied sources for the set of arguments outlined in his press conference. K.C. Pant, the general secretary of the Congress, who had pressed for a more robust nuclear policy since 1964, changed his stand, maintaining in a debate on All India Radio that India should not decide politically to go in for nuclear weapons at that point.[62] Pant's view ran parallel to the argument being made by the Indian envoy to the UN for the rights of non-nuclear states to conduct peaceful explosions and for non-proliferation in general. Years later, Pant was to admit to Perkovich, echoing Vikram's effort to cool down the rhetoric, that the intense internal debate on the subject had been both unnecessary and counterproductive.

In November 1966 came an even more weighty show of support. Major General Som Dutt, director of the Indian Institute for Defence Studies and Analyses, a premier institute for strategic and security studies that had been set up in 1965, presented a paper at the International Institute for Strategic Studies in London in which he maintained that the cost of nuclear weaponization far outweighed the potential benefits for India.

The strength of Dutt's arguments stemmed not so much from his position in the army (retired military chief J.N. Chaudhuri was to reach similar conclusions around the same time but the army had never been involved in formulating nuclear policy) but from his study of multiple aspects such as direct security threats, effectiveness in war, India's relations with other nations and so on. Putting them together, Dutt found that the development of a rudimentary capability would deprive India of her moral stature and invite the wrath of the superpowers. A full-fledged arsenal if developed, he believed, would end the scope of any understanding with Pakistan without affecting China's ambitions in South Asia; it would encourage a pact between the two, in fact. As Perkovich points out, this was a 'dispassionate and realistic' assessment that looked outwards and not inwards as Bhabha's rhetoric had done.[63]

By the end of 1966 the clamour for nuclear weapons appeared to have died down. On 16 December, India signed an agreement with Canada that promised assistance on design and construction of a second power reactor in Rajasthan (RAPP II). The tougher safeguards imposed by the Canadians and agreed to by India reflected, according to Perkovich, the difference between Bhabha and Vikram and also Canada's growing interest in non-proliferation. But Vikram also negotiated a provision for maximizing Indian components. Two days later, India announced plans to build its second plutonium separation plant and its second heavy water production unit. On 28 December, China conducted its fifth nuclear test, evoking little comment in India.

In the international arena, however, the debate over nuclear weapons was heating up. It was becoming increasingly evident that the emphasis of the superpowers was on stemming the spread of weapons through the Nuclear Non-Proliferation Treaty (NPT) rather than discussing measures for disarmament. President Lyndon Johnson of the US even offered to provide peaceful explosives at low cost with safeguards to non-nuclear weapon nations. India was loud in its criticism on both counts: a ban without disarmament was unfair and the US offer reeked of a colonial attitude that sought to make developing nations markets rather than manufacturers of technology. By virtue of the philosophical questions it had raised, India was becoming central to the debate.

Within the country, the focus shifted from the question of whether India should produce weapons to whether India should sign a treaty relinquishing the right to produce them. On 1 March, a group of eminent Indians from both the pro- and the anti-bomb lobbies issued a statement urging the Indian government not to sign the treaty being shaped by the superpowers. Three weeks later the Lok Sabha expressed hope that the treaty could be improved.

Vikram was extremely perturbed by the debate. Rules of secrecy forbade him from discussing certain matters related to atomic energy with anybody. Even his family members and closest associates were not privy to the workings of his mind at the time. The only way to gauge his intentions on the controversial subject of nuclear weapons is by putting together his random utterances, the interpretations of those in a position to observe him and, of course, his actions themselves.

A handwritten note to himself dated 15 February 1966 indicates that his concerns predate his chairmanship—it mentions 'C.S. Jha', who was foreign secretary at the time, and lists among other points, 'Discussion on Non Proliferation' and 'Restraint has to be shown by haves as well as have nots'.

In 1967, as chairman, he was in a more influential position to affect the course of events. At the time, L.K. Jha was principal secretary to the prime minister. In 1958, when Vikram was running Sarabhai Chemicals, Jha had been special secretary in the commerce and industry ministry. As such, Vikram already knew him well. Now Vikram met with him to discuss the possibility of an alternative which would help fulfil the objective of non-proliferation without a discriminatory treaty but by a guarantee of some kind that would make non-nuclear powers feel secure from nuclear threats. 'Time and again,' says Jha, 'we met to ponder over this problem, and I am not being modest when I say that it is he who was responsible for evolving an alternative approach, while my role was one of injecting comments and suggestions.'[64]

The 'alternative approach' which Vikram evolved and which both he and Jha were to proceed to try and sell hinged on the fear of nuclear blackmail rather than nuclear attack. The former, they believed, was the 'real danger' for many non-nuclear states as even an implied threat of the use of nuclear power could be an instrument of coercion. The issue, Jha points out, also had practical implications for India vis-à-vis nuclear China which was making claims on Indian territory.[65]

Vikram and Jha decided that any 'assurance or guarantee' they could wrest would have to be multilateral in character, with both the superpowers subscribing to it. The emphasis was to be on immediate support, the declaration of which would possibly serve as a deterrent to the aggressor. Vikram hoped to convince the nuclear haves that such an assurance might dissuade non-nuclear powers from incurring the expenditure and risk of going nuclear.

Their first move was to convince the Indian government. A similar arrangement had been hinted at by Shastri and it was widely condemned in India as a sell-out. It says something for Vikram's clout that the government, despite the Shastri example, considered his proposal seriously. A committee of secretaries and then a cabinet committee pondered over it. And finally the duo was authorized to go to various state capitals, armed with a letter from Prime Minister Indira Gandhi.

Their travels took them to Moscow, Washington, London and Paris. There were meetings and discussions with heads of government as well as cabinet ministers in charge of defence and foreign affairs. The response was not encouraging. There was, according to Jha, 'no frontal opposition' to the approach which Vikram had initiated. But, he admits, there were insurmountable problems all the same. Differences over Vietnam apparently made the Soviets reluctant to sign any kind of joint declaration with the US. The US President, meanwhile, had doubts about getting Congressional support for any move threatening to enlarge the country's military commitments beyond the UN charter. The British and the French offered to support any proposal which the two superpowers agreed on but maintained that without their agreement the proposal would be 'devoid of life'.[66]

On 18 April, Vikram met with US Defence Secretary Robert McNamara and told him that the fact that the NPT as it existed was not saleable in India did not indicate a 'secret desire to build the bomb'.[67] It is unclear whether Vikram was completely sincere about abjuring India's right to acquire technological know-how in return for a guarantee. His position, in many ways, was a hark back to the Nehruvian strategy of ambiguity but whether it was meant to run parallel with developing an Indian capability is not known. Perkovich makes the shrewd observation that Vikram's proposal, if accepted, would have taken the NPT off the table; by leaving the matter of peaceful nuclear explosions unaddressed, it would '[free] India to do as it wished'.[68]

The manner in which Vikram spoke about the ongoing negotiations and his distress at the manner in which they were proceeding, however, do tell of a heartfelt commitment to a nuclear-free world. To McNamara he said: 'The developing international nuclear situation possesses the characteristics of a Greek tragedy in which the actors are drawn inexorably to fates which they are seeking to avoid.'[69] Mallika, once telephoning him on one of these trips, found him extremely disturbed. 'People don't seem to understand that the nuclear way is the wrong way to go,' he said to her agitatedly. He was convinced, his daughter claims, that 'strength was not in being macho. India had to show the moral path.'

The talks did not provide India with the watertight guarantees Vikram was seeking. In May 1967, India decided it would not be party to the treaty. At the same time, it would not produce weapons. The position was reiterated by Defence Minister Swaran Singh in October 1967.

While all these dramatic events were taking place in Vikram's life, he was getting accustomed to a major change in his domestic arrangements. The chairmanship of the AEC had necessitated a shift to Bombay. Initially, he moved into Kashmir House, a family-owned property in the posh residential area of Malabar Hill. Kamal had built a penthouse for him to use on his frequent trips to Bombay for business. He lived alone. Mrinalini, busy with her dance school, had opted to stay on in Ahmedabad.

There was some family close at hand, however; his sister Gita lived with her family on the floor below his. On a financial level it is unclear what Vikram's relationship with his siblings was. After his resignation from Sarabhai Chemicals he never attempted to interfere in the business or even enquire about its functioning. A flow chart among his handwritten jottings, however, shows him mulling over 'estate duty' and 'Ambalal's estate', indicating that he was not totally cut off from the family's financial affairs. On a personal level, he maintained the warmest relations, as Gita testifies.

'Every morning,' Gita recalls, 'he would whistle to call me up. I would go, we would chat while he exercised and got dressed. We would have breakfast and then he would be gone. It would all be very quick but we got some time together. He liked keeping the family around though ever since he got involved in public life he had no time.'

His colleagues from the AEC, such as Professor Yash Pal and Ashok Parthasarthi or fellow scientist M.G.K. Menon, would come by with their wives in the evenings. Despite the company, Vikram had for all practical purposes a lonely private life. Kamla was busy with the IIM-A and he confessed to U.R. Rao that he missed his son. Kartikeya had gone to Cambridge to study mathematics and physics but had decided against science as a career choice. If Vikram was disappointed that his son would not follow in his footsteps he did not show it, though he did insist on Kartikeya finishing his tripos at Cambridge.

A source of solace at this time was his growing closeness to his daughter. In her teen years, Mallika had experienced a gradual thawing in her unforgiving coldness towards her father. After years of name-calling and lashing out, she seemed to be softening her stand. An incident at school helped break the ice. 'Two boys fought over me and papa was called in,' she recalls. Vikram was apparently amused by the fact that his baby was growing into a young woman. She remembers him giving her a talk on 'society' and 'societal norms'. 'If you follow your own beliefs and stick your head above the crowd,' he told her, 'then you must prepare to be stoned.'

Talk of behaviour eventually led to the subject that had lain like an open wound between the two. According to Mallika, Vikram never attempted to defend himself on the matter of Kamla, merely telling her, 'You don't choose the people you love.' Even if he was to cut his lover out of his life, he explained, her memory, like that of an amputated limb, would always be there. 'My home is with you, amma and Kartikeya. Isn't that good enough?'

Mallika was not assuaged by his response but some of the tension seemed to dissipate. On weekends, when Vikram was in Ahmedabad, they would spend time together, having long conversations about life, going to classical music concerts and catching a late-night snack. Padmanabh Joshi once went with them for pani puri to the city's famous Manek Chowk. 'Vikram would never order but nibble from other people's plates. And, of course, he would never be carrying any money!' Thanks to their growing closeness, Mallika claims she found herself developing an almost telepathic connection with her father that helped her cope with his frequent absences. 'Wherever he was in the world, if he was depressed, I would sense it and I would call to cheer him up.'

In August 1968, Vikram burst into the spotlight as Scientific Chairman of the United Nations Conference on the Exploration and Peaceful Uses of Outer Space. The conference in Vienna was a much-publicized event. In film footage Vikram is prominent, handsome in a crisp bandhgala, making his way with a smile and a modest stride past the forest of cameras to the venue.

His address at the conference was delivered in his usual direct, unembellished style. He spoke of his ideas for space technology and its applications in India, rounding it off with what was becoming by now a familiar theme in his speeches, the need for global interdependence. 'It is important to note a fundamental aspect of human development that knowledge cannot for long be contained within artificial boundaries and one has to learn to share rather than control harmful effects through withholding transfer of technology or knowledge,' he said. Pointing to Hiroshima, which, by confirming that the device worked, guaranteed its proliferation, he concluded that 'restrictions on the transfer of technology which are involved in the peaceful uses of outer space merely jeopardize the security of the world through retarding the progress of nations'.[70]

At PRL and at Rossi's lab, he continued to work on his cosmic rays project. By the late 1960s artificial satellites and deep space probes had confirmed the qualitative validity of Parker's model and provided direct information on the direction of the magnetic field lines near the earth. Eventually, they would also detect the rotating shocks predicted by Vikram. At the time though he was involved in building physical models that would account for the observed anisotropies, a gargantuan task of reducing and analysing increasingly precise and comprehensive observational data.

He continued to visit Thumba once a fortnight, spending a packed and fruitful forty-eight hours. Abdul Kalam describes the average schedule on such trips:

> The day starts with witnessing of a Rohini-100 motor flight test. It fails. He tells the Project Leader: 'don't give up'. Meanwhile, he discusses with John the plan of the SSTC buildings. He gets five minutes and finalizes with Murthy and Gupta the single axis control flight of the RH-125 test plan, linking the inauguration of the SHAR range. He witnesses in Thumba the same day a two-stage successful rocket flight...his next engagement is a four-hour review session on a preliminary design study of the SLV3.... Then Sarabhai visits the gyro laboratory and is shown the precision components by Gupta...[71]

The schedule winds on with Vikram eventually leaving with forty-five reports of 6000 pages collected through the day. 'It was like a resourceful farmer harvesting loads of grain from his selective seedings,' Kalam concludes.

7

THE TOUGHEST BATTLE

I.K. Gujral, former prime minister of India, recalls the first time he met Vikram Sarabhai. 'It was in 1967-68. I was minister of state for communications. The Americans had offered to loan us a satellite for a year and we had to build an earth station. A decision had been taken to give the contract to the Canadians. Vikram came to see me in great agitation. He was very upset with the decision to bring in outsiders to build the earth station. "Where will the Indians experiment if not in India?" he asked me. "Will the Canadians ask us to build it for them?"'

P.N. Haksar, who had taken over as principal secretary to the prime minister from L.K. Jha in 1967, had also felt the full force of Vikram's disappointment. 'Vikram was diffident, nervous, angry, red in the face, and trembling almost,' he recalls.[1] It was unusual, to say the least, for Vikram to have let his customarily controlled demeanour crumble. But a conversation Haksar had with him even prior to this incident indicates that around this time Vikram's immense patience might have been wearing thin.

'You know it is all very well for me to hold forth and have a design and a vision of India,' Vikram had apparently said to him, 'but it has to be translated to this rotten system of government of India and its bureaucracy.' The solution Vikram had proposed to Haksar was that the two of them could collaborate. Vikram would pour out his frustration over bureaucratic impediments to Haksar and the latter, with his enormous experience, would come up with possible ways out including, 'first or second approximations to the solution'. Haksar clearly accepted Vikram's proposal for that, he maintains, was 'the kind of partnership we had'.[2]

Anyone familiar with Vikram's ideas and passionate advocacy of indigenization and self-reliance would have understood his distress in the case of the earth station. As head of the electronics committee he had suggested numerous practical guidelines regarding research and development, efficiency of operations, exports and so on. His recognition of interface problems between development and production would lead to the establishment of the Electronics Prototype Engineering Laboratory at BARC. And his vigorous canvassing on the importance of the subject would result in the setting up of a separate ministerial wing for electronics.[3]

He believed strongly in exposure to sophisticated technology of the West; in fact, he was of the opinion that India's first satellite should be built and launched from abroad to avoid delay in disseminating developmental communication and to give Indian engineers experience they could then apply back home.

At the same time he was implacably opposed to the import of obsolete technologies from abroad. He wanted Indian technology to be as current as that of the West and produced as economically as possible. He believed that developing countries were actually at an advantage in that they could 'leapfrog' the stages of trial and error through which the advanced countries had passed. For this, however, it was important that every opportunity that presented itself at home be exploited. To find his own government standing in the way of his assiduously laid plans for indigenization could not but have been a hurtful experience.

As it happened, his customary zeal ensured that he saved the situation: the government was forced to relent and let him build the earth station after he had rushed around piling up the forceful intervention of Haksar, Gujral and then, to leave no stone unturned, the prime minister herself.

Red tape, however, was just one of Vikram's gargantuan concerns at the time. If, he, usually so calm, self-assured and determined, was fussing and fretting in a manner more suited to an anxious mother-to-be, it was perhaps also because he was, in a sense, about to give birth. The dream he had nursed, pursued and relentlessly described in private conversations and public speeches over many years, the dream of using space technology to better the lives of the poor by transmitting to them information about health, sanitation, agriculture and so on, was about to materialize.

The process had already been set in motion. Soon after assuming charge as chairman, AEC, Vikram had kicked off a study by the DAE on the cost and significance of a synchronous satellite to link together isolated rural communities and distant centres of population in India through a powerful national system for mass communication using television.

In 1967, a 'National Study Group' with members such as U.R. Rao and Kiran Karnik, a bright young graduate from IIM-A, who had recently joined the AEC, conducted a dry run for rural development television in collaboration with All India Radio, the Indian Agricultural Research Institute and the Delhi administration. The experiment, called Krishi Darshan, involved beaming material to community television sets placed in eighty villages around Delhi. The group also looked into matters of programming and test marketing, for Vikram was keen on monitoring the impact of the new medium to ensure its best use.

Alongside this exercise a comparison was made of the costs of four systems: conventional rebroadcast stations with terrestrial microwave interconnections, direct broadcast from a synchronous satellite, conventional rebroadcast stations with satellite interconnections, and a hybrid system involving direct broadcast to some areas and five rebroadcast stations for the densely populated regions. The last alternative was found to be most economical with five lakh villages being covered for an amount of Rs 160 crore.

A national programme for television, Vikram maintained, would be of great significance to 'national integration, for implementing schemes of economic and social development and for the stimulation and promotion of the electronics industry'.[4] He had envisaged the programme in phases. Phase one, from 1969 to 1973, was to lay the foundation by providing experience in design, development and fabrication of equipment, establishment of management systems and software skills. Phase two, from 1974 to 1976, was to involve progressive coverage through community sets which, in his projections, would cover 98 per cent of the population.

E.V. Chitnis and Pramod Kale had already been put on the job of getting familiar with the technology of satellite transmission with visits to facilities in the US, Japan and elsewhere. Over the next few years, Vikram would pull strings with heavyweights such as Robert McNamara and the Ford Foundation to get funding and access to high security installations. Chitnis would also participate in studies with General Electric, Hughes and MIT on evolving a model for an India-specific satellite that could perform the many functions Vikram had in mind.

Next, Vikram pulled off a startling coup that would help the country kick-start phase one of his pet project. He managed to convince the Americans to loan their advanced communications satellite, the ATS-6, to India for a year. The agreement which would be formally signed on 18 September 1969 between NASA and Vikram, as secretary of the DAE, would enable the transmission of locally produced educational content to 2400 villages in the most backward regions of India. The programming would be Indian and the signals would be transmitted from the Experimental Satellite Communications Earth Station at Ahmedabad and from the new earth terminal for the Overseas Communication Service to be installed near Delhi. The DAE would make the hardware including the ten-foot chicken mesh antennas and community television receivers.

SITE would be the world's first experiment in direct broadcasting by satellite. And it would enable India to lay the foundations for a future countrywide development-related communications network. Vikram's vision was about to propel a mechanism filled with vast possibilities.

❧

Despite the magnitude of the satellite communications project, Vikram's mind was running along many simultaneous tracks. A flow chart he doodled on the stationery of the Ashoka Hotel with lines connecting DAE, INCOSPAR, AIR, Tel, Delhi, Krishi Darshan, I&B, DAE, Advisory Body, UNESCO is an approximate reflection of his busy mind at the time. Even as plans for television were being mooted, Vikram was thinking seriously of atomic energy as well. In fact, he was proposing a revolutionary scheme for taking the atomic energy programme forward by setting up 'agro-industrial complexes' around nuclear power stations.

The process of researching the scheme had begun two years previously when Vikram had initiated a study at the DAE to explore the implications of abundant low-cost power to agriculture. A number of major electricity-consuming outlets such as electro-chemical and electro-thermic processes and pumping of underground water through tube wells had been examined in addition to desalination of water to ascertain if, by a careful choice of energy-consuming projects related to a low-cost energy-producing centre, fresh inputs could be provided for economic development and a balanced load within the grid system.

In areas with abundant underground water such as the western Indo-Gangetic region of Uttar Pradesh it had been found that the use of low-cost energy for lifting water along with modern agricultural methods could make a crucial difference to the profitability of farming and would have a major impact on the country's economy. In specific terms, Vikram envisaged setting up two nuclear reactors of 600MW capacity in the region, a fertilizer plant with a capacity of 4500 tonnes per day and an aluminium plant with a capacity of 150 tonnes per day with 200MW being used for lift irrigation through 36,000 tube wells.

The total investment, Vikram calculated, would be Rs 429 crore. With this, 72,000 hectares would be irrigated, producing 4.5 million tonnes of cereals and 700,000 tonnes of pulses. The per capita income of people engaged in the project would increase by Rs 1400 per annum and the project would contribute Rs 486 crore to the gross national product (GNP). Moreover, a substantial part of the fertilizer and food produced would be available for use outside.[5]

Vikram's concern about boosting agricultural productivity was not as far removed from his function as atomic energy chief as it might have seemed. The much vaunted Green Revolution propelled by the various Indian Agricultural Research Institutes had boosted production levels dramatically in the late 1960s. But India was still in a precarious position as far as its food supplies was concerned. Memories of what was referred to, with a touch of black humour, as its 'ship to mouth' existence—in the late 1950s and early 1960s the country had to resort to large-scale import of food—were still fresh. Reliance on Western powers for food supplies made it vulnerable to blackmail and was a perfect example of the 'internal' security angle Vikram had referred to in his first press conference as chief of the AEC.

The agro-industrial complex proposed by him had the

potential to strengthen the country and to provide a boost to the energy programme. Itty Abraham found it a 'truly technocratic vision' that sought to 'force an engagement between man and machine' and which, by 'moving atomic energy away from the industrial grid and into the lived texture of people's existence', would provide a more 'sustainable future for the programme'.[6]

There is no doubt that in both his programme for television and in his vision of agro-industrial complexes, Vikram was motivated by a compelling need to uplift the backward. As he mentioned in a paper 'Television for Development':

> Should one concentrate on providing the benefits first to urban communities and progressively go to rural areas? ... I would submit that the answer to this question can be clearly stated. It is that we should consciously reach the most difficult and least developed areas of the country and, because they are in this state, we should reach them in a hurry.[7]

Yet, Abraham cautioned that the vision was 'less liberatory' than it seemed:

> Even as it seemed to recognize the existence of society for the first time, this conception in no way diminished the power and reach of the state in controlling the lives of its people.... Sarabhai may have recognized society, and indeed may have been driven by a greater sense of the need to overcome poverty and underdevelopment, but there was no room for local knowledge or non-expert thinking within this system.[8]

The concern was echoed by Raj Thapar, one of the people approached by Vikram to evaluate the programming for Krishi Darshan. Thapar confessed to being baffled by the selection of urban people like herself to appraise content meant for a rural audience.[9]

Others had different reasons for experiencing disquiet about Vikram's aims. Abu Abraham, cartoonist and columnist, interviewed Vikram in 1971, and was struck by his clear preference for providing information over literacy. 'I found it strange,' says Abu. 'Literacy gives people choice. If you educate people entirely on information they are at the mercy of the government which holds power over the medium.'

One could add certain other factors in this regard. It is striking, for instance, that few scientists working for the space programme had actually even seen a television set. Radio was just about becoming a mass medium in India with the introduction of the transistor, but the attractions or otherwise of television were still unknown. It is doubtful if even Vikram, who travelled extensively in the developed world, had actually watched television as a mere viewer.

It is again significant that there was no evidence of Vikram's own familiarity with the rural masses whose lives he showed such keenness to impact. His life was lived in cities. Apart from a bullock cart passed on a family holiday, there is no mention in his speeches or in the reminiscences of his associates and his family of any direct experience of village life or rural folk or of any extensive time spent in a backward area.

It could, of course, be argued that the preoccupation with the grand technological sweep was the fi st step and it is entirely possible that Vikram, with his interest in market research and 'feedback loops'[10] would have shifted focus to the small man on the ground. He talked of channels in different languages; his ideas would inspire the setting up of a popular local channel in Kheda district in Gujarat. That he was acutely conscious of potential ground-level problems such as receptivity and maintenance was also clear from his comment quoted by a colleague, B.S. Bhatia: 'Even if I have to deploy a helicopter for set maintenance I will do it.'[11]

Vikram's impact on communications was to be evident in the fact that many decades after his death his vision still forms the basis for discussions on ideal formats for Indian television. Yet, given television's complete departure from these early aims, falling prey first to government propaganda and later to the thirst for entertainment, it does seem relevant to wonder if Vikram, humanitarian that he was, had an insufficiently realistic view of human fallibility.

On the other hand, it is also possible to speculate that he had faith in his ideas that went beyond teething problems and distortions. Take, for example, his comments on 'real advanced technology providing freedom without monolithic structures' in the documentary *India and Science Today* produced by Michael Treguer for French television. Likening television to a computer, he pointed out that the choice was between getting one large-sized machine for many to cluster around or to have several terminals connected to a mainframe. With a delivery system, he suggested, information could be delivered to the farmer, leading to the development of life at various levels instead of encouraging 'obnoxious large conglomerates [cities]'. It could be said that that is precisely what the internet has brought about.

A scribbled note to himself provides the information that Vikram spent $90.25 on entertainment (New York, Boston, etc.) and $16.30 on car rental between 10 and 25 March 1969. Other notes of the time reveal that he had travelled to Martha's Vineyard to meet Dr Weisner, spent 24 francs in France, met the president of AECL, Lorne Grey, in Ottawa, 'Mehta' in Montreal, Ramanna at the Park Sheraton in NY, Dr Desai in DC, and Chandra in Chicago. Yet another note reminds him to take back Erinmore tobacco and tablets for Haksar from Vienna.

Clearly there was no let-up in Vikram's schedule. Given his peripatetic lifestyle, the people Vikram saw most of through the latter half of the 1960s were his staff, in particular, his two personal secretaries, N.V.G. Warrier and K.R. Ramnath. Both were utterly devoted to their boss and had adapted themselves totally to his eccentricities. They would keep up with his long hours, arrange last-minute reservations, keep track of his hectic schedule and personal expenses, and often travel with him taking dictation along the way. Vikram was solicitous as always of their needs. 'He knew the number of shirts I had, my tastes in food and would order for both of us on flights,' says Warrier in an interview with the *Illustrated Weekly of India.*[12] On their part they watched out for him like eager hawks, arranging jugs of water for him at airports and ensuring nothing offended his extreme fastidiousness about hygiene.

At times their concern veered towards overprotectiveness. Such as the time they put Vikram down as a teetotaller for a forthcoming trip to Australia. 'Sir, I have not seen you drinking,' Ramnath explained fearfully when Vikram queried him. 'It's all right. On occasions, I have no objection to taking a little wine,' Vikram had to clarify.[13]

The other person who loomed large, literally, in his life at the time was a burly Tamil IAS officer called T.N. Seshan who had been put in charge of the AEC secretariat in August 1968. Given the way the power scales were tipped in favour of the scientists, most bureaucrats gave the DAE a wide berth. But Seshan had some interest in the subject, having written a dissertation on the economics of nuclear energy. Loud and of a stubborn temperament, Seshan was soon to develop a warm rapport with his boss.

These comprised Vikram's support system, individuals he could completely rely on in the somewhat thorny environment he found himself in at the DAE. And he was in need of support, for he had fairly dramatic plans for the department, plans he would give clear shape to in the path-breaking ten-year profile, a projection for the decade 1970–80. These included the building of 500MW enriched uranium reactors, the development of gas centrifuge technology for uranium enrichment and the speeding up of the fast breeder reactor programme. If passed, the plan had the potential to give India 43,000MW of installed nuclear power by the year 2000.

P.K. Iyengar, a physicist who would go on to head the AEC, believes Vikram's plans for enriched uranium and fast breeder reactors indicated 'vision and daring'; many of his colleagues did not share his assessment. Unlike at the space programme where Vikram's ideas were invariably received with warm enthusiasm, at the atomic energy department Vikram had to tiptoe around strong opinions and established hierarchies.

M.R. Srinivasan, a senior-level engineer, for instance, was alarmed at Vikram's excitement over a molten salt reactor at the Oak Ridge National Laboratory in the US and writes of the 'relief of the more practical engineers and technologists' when a team appointed to study it was wound up.[14] Sethna and Ramanna were dismissive of Vikram's plans for building 500MW enriched uranium reactors.[15] Personality clashes rose to the fore when Vikram tried to restructure the AEC. And at the newly set up Electronics Corporation of India Limited (ECIL), A.S. Rao, the senior scientist in charge, adamantly opposed Vikram's proposal to set up foreign collaborations and adopt the commercial route.[16]

While there could have been genuine differences and reservations on technological grounds, the lukewarm and at times uneasy response of the AEC scientists to Vikram's ideas indicated a tension that may have arisen from fear. The former seemed to lack Vikram's instinct for exploration and were afraid of where it would lead. As Abraham observes, the period of 'technical and institutional innovation' starting with Bhabha was to end with Vikram's death; their successors being inclined only towards strategies of 'institutional maintenance'.[17]

Some of Vikram's other initiatives met with greater success. He tried to bring his interest in management to the DAE, organizing studies with Kamla and holding seminars. For most of the staff, it was their first experience in management training. 'We benefited immensely,' writes M.R. Srinivasan.[18]

But probably the most critical impasse was over the apparent divergence on the matter of nuclear weapons. The gulf, according to Abraham, was just too wide. The Trombay scientists just could not accede to 'his sharply divided worlds of meaning, internal from external'. For them, success in mastery of technology was not measured by the welfare they would provide but by the admiration they would evoke, to which end national development had to be 'reconfigured to mean national security, and the explosion of an atomic bomb was to be the index of security'.[19]

In practical terms though not much headway had been made on designing an explosive at the time Vikram took charge. After Shastri's go-ahead, separate groups had been formed to work on different functions and some sparse research had been conducted on explosions and plutonium extraction. Apart from insufficient know-how, what made the possibility of a test distant was that there was simply not enough fissile material.

Sethna claims that Vikram on assuming office wound up the SNEPP and asked for all papers to be handed over to him. It is suggested that the AEC scientists continued, however, surreptitiously or openly—since Sethna's claim has not been corroborated—to work on the project. In 1967, Ramanna called R. Chidambaram, an experimental physicist, and asked him to work on a design.[20] Chidambaram and his colleague P.K. Iyengar at BARC apparently set to work with Dr B. Nag Chaudhuri, the director of DRDO, engaging about fifty to seventy-five scientists and engineers.

If Vikram had wound up SNEPP, then the actions of Ramanna and his colleagues were evidence of insubordination. But it is possible that Vikram knew, either because he had been informed or had discovered it for himself, and had chosen to say nothing. The explanation given to Perkovich by an unnamed former official is that Vikram could have stopped it if he had wanted to but was too gentlemanly and did not wish to enter into this particular fight.[21] Other, more complex explanations, cannot, however, be ruled out.

ঌ

Though the AEC job was proving a tough nut to crack, it did not alter Vikram's style of operation. He continued to enjoy his little pleasures such as the boat ride from the Gateway of India where the AEC had its headquarters to Trombay. Bhabha had acquired the boat, originally owned by British royalty, from the navy at a throwaway price. K.R. Ramnath claimed Vikram enjoyed the ride so much that he would take it even when the waves were high, apologizing profusely to all present for the inevitable drenching.[22]

He continued also to keep as many balls up in the air as he could. At any given time, Seshan describes, 'there would be three or four meetings happening in his room, one on the sofas, one around the main table, one impromptu in a corner. He would be like a grandmaster moving from one to another, never losing his temper.' Despite the trepidation with which some of his ideas were received, his legendary charm soon infected the AEC's vast staff. While Bhabha had an imposing presence, Sarabhai's was an endearing one. Claims M.R. Srinivasan, '...he made friends easily, and even the younger colleagues talked to him about their problems.'[23]

One person, however, remained implacably opposed to Vikram. Homi Sethna, who as head of the BARC was in a crucial administrative position, had, in fact, grown increasingly agitational, leading him to adopt an obstructive position on all matters ranging, as Seshan observes, from 'a management proposal to the annual budget'. 'You could touch and feel Sethna's animus, it had a palpable quality,' Seshan claims. 'He would confront Vikram directly and ask him "what is your legitimacy?"' adds Ashok Parthasarthi. Their stand-off soon became common knowledge in the corridors of BARC. Vikram was the head but Sethna was in the driver's seat for research and personnel and the friction was taking its toll. Yet, Vikram did not confront Sethna.

Time and again, his colleagues and staff watched in amazement as he tried to defuse the sparks of yet another ugly encounter. 'Meetings were a nightmare,' Seshan recalls. 'If I had to ask a question, Sethna would fly into a rage but Vikram would step in immediately and say: "Homi, let us go to your room and discuss the ground rules." Then he would come back and say, "Seshan, do not ask any questions."' Alternatively, Vikram would ask members of his team to prepare memoranda to counter Sethna's position. But he would not take him on.

Two contradictory interpretations have been offered to explain Vikram's apparent unresponsiveness in the face of Sethna's blatant hostility. There are those who believe that he did not quarrel, pull rank or counter Sethna because he had a problem dealing with aggression. Kamal Mangaldas, for instance, believes that the Sarabhais tend to lack a certain robustness in dealing with differences, as seen in the high incidence of failed marriages in the family. Prakash Tandon found Vikram 'rather naïve', especially about people; 'he judged them as he saw himself'.[24]

Most of Vikram's friends claim he was a man who did not know how to say 'no'. U.R. Rao even has a story about a scientist who slapped a man for getting fresh with his wife and when Vikram was asked what he would have done in his place, he 'smiled and said "probably nothing"'.

There is, however, another hypothesis offered to explain Vikram's unusual behaviour and that is his dealings with aggression were marked not by faint-heartedness but by restraint. His colleagues often mention watching him 'bite his lip' and staying silent, suggesting that he was able to control his emotions and was not incapable of them.

U.R. Rao maintains that any suggestion that the directorship of BARC should have stayed with the AEC head as was the case in Bhabha's time instead of being given to Sethna would earn a firm rebuke from Vikram: 'Scientists and engineers should learn to work together.' Seshan believes that 'knowing [Vikram] he would have tried to make an ally out of him [Sethna] instead'. Mallika, too, from her conversations with her father, believes 'he always felt people had a right to disagree and you could set an example, talk, educate people into thinking there are options. But you couldn't be aggressive.'

There are several examples of Vikram meeting opposition with patient explanation. With unpredictable results. Once at Sarabhai Chemicals he insisted on giving a detailed exposition of company policy to an antagonistic newspaperman instead of the dressing down his colleagues had planned. 'The paperwallah was only hoping to squeeze out an advertisement and was dazed by the response,' K.J. Divatia chuckles. Seshan too recalls innumerable occasions where Vikram met tedious and sometimes flagrantly ridiculous queries from members of parliament with detailed presentations much of which went right over his esteemed listeners' heads.

One can see in this approach a touch of the scientist. As Kalam writes: 'When there were alternative courses of action before us, whose outcome was (*sic*) difficult to predict, or to reconcile varying perspectives, Prof Sarabhai would resort to experimentation to resolve the issue.'[25] Then again there is the question: could it work? And, second: was it appropriate in all circumstances? Was Vikram trying to pull off the impossible? In his personal life, instead of opting for a choice, he was seeking a resolution that would include his wife and his mistress—two passionate and independent women—and keep all in perfect harmony. Was his effort to win Sethna over a similar attempt at reconciling the irreconcilable? More to the point, was it really worth the effort and the attrition?

Those who hold the view that Vikram was totally and adamantly opposed to the manufacture of nuclear weapons by India would have been hard put to explain his actions from 1968 onwards.

Early in 1968, Vikram sent a delegation under P.K. Iyengar

to the Soviet Union after persuading the Soviets to allow the delegation to visit its nuclear facilities. Iyengar returned extremely excited about a pulsed reactor he had seen in Dubna. A similar reactor, he suggested, would provide insights into explosives technology without raising suspicions since India's long-term plans involved fast breeder reactors with plutonium at the core. Vikram not only attended a seminar on the subject but sanctioned a sum of rupees ten lakh to begin work on a design for what was to be known as the 'Plutonium Reactor for Neutron Investigation in Multiplying Assemblies (Purnima)'. A site was selected next to the plutonium reprocessing plant in Trombay. 'That's when I knew he was in favour of acquiring the physics,' exults Iyengar.

In December 1968, Vikram received an interesting visitor. K. Subrahmanyam was a young deputy secretary in the defence ministry with a keen interest in defence policy. On at least one count, his views matched Vikram's: India was not ready to go nuclear. In 1967, Subrahmanyam had presented a paper at the International Institute for Strategic Studies conference in Elsinore in which he had maintained that India, unlike China, had a long way to go before it could become a nuclear power. In his assessment this was not likely to come about till the 1980s. But unlike the widespread impression of Vikram as a dove on matters of nuclear policy, Subrahmanyam was categorically and avowedly pro-nuclear. It must have been a charged encounter. T.N. Seshan had fixed a meeting at Vikram's office in the AEC headquarters for forty-five minutes but the conversation went on for two hours.

It was not the last time they talked. In the following weeks, Vikram called Subrahmanyam several times on his frequent trips to Delhi and invited him over for a chat. And each time Subrahmanyam received the impression of Vikram as an unusually open-minded man but one who did not share his keenness on a nuclear weapons programme for the country. Sometime in the early months of 1969, however, he had reason to review his assumption.

Subrahmanyam, who by then had taken over as head of the Institute of Defence Studies and Analyses from Som Dutt, was travelling to Vienna en route to a summit in France and ran into Vikram on the flight. Vikram launched into a dialogue that continued for hours in the narrow aisle separating first class from economy. At some point Subrahmanyam recalls raising a tricky question. He had heard from his sources that a bitter battle was under way between the DRDO and AEC's BARC to procure a contract to develop the phased array radar, an instrument for detecting invading missiles. 'If you are not keen on this sort of militarization then why is BARC vying for this contract?' he asked Vikram. Surprised, Vikram retorted with an answer Subrahmanyam recalls vividly: 'Who am I to shut off all these options for future generations? I am only saying at present I am not for the bomb.'

Sethna is of the opinion that Vikram changed his stand on nuclear weapons, turning more pro than anti, after the failure of his mission with L.K. Jha to convince the superpowers of his alternative approach to the issue of non-proliferation. Kartikeya feels he never quite made up his mind on the subject. The other explanation is, of course, that while as a humanitarian he opposed atomic weaponry, as a scientist he did not believe in curtailing technological prowess. In an October 1969 paper, he provided an inkling of the philosophy underlying the coexistence of such contradictory views:

> Gandhi's assertion that non-violence provides the best path was clearly dependant on the assumption that there is 'good' in everyone. Certain societies have a philosophical and religious base which accepts divinity in all creation.... The Freudian assertion of love and hate coexisting represents the contemporary interpretation of the same principle. Physicists were locked in bitter controversy over the nature of light—whether it consisted of corpuscles or waves—till they realized that the seemingly contradictory observations were

> manifestations of the same phenomenon. Just as the superposition of states provided a framework for comprehending many aspects of natural phenomena, so is an understanding of ambivalence crucial if we are to have a humanistic positive view of life—to give and receive the trust which is fundamental to action.[26]

Vikram's focus, however, continued to be on the energy side where he had set several projects in motion. One of these was the fast breeder project. Bhabha had envisaged overcoming the problem of India's insufficient uranium ore with a three-step programme starting with natural uranium reactors proceeding to converter-type reactors and leading up to the fast breeder reactor.

The fast breeder reactor was a reactor that produced more fuel than it consumed. Enrico Fermi, designer of the world's first nuclear reactor, had declared that a country that could master fast breeder technology would have solved its energy problems. Two decades after his assertion, however, no country was in a position to make that claim. France was one country that had tried, with the setting up of an experimental fast breeder reactor, 'Rhapsodie'. In April 1969, Vikram sought its help in building India's first fast breeder reactor. At the same time, a Reactor Research Centre was established in Kalpakkam in the south to look into various aspects of fast reactors.

In May 1969, Vikram went to Sriharikota, eighty kilometres north of Madras. The strip of scrubland in the middle of the Pulicat Lake—so wild that when Vikram first visited it, a makeshift track had to be created with leaves—was to be India's satellite launching station. Chitnis and Kale had found it. The Americans had quoted a sum of Rs 50 crore, half payable in dollars, for developing it. But Vasant Gowarikar, rising to the challenge subtly thrown by Vikram as they were driving around Ahmedabad one day in his Herald, promised to do it for less and eventually managed, he claims, to do it in Rs 8 crore with a foreign component of a trifling ten per cent.

In August 1969, INCOSPAR was reconstituted to create the Indian Space Research Organisation (ISRO), the apex body of the space programme with Vikram as chairman. On his visits to the space centre, Vikram did not stay in the city as his colleagues did but in an elegant, solid stone building overlooking the crashing waves of Kovalam. Designed by a French architect, the imposing structure was a royal residence before being turned into a guest house. It had a garden, stone steps and a wide staircase that flared into two as it wound upwards to the top floor where Vikram stayed on his visits. His favourite room had a high ceiling and long narrow windows facing a balcony. Every morning he took a swim in the sea, racing over the sand and plunging into the water in one speedy motion, before setting out for work.

In Thumba, work on the satellite launch vehicle (SLV) was proceeding apace. A design had been selected, based on the American Scout model; it was the third of four options presented, earning it the nickname SLV3. Vikram had broken up the project into four parts and put each one under a different leader: Gowarikar, A.E. Muthunayagam, M.R. Kurup and Kalam. The absence of a group leader meant he had to take on the role, leading his detractors to maintain that he had some difficulty giving up control.

Later that year, Vikram ran into a young professor from the Indian Statistical Institute in Delhi. Kirit Parikh, who also had a degree in engineering from MIT, had just married a physicist from TIFR. He saw Vikram on a flight, introduced himself and asked if he could help his wife find a job in Delhi. 'Why don't you come to Bombay instead?' Vikram responded. The meeting resulted in Vikram setting up the Programme Analysis Group (PAG) with Parikh as director. Keen at all times on bringing a commercial approach to his activities, Vikram expected PAG to analyse the activities of the DAE from an economic and marketing perspective. One of PAG's earliest projects, for instance, was to study the viability of a proposed onion irradiation plant in a small town in Maharashtra. Later, the PAG made feasibility studies of power plant sites and so on.

The close of 1969 saw him working round the clock to ensure the timely inauguration of the country's first nuclear power station—a project launched by his predecessor—in Tarapur.

While Vikram was playing a balancing act between the peaceful and non-peaceful uses of nuclear power, a major political transition was taking place in the country. The Congress Party, riven with factionalism, had split down the middle. And Indira, in a fighting bid to hold on to her position, had announced a series of populist measures such as the nationalization of banks and the abolition of the privy purses of former princes.

With an air of uncertainty hanging over the capital, bitter communal riots broke out in Ahmedabad. Vikram was still commuting regularly between the two cities. He would spend most weekends in Ahmedabad, dropping in for a salad lunch at PRL on Saturdays. The violence in his home town disturbed him and, as P.K. Iyengar recalls, his solution was typically quirky. 'They should put something in the water supply,' Vikram suggested, 'to make everybody go to sleep for a few days.'

There were other things on his mind at the time, such as the upcoming fourteenth general conference of the International Atomic Energy Agency (IAEA). The IAEA had been set up in Vienna in 1957 to assist in scientific and technical cooperation in the peaceful use of nuclear technology worldwide. It was a crucial time following as it did the protracted battle over the NPT. (The NPT had come up for signing in June 1968; India, as expected, refused to sign.) The international community had changed its stand on 'peaceful nuclear explosions'—explosions for developmental purposes as against weapons for destructive purposes though the technology for both was essentially the same. In fact, the Americans and Soviets were propagating peaceful nuclear explosions in a big way. From 1970 onwards, the IAEA was to hold a series of panel meetings on the subject with presentations from the US, the USSR and France.

Vikram was to preside over the Vienna Conference in 1970. Leena and Sarla decided to pay him a visit. He had a terrible cold on the day they were there, Leena recalls. But he worked late into the night and took them around the famous Vienna Woods the following day. He also procured the assistance of friend, industrialist and a board member of the AEC, J.R.D. Tata, to fly down an Indian feast from his hotel, the Taj Mahal in Bombay, on an Air India flight as a treat for the delegates on the last day of the conference. There was music and dancing as well at the closing ceremony.

R. Chidambaram made a presentation on underground copper mining at the conference. In an interview three decades later, Chidambaram claims that a detailed report on peaceful nuclear explosion applications had been handed by Ramanna to Vikram. After the conference, Chidambaram met Vikram and briefed him further and the latter's response appeared to be 'positive'.[27] Chidambaram mentioned to Vikram that he needed help to make high-speed detonators to trigger the chemical explosives needed to compress the plutonium in the device and Vikram asked him to meet Kalam in Trivandrum.[28] The subtext of the exchange is very clear. If Vikram was not already aware that Ramanna and his colleagues were working on an explosives design, he did now. And he appeared to be encouraging.

However supportive Vikram may have been of efforts to obtain technological know-how, the hawkish mood once again building up in the country could not have been to his liking. Following the controversy over the NPT, the pressure was apparently building from the atomic energy establishment and concerned elites. In March 1970, the Consultative Committee on Foreign Affairs and Atomic Energy persuaded the government to take a fresh look at the cost. Vikram obligingly asked N. Seshagiri of TIFR to conduct a cost-benefit analysis. Seshagiri claims Vikram's hope was 'that the result might show that the cost of a viable nuclear arsenal could not be justified even if [peaceful nuclear explosions] were included'.[29]

Meanwhile, the same month, China launched a long-range rocket carrying a satellite into orbit, raising the alarming possibility that nuclear warheads would be aimed at distant targets. The Indian Institute of Public Opinion conducted a study in August and found that the response in some circles 'bordered on the panicky'.[30] Sixty-nine per cent of the people polled in cities felt India should go nuclear. Yet, when asked if the move should be at the cost of a drastic cut in development expenditure, 54 per cent changed their minds.

Those in favour of the bomb, however, sought to exploit the Chinese act. In May 1970, the Indian Parliamentary and Scientific Committee had organized a meeting of eminent scientists, academics and politicians in Delhi which urged the government to produce weapons immediately. The most intense advocates came from two opposite ends of the spectrum: the right-wing Jan Sangh and the left wing of the Congress. Among the arguments put forward in support of the programme one was that it would create jobs and two, that it would enhance the country's power and prestige.

There were still voices of dissent. Former commander-in-chief of the Indian Army, K.M. Cariappa, warned that it would be suicidal for India to go nuclear as such a move would 'shatter our economy and jeopardize our development plans'. A similar view was expressed by P.V.R. Rao, a former secretary in the ministry of defence.[31] The short-term interest was pitted against long-term ones. And there were at least some at the AEC who appreciated Vikram's wariness. Iyengar believes that Vikram was 'a shrewd businessman who knew what it would mean economically to incur the wrath of the US. He knew the consequences, so he was much more careful.' On 17 May 1970,

Vikram announced that India would not seek nuclear weapons but would retain the option of conducting nuclear explosions for peaceful purposes. Eight days later, he released 'Atomic Energy and Space Research: A Profile for the Decade 1970–1980', a ten-year plan for atomic energy and space in India.

The plan, or Sarabhai Profile as it came to be known, made waves for various reasons. In every way, except in its belief in the applicability of atomic energy, it marked a departure from the old culture. One, it laid down in cold print the aims and possibilities of the programme. It also confessed the inadequacies of the existing political economy on which it depended for manufacturing and human resources, correcting, as Perkovich is quick to point out, 'the misleading assumption of the 1950s that increased provision of power would directly raise per capita gross national product'.[32]

Vikram admitted that the programme had slipped badly vis-à-vis earlier targets and announced a further scale back—from 8000MW envisaged for 1980-81 to 2700MW—but in conjunction with a plan to fuel one additional 400–500MW fast breeder reactor every other year in the 1980s. The new plan called for an expenditure of Rs 1250 crore which, to put it in context, was slightly more than the defence budget and amounted to a 30 per cent increase in DAE funding. The plan also listed specifics such as staffing requirements, alternative schemes of power generation with cash flow analyses and so on. The accrued benefits for a speedily growing population were likely to be enormous and included spin-offs in agriculture, food preservation and medicine. Above all, as the plan put it, 'We would need a very strong base of science, technology, industry and agriculture not only for our economic well-being but for our national integration and for ensuring our security in the world.'[33]

The second part of the profile dealt with space and for Kalam it was akin to the 'romantic manifesto of a person deeply in love with the space research programme in his country'.[34] It hinged on the early ideas of using satellites for television and developmental education, meteorological observation and remote sensing for management of natural resources. To this had been added the development and launch of satellite launch vehicles and satellites. The active international cooperation of the early years was virtually eased out with the new emphasis being on self-reliance and indigenous technologies. Vikram envisaged the development of a wide range of spacecraft subsystems and technological spin-offs like gyros, transducers, telemetry, adhesives and polymers for non-space applications. It showed that Vikram had intended the space programme to be a vehicle for the country's economic and technological development.

The plan's value according to Perkovich was that 'Sarabhai offered a more realistic and systematic assessment of the past, in order to build support for a somewhat more feasible, yet still demanding, agenda for the future'.[35] Many, however, perceived in it a long-term preparation plan for nuclear arms. A 1982 seminar conducted by the Delhi-based Centre for Policy Research observed that 'the perceptible goal of the Sarabhai nuclear programme was to acquire for India a balanced nuclear infrastructure and to enable it to emerge as a threshold nuclear power' and pointed out that the 2700MW programme would produce 1000kg of plutonium, 'a figure of military significance considering that India already had a plutonium separation plant'.[36] The plan was resoundingly silent on the subject of peaceful nuclear explosions. Yet, the *Guardian*, London, maintained on 27 July 1970 that the plan gave the impression 'that it is a firm step towards nuclear weaponry'.[37]

The plan was apparently released to national approbation, but was adopted by the government almost a year later, in 1971, after Indira's massive victory in the general elections.

In the midst of all his myriad official duties Vikram was, as always, managing to find time for a variety of engagements on the side. Neil Armstrong, the first man on the moon, came to Bombay and Vikram went to TIFR to gaze upon a bit of moon rock and meet the American astronaut. He also lent his name to a cause which led M.R. Srinivasan, whose wife Geetha was a family friend of Mrinalini's, to describe him as an 'amiable man' but one who espoused 'controversial programmes'. Srinivasan's reference was not, as one would have thought, to the nuclear programme but to the concept of population control.

It was a subject which clearly interested him for he had long discussions on it with his sister-in-law Lakshmi Sehgal who practised medicine in Kanpur. Srinivasan was apparently a trifle taken aback by Vikram's espousal of male sterilization and claimed there were many who felt he should not have been lending his name and support to such a programme. The criticism did not bother Vikram who was 'convinced that India had to find an answer to its population explosion'.[38]

He even managed to squeeze in family time. He took Mallika with him to his laboratory in Gulmarg after her final year school examination and taught her to play golf on what was said to be the highest golf course in the world. When his son and daughter-in-law—Kartikeya had married his childhood sweetheart Rajshree in 1968—fell ill in the US, he took leave to look after them. And when Mrinalini was invited to Venice to participate in *Creatures of Prometheus*, a ballet to celebrate the centenary of Beethoven, Vikram turned up with Mallika to watch from the royal box. 'Somehow, he was always around,' claims Kamal Mangaldas.

This omnipresence took its toll. According to Itokawa, Vikram launched a system of two-hour sleep breaks to deal with his hyperactive lifestyle.[39] Once a month, more or less, depending on how often his protesting body demanded it, he would declare a break, bringing all activity to a standstill around him with all his colleagues taking care not to disturb him.

In October 1970, Kartikeya's wife gave birth to a boy in a Bombay nursing home and Vikram was reportedly 'over the moon'.[40] He was even happier when Kartikeya, who had to be in the city for a study project, moved in with his family for a few months. By then Vikram had moved out of Kashmir House to a new building constructed by the AEC on Little Gibbs Road, just a short distance away.

Visitors claim he had done up the flat beautifully with spot lights in the ceiling and tasteful furnishings. Vikram had been exceedingly keen on an attached roof garden and had mentioned the same to I.G. Patel, his old friend from Cambridge who had become secretary and finance member in the AEC. Patel told him to 'add a couple of extras' to the plan to get it past the austere eyes of Morarji Desai who was then finance minister, and got him a roof garden.

But even as Vikram played with his infant grandson amidst the terrace greenery in the mild Bombay winter, ominous clouds were beginning to gather on the horizon. In December 1970, Indira dissolved parliament and called for elections. The campaign, fought on the populist slogan of 'Garibi Hatao', brought her back to power in March 1971 with 350 seats in a house of 518.

Vikram enjoyed an undeniably strong rapport with Indira till the late 1960s. At the professional level it was evident in the consonance between their public utterances on certain issues. On 24 April 1968, in an echo of Vikram's press conference, for instance, Indira said to the Lok Sabha: 'We think that nuclear weapons are no substitute for military preparedness involving conventional weapons... [it] may well endanger our internal security by imposing a very heavy economic burden.'[41]

Around this time, Vikram was taking Kalam and Narayanan to the distant airfield to discuss RATO systems for military aircraft. Following the meeting, Kalam reports, Vikram went to the prime minister's house for breakfast. The same day, an announcement was released to the press about India developing the RATO, suggesting a prior discussion. Describing Vikram as 'the most dynamic of the Sarabhai clan', Raj Thapar said he was seen 'frequently in Indira's entourage, literally running behind her'.[42]

By the end of the 1960s things had begun to change. Politically it was clear that Indira was winning the battle against the old guard in the party. With experience she had grown more confident and the overwhelming support of the electorate was to give her an even greater rootedness. But the machinations and power play had changed her and made her increasingly suspicious and intolerant of others. Raj Thapar vividly describes the transformation as one by one she alienated her old friends and advisers. P.C. Alexander, who was to be her principal secretary in the 1980s, observed that she 'was one of the loneliness [*sic*] leaders in contemporary history... [I] always had the feeling that she never trusted any person completely or unreservedly'.[43]

Raj Chengappa maintains that the seed of a schism between Indira and Vikram was laid in the late 1960s itself. According to him, senior scientists of the atomic energy fraternity, concerned about any bargain that the Sarabhai–Jha team might have struck with the superpowers, had maintained links with the prime minister and her advisers directly, cautioning them about the danger of giving up India's nuclear options.[44] Such an exchange, if it did take place, would have been of extremely questionable propriety. But the scientists at AEC, as shown time and again, considered themselves the keepers of India's security. Vikram had failed completely in his effort to change that mindset and push nuclear defence policy where he felt it belonged, in the public arena.

On the other hand, it is conceivable that Indira, with her growing tendency to play people against each other, could have given a patient ear to the scientists' anxieties. Perhaps the reservations she had expressed earlier about a weapons programme were never based on conviction. Her advisers too had changed. The moderate L.K. Jha had become governor of the Reserve Bank; his successor P.N. Haksar and G. Parthasarthy, Indira's adviser on foreign policy matters, were markedly more hawkish in their views.

The issue that seemed to be exercising the anti-Vikram lobby, if disparate individuals with a common cause could be called that, though was not a weapons programme—on which Vikram's views were ambiguous—but the desirability of a demonstration. What the politicians, bureaucrats and senior scientists at the AEC wanted was a show of India's might. And there was no question of Vikram's stand on that. At the very outset Vikram had made his views on a demonstration clear, going so far as to call it a 'paper tiger'. Yet, once again the demand was surfacing. And this time both the know-how and the requisite fissile material were closer at hand.

There are signs that Indira was seeking military assertion in other ways. In November 1970, she had asked the DRDO to launch a feasibility study on building a long-range ballistic missile. Two months before that she had apparently asked for a similar study on a nuclear-propelled submarine. As Chengappa observes, 'Mrs Gandhi had laid plans for India to join the big boys' club.' But crucially, he maintains, some time in mid-1970 she had also asked Vikram to prepare for a nuclear explosion.[45]

This appears to be accurate because the *Morning Herald*, Sydney, 27 July 1970, quotes Vikram as asserting that India was capable of conducting underground nuclear explosions and that it was internationally entitled to do so as a non-signatory to the NPT.[46] Those who knew Vikram well maintain that he would not have disobeyed a direct order from the prime minister. The US, clearly perturbed, sent an aide-memoire in November 1970 indicating that using plutonium from CIRUS, the Canada–India research reactor, would violate the US–India nuclear cooperation agreement.

Privately, however, Vikram appears to have been torn apart. Kamla maintains that he was under tremendous stress at the time, particularly with regard to the prime minister's advisers. I.G. Patel noticed a diminishing warmth and trust on Indira's side towards Vikram. There is a suggestion that Vikram was deeply concerned about the potential fallout of these factors on his beloved space programme. Funds allocated under the Fourth Plan (1969–74) were half of what he estimated the space programme would need for the same period in his ten-year plan.

Characteristically, however, Vikram concealed his mounting agitation under an appearance of liveliness. In May 1971, he took a rare holiday with his family in Manali. A small house was rented in the valley and Vikram appeared to relax completely, playing golf, wandering in the town, eating noodles and playing with his grandson. There were security men in the bushes—he was the AEC chairman, after all—but, according to Mallika, they unwound too, flirting with her and teaching her to fire a pistol.

But the clock was ticking. The cost-benefit study on explosives that Vikram had commissioned from Seshagiri became available in 1971. The outcome could not have been to his liking; it showed that peaceful nuclear explosives for engineering purposes would be economically viable though weapons might not. The pressure was growing. Still, he did not show it outwardly. He travelled to Thumba and to Ahmedabad and though the perceived tussle over the bomb was well known enough for his colleagues to whisper about it, Vikram did not say much.

'It was this Gandhian thing of self-sufficiency,' says Mallika. 'Look inside. Churn the depths of your spirituality. Mridulaben was also like that. Not being self-reliant was considered a weakness, a flaw in character.' And yet, inside Vikram was crying for help. Some time roughly between June and November of 1971, Mrinalini describes him getting up from his sleep suddenly in the middle of the night. 'He went to the window talking incoherently about his work,' she recalls. 'I woke up and soothed him, gently patting him on the back like a child till he calmed down. It was disturbing. Such a thing had never happened before.'

Few would have guessed at the battle that was raging within as Vikram announced at the Fourth International Conference on Peaceful Uses of Atomic Energy in Geneva that his scientists were developing nuclear explosive engineering (a term he preferred to 'peaceful nuclear explosives') as a top priority. His handwritten notes of the meeting, taken in a small brown notepad of 'The Abbey on Lake Geneva', are customarily detailed and betray no agitation.

A few weeks before that he had made an intriguing confession to Subrahmanyam and Sisir Gupta (later professor of international relations at the Jawaharlal Nehru University). Over dinner he had told the two men that 'in the New Year of 1972' the French had invited him to Morovia to watch the French nuclear test. Subrahmanyam drew the obvious conclusion that Vikram had decided to cooperate fully with the pro-demonstration lobby.

After the Geneva Conference, Vikram stopped over in France to meet André Giraud, administrator-general of the Commissariat á l'Energie Atomique, to seek his cooperation in developing a 500–600MW heavy water reactor in India. The growing closeness to France was probably a preparatory move. France had not signed the NPT and was openly critical of US hegemony, unlike the Canadians who were seen as kowtowing to the US, and had already written a letter to Indira similar to the one sent by the Americans warning India about flouting guarantees.

Indira wrote back disputing the Canadian interpretation of guarantees but added that a peaceful nuclear explosion was a 'hypothetical contingency'.[47] She had another, far more urgent problem looming in her backyard. In October 1970, Pakistan had conducted its first democratic election, sparking off a long-standing demand for regional autonomy in East Pakistan. Negotiations over power sharing had failed and the military regime under General Yahya Khan had responded with the use of force against the Bengali population of East Pakistan. Civil war had broken out and, since March 1971, refugees had been pouring into India through the eastern border from East Pakistan. In the months that followed, the influx crept to the one crore mark, putting a great strain on India's resources.

As hints of military action by India against West Pakistan began to make the rounds, Vikram busied himself visiting suitable sites in the Indo-Gangetic plain for his proposed agro-industrial complexes. It is not possible to confirm that the following is exactly what took place. But those in a position to observe proceedings in the matter claim that whether Vikram sensed it or not, the impasse at the AEC was finally reaching a head. Vikram had completed five years in office and Sethna was reportedly getting restive. At the same time, Indira had been persuaded by her advisers to hive off the space programme from the DAE and make it independent. The plan was that Vikram would be asked to choose and his breakneck schedule would be the reason given for the enforced decision. 'You will die if you go on like this,' is what Indira is supposed to have told him.[48] Vikram's potential successor at the space department had already been selected in case he was distraught and furious enough to sign off both.

There are some who disbelieve this story on the grounds that Indira would not have made a move that would seem so much like a vote of no trust; that she would not have gone so far as to humiliate Vikram by making him choose his own demotion. There is also the fact to be considered that Vikram's relentless schedule was a cause of worry to all who cared for him. Haksar claims, 'I often used to tell him that since he had so much to do and so far to go why was he missing aeroplanes by the skin of his teeth?'[49]

It has been suggested that Indira, if she did ask him to choose, was taking a practical view of the matter. Seshan believes Indira did ask Vikram to choose and that 'it broke his heart to make a choice'.

Vikram in his usual tight-lipped fashion gave no indication to anyone by behaviour or speech that such a choice had been put to him. But that could also perhaps be at least to some extent due to the fast evolving situation on the military front: on 3 December 1971, Pakistan, anticipating an attack from the Indian side, bombed Indian airfields. The next day, India hit back.

Through the brief war Vikram continued working his usual hours unmindful of dusk-time restrictions. Seshan remembers that the two of them were at Bombay's Marine Drive one evening when the warning siren sounded out. 'We had to get out of our car and lie flat on the kerb with our briefcases over our heads.'

Vikram managed to make a contribution at the battle front as well. Hit by an inspiration, he suggested that the sounding rockets developed for use in the space programme could be used as makeshift missiles against the enemy. Though devoid of any guiding mechanism, the rockets with a payload of 20–25 kg each could cause serious damage. Apart from which, the very sight of the flaming crackers bursting out of nowhere could be a terrifying one. K.F. Rustomjee of the Border Security Force agreed to deploy them.

The war lasted thirteen days. Pakistan surrendered to the Indian army on 16 December 1971, but not before the US signalled its pro-Pakistan tilt. The Western press had reported General Tikka Khan's atrocities in vivid detail but Nixon, while refusing to take sides, sent a fleet of ships headed by the nuclear warship *Enterprise* to the Bay of Bengal ostensibly for the protection of US nationals who had long been evacuated.

As the war wore on, Mrinalini found herself getting worried about Vikram. 'He looked tired. Even though he did not confide his work problems to me, I knew instinctively that he was under great strain. I wanted to be with him.' She was right in assuming that something was wrong. Vikram himself confessed in a roundabout way that something had been worrying him. One day, he told her, he was running to the sea in Kovalam and he came across a snake with its hood raised. Unable to break his stride he claimed he jumped right over it. 'I think,' he concluded from the incident, 'the problems I have are over now.'[50]

It is an interesting touch of superstitiousness and a throwback to his father. Ambalal, when he took over the family business, had apparently been confronted with a serious problem, deliberately created by mischief makers at work. The solution to the problem and its location were said to have come to him in a dream.[51] In Vikram's case, the truth was less clear.

In late December, Vikram invited Gita and her daughter Pallavi over for dinner. Pallavi had just passed an examination and Vikram was full of questions about how she saw her future. They ate out on his terrace garden. 'It was not a dinner, it was fine dining!' Pallavi recalls. 'He made a real occasion of it. He was very focused, he really knew how to make someone feel special.'

Around Christmas Eve Vikram travelled to Ahmedabad. He made it a point to drop in on his mother. Always affectionate, after his father's death he had become even more particular about checking on her, claims his sister, Leena. They chatted for a while. Presumably, Sarla chided him for working too hard. He told her of his longing to retire and sit by the side of an aquarium at the Community Science Centre and teach science to children.

But retirement seemed a long way away. On Sunday, 26 December, he returned to Bombay, exhausted, but prepared to leave for his routine trip to Thumba. The house in Bombay would have been empty, for Kartikeya and his family had gone back to the US, but for once Mrinalini and Mallika were in town. His daughter, who had grown into a lissome young woman with the delicate features and fine complexion of the Sarabhai clan, had been offered a role in a film by a Bombay film-maker. Her decision to accept had evoked strong reactions in the conservative circles of Ahmedabad just as Mrinalini's decision to dance had two decades earlier.

It might have been that afternoon that Vikram and Mrinalini

took their young daughter for lunch to the Sea Lounge, a fine restaurant overlooking the Bombay harbour, to boost her morale. Vikram's travel plans were in a state of flux. A cabinet paper had arrived from Delhi informing him of a meeting on SITE. He was alerted late in the day and it was midnight when Warrier phoned Ramnath to ask him to book him on to the early-morning flight. Ramanna travelled with Vikram to Delhi.

A week before Vikram had been declared fit after a thorough check up by his physician Dr R.J. Vakil. On the flight Ramanna recalls him talking about a blood pressure problem and his keenness to learn special yogic exercises to control it. 'This was surprising,' observes Ramanna, 'coming from a man who owned pharmaceutical firms which manufactured large quantities of allopathic drugs.'[52]

Vikram returned from Delhi the same day all set to leave for Thumba the next morning. Mallika begged him not to go. The new year was approaching and she was keen on celebrating it with her family in Ahmedabad. Vikram promised to be in Ahmedabad three days later. Father and daughter left the house at the break of light the next day, one, to catch a flight south, the other for an early-morning shoot.

The next couple of days—28 and 29 December—passed in a flurry of activity for Vikram. From various accounts it seems likely that he might have spent the whole of 29 December at the guest house. He had lunch with R.D. John and the head of TERLS, H.G.S. Murthy. In the afternoon he met with the chemicals group. The meeting went on for a few hours. U.R. Rao recalls being disappointed by the progress revealed though Vikram did not appear to share his dejection, saying merely, 'We have to build the chemicals group.'

A meeting then may have followed with Gowarikar, Suresh Thakur, who was director of administration at PRL, and ISRO's Y. Janardhan Rao, A.E. Muthunayagam and M.K. Mukherjee. E.V. Chitnis was probably there as well. After the meeting, the group broke for dinner. A young couple who was holidaying on the premises went by. Gowarikar recalls Vikram waving to them cheerily and confirming that he would be joining them at six the next morning for a swim.

After dinner everyone converged again upon Vikram's room to resume the lively conversation that had started in the dining room. Vikram appeared to be in robust spirits and nobody noticed any signs of ill health except Gowarikar who, when he went in to talk to Vikram alone for a few minutes, found him lying on the floor with his hands under his head. 'He always sat very comfortably but I had never before seen him in that position and I mentioned it to my wife when I got home that night.'

The evening broke up probably a little after ten. Vikram's secretary, Warrier, went to his room in the annexe to the guest house at the back. Vikram promised to pick up Thakur on his way to the airport for both were travelling to Ahmedabad together. Just then Kalam called from Delhi where he had attended a meeting of the missile panel. Vikram heard him go over the salient points, then instructed him to wait at Trivandrum airport on his arrival the next morning so that they could confer on the SLV3 before Vikram's flight to Bombay.

Dawn broke over the sandy parapets of the Kovalam guest house on 30 December. The sea lapped gently at the empty shore. An hour or two later, Nadesha Paniker, the room boy, rang the bell of the suite on the top floor. Receiving no response, he tried the handle. The door was locked from the inside. Just then the cleaning lady, Mrs Shandamma, turned up. One by one both went out to the strip of balcony that ran along the length of the room. Through the long windows they saw a sleeping figure under the mosquito net.

Both were aware that it was Vikram. He was their most frequent guest and generous with tips ('He would line the staff up after every visit and give us each a tip, rupees five sometimes or rupees ten.').[53] Familiar with his habits they were surprised that he was still asleep. They pressed the bell again and banged on the door. There was still no response. Mrs Shandamma informed the steward who sent for Warrier. The manager joined them with the key.

The large room was uncluttered and clean. Under the net Vikram lay still, a book open on his chest. A doctor had been sent for and he said Vikram had probably died a couple of hours before.

'His face was so fresh,' says Mrs Shandamma. 'He looked like he was just sleeping.'

8

A 'HEROIC' DEATH

At the present time many implicitly carry a conviction that life is unique on earth. If and when this proves to be wrong, I would like to suggest that a very fundamental transformation will occur in the way man looks at life and nature.

—Vikram Sarabhai[1]

A.P.J. Abdul Kalam found a pall of gloom hanging over Trivandrum airport when he got off his flight from Delhi. An aircraft ladder operator, choking with emotion, told him about Vikram's death.[2]

In Bangalore, the head of Hindustan Aeronautics, Air Marshal Mehra, was at the airport waiting to meet Vikram for a brief discussion when the flight from Trivandrum halted en route to Bombay. His houseguest, Prakash Tandon, chairman of Hindustan Lever, had joined him on an impulse to say hello to his old friend.[3] The airport manager gave them the sad news even as they were joined by S. Ramaseshan who, having heard, had hurried to the airport to pay his last respects.

In Baroda, Anil Majumdar, a senior executive at Sarabhai Chemicals, entered his office at nine and almost immediately received a phone call from a journalist who told him about the information coming over the teleprinter. A little while later, workers began trudging out of the factory gates in a melancholy fashion.

In Ahmedabad, Leena was preparing for a school advisers' meeting that she expected her brother to attend. The phone rang. It was Sarla, saying, '*Vikram nathi.*'

At Bombay airport, Mrinalini and Mallika clutched each other in grief as they waited for the special air force plane that was bringing Vikram's body. The city's mayor, Hemchandra Gupta, and industrialist J.R.D. Tata were also there along with a vast throng of friends and admirers. The next day, the country's leading English-language daily the *Times of India* would carry, amidst news of Bangladeshis celebrating their leader Mujibur Rehman's release, a large photograph of the coffin with a face barely visible underneath the garlands and the white sheet with the headline: 'Space Research Pioneer Vikram Sarabhai Dead'.

In Ahmedabad, on 31 December 1971 at 8.10 a.m., the body with a tilak on the forehead was placed inside a black Dodge station wagon accompanied by Mrinalini and Sarla Devi. Many had turned up at The Retreat to pay their respects the previous day. M.R. Srinivasan joined his colleagues from the DAE, including T.N. Seshan, on the overnight train to Ahmedabad. I.G. Patel who had been planning a holiday in Kovalam at Vikram's invitation in the near future was with the governor of the Reserve Bank in Bombay when the news trickled in. Both set out for Ahmedabad as well.

Condolences flowed in. Indira Gandhi, who would pay a private visit to the family, confessed to being 'deeply grieved'. M.S. Swaminathan, director of the Indian Agricultural Research Institute, said it was 'a great loss'. U Thant and Kurt Waldheim, the incoming and outgoing secretary-general of the UN respectively, had written as well.

P.N. Haksar, the prime minister's principal secretary, who had often asked Vikram to slow down his pace would later say, 'I now understand that somewhere deep down within his subconscious there must have been a feeling that life is uncertain...within the short period of time which stretches between the hour one is born and the hour one dies...a man must do his best and Vikram was hastening.' Describing his death as 'heroic', Japanese space technologist and friend Hideo Itokawa wrote that 'his ability went beyond his living power'.

There were murmurs of international foul play. Kamla, whom Mrinalini had informed and who confessed to being overwhelmed by the family's 'generosity' towards her at the time, would later claim that Vikram had told her that he was being watched by both the Americans and the Russians. Bhabha's death had sparked off similar speculation. But no post-mortem was performed on Vikram's body.

The Dodge, preceded by a pilot car and followed by a stream of automobiles, took seventy minutes to traverse the fifteen-kilometre distance to the Sarabhai family's Kotarpur farm at Hansol village.

The priests were already at the picturesque farm chanting shlokas. The gates had been shut for what was meant to be a private event but Mridula flung them open saying he was a public figure. And, as family friend Navroz Contractor recalls, 'Half of Ahmedabad flowed in.' There were people from the IIM-A, ATIRA and all the various institutions set up by Vikram. There were workers from the Sarabhai group of companies and their families. But there were also ordinary people who had somehow been touched by Vikram. The crush of photographers made his nephew, Kamal Mangaldas, uncomfortable. 'I was angry with the jostling but I was told to bear it because he had been a national figure.' Pallavi Mayor says, 'I never realized what a big shot my uncle was till then.'

The mood was understandably sombre. Many wept openly. Warrier's wails were heart-rending. Every female employee from PRL had insisted on attending. The occasion proved too much for some though, who fell unconscious and had to be revived.

Vikram's mother was there, of course. Vikram's associate from PRL, Rastogi, recalls that the winter cold had solidified the ghee and Sarla kept telling the priest as he broke chunks for the pyre, 'Apply it gently, he can get hurt.'

The body was laid on a charpai. Wreaths had been placed on behalf of the Indian Air Force, and the union and state governments. Family members milled around in pristine white. At 10.30 a.m., Mallika stepped forward to light the pyre. The decision that she should perform the task had been made on a purely practical basis; Kartikeya, who would traditionally have been expected to light the pyre, had not been able to make it home from America in time. The resonances, however, were historic; it was a rare occasion that a woman had lit the funeral pyre. 'I received thousands of letters praising me later,' Mallika says. 'At the time it just seemed the natural thing to do. Had my brother been there, we both would have done it.'

Some days later Vikram's ashes were scattered in the Indian Ocean at Thumba.

That year the rains were especially ferocious. The Sabarmati swelled and flooded its banks. Its waters washed away the remnants of the pyre at Hansol where Vikram had been cremated. So great was the force of the river that it even trickled into Chidambaram. Vikram's private den down the slope, the glass-fronted Ghoghu, found itself submerged in water.

In 1974, a moon crater was named after Dr Vikram Sarabhai. The International Astronomical Union at Sydney, Australia, decided that crater BESSEL in the Sea of Serenity would be known as the Sarabhai Crater.

NOTES

Unless otherwise specified, statements or information attributed to the following are drawn from interviews with the author between April 2001 and December 2003: Pranlal Patel, Leena Mangaldas, Kartikeya Sarabhai, Usha Dhumketu, Khushwant Singh, Navroz Contractor, U.R. Rao, Gita Mayor, Arvind Lalbhai, Prabhaben Lalbhai, Mrinalini Sarabhai, Ashis Nandy, Lakshmi Sehgal, T.N. Seshan, Kamal Mangaldas, Mallika Sarabhai, Dwijendra Tripathi, Pramod Kale, Kekoo Gandhy, S.M. Chitre, Abu Abraham, S. Ramaseshan, Dr P.K. Iyengar, M.S. Sastry, Dr Kirit Parikh, Vinodini Mayor, Alaknanda Patel, Praful Bhavsar, R.G. Rastogi, E.V. Chitnis, M.M. Gharia, Kamla Chowdhry, Jahar Saha, I.K. Gujral, Dr I.G. Patel, H. Kumar Vyas, Dr K. Kasturirangan, Dr Vasant Gowarikar, G.D. Zalani, Pallavi Mayor, Ashok Parthasarthi, Gopal Raj, Homi Sethna, Padmanabh Joshi, K.J. Divatia, Nadesha Paniker, K. Subrahmanyam and Mrs Shandamma.

Vikram's handwritten notes refer to a collection of loose sheets and notepads with his scribblings between 1965 and 1971, sourced from the Dr Vikram Sarabhai Archives, Nehru Foundation for Development, Ahmedabad.

1. THE CRUCIBLE

[1] See, for instance, *The Ahmedabad Chronicle—Imprints of a Millennium*, Vastu Shilpa Foundation for Studies and Research in Environmental Design, Ahmedabad, 2002.

[2] *Haft Iqlim* (1593) by Iranian author Amin Ahmad Razi at Akbar's court, quoted in 'The City of Beauties in Indo-Persian Poetry' by Sunil Sharma. Refer http://www.cssaame.ilstu.edu/issues/24-2/sharma.doc and http://www.egovamc.com/A_City/ahmedabad/history.asp.

[3] Kenneth L. Gillion, *Ahmedabad*, pp. 5-6.

[4] Ibid., p. 87.

[5] Ibid., p. 4.

[6] Achyut Yagnik and Suchitra Sheth, *The Shaping of Modern Gujarat*, p. 37.

[7] Erik H. Erikson, *Gandhi's Truth*, p. 258.

[8] Leena Mangaldas, *Akhand Divo*, p. 7.

[9] Kenneth L. Gillion, *Ahmedabad*, p. 86.

[10] Erik H. Erikson, *Gandhi's Truth*, p. 298.

[11] Lawrence A. Babb, *Ascetics and Kings in a Jain Ritual Culture*, pp. 5-6.

[12] Letter written by E.M. Standing in 1921, quoted in Aparna Basu, *Mridula Sarabhai: A Rebel with a Cause*, p. 26.

[13] See the early chapters of Jan Breman and Parthiv Shah, *Working in the Mill No More.*

[14] Arun Gandhi, *Kasturba: A Life*, p. 196.

[15] M.K. Gandhi, *The Story of My Experiments With Truth*, p. 329.

[16] Dwijendra Tripathi, *The Dynamics of a Tradition: Kasturbhai Lalbhai and His Entrepreneurship*, p. 171.

[17] Erik H. Erikson, quoting Gulzarilal Nanda, in *Gandhi's Truth*, p. 86.

[18] Paper presented at the Gandhi Centenary Conference on Science, Education and Non-violence at Gujarat Vidyapith in 1969, Dr Vikram Sarabhai Archives, Nehru Foundation for Development, Ahmedabad. Also in Vikram Sarabhai, *Science Policy and National Development*, p. 165.

[19] 'The Two Cultures', BBC interview, 1970, reproduced in Padmanabh K. Joshi (ed.), *Vikram Sarabhai: The Man and the Vision.*

[20] Leena Mangaldas, *Akhand Divo*, p. 11.

[21] C.J. Bhatt, 'The Boy Vikram', in Padmanabh K. Joshi (ed.), *Vikram Sarabhai: The Man and the Vision*, p. 24.

[22] Privately circulated reminiscences of E.M. Standing, Dr Vikram Sarabhai Archives, Nehru Foundation for Development, Ahmedabad.

[23] C.J. Bhatt, 'The Boy Vikram', in Padmanabh K. Joshi (ed.), *Vikram Sarabhai: The Man and the Vision*, p. 24.

[24] Copy of letter written home by Miss Williams in 1926, Sarabhai Foundation Archives, quoted in Aparna Basu, *Mridula Sarabhai: A Rebel with a Cause*, p. 20.

[25] J.S. Badami, 'My Student, Employer and Friend', in Padmanabh K. Joshi (ed.), *Vikram Sarabhai: The Man and the Vision*, p. 28.

[26] Vikram Sarabhai in *India and Science Today*, a documentary produced by Michael Treguer for French television.

[27] Privately circulated reminiscences of E.M. Standing, Dr Vikram Sarabhai Archives, Nehru Foundation for Development, Ahmedabad.

[28] Khushwant Singh in the preface to Aparna Basu, *Mridula Sarabhai: A Rebel with a Cause.*

[29] M.O. Mathai, *Reminiscences of the Nehru Age*, p. 201.

[30] J.S. Badami, 'My Student, Employer and Friend', in Padmanabh K. Joshi (ed.), *Vikram Sarabhai: The Man and the Vision*, pp. 28-29.

[31] Prahlad C. Patel, *Viral Vibhuti Vikram Sarabhai*, pp. 6-7.

[32] M.K. Gandhi, *My Experiments with Truth*, p. 342.

[33] Aparna Basu, *Mridula Sarabhai: A Rebel with a Cause*, p. 27.

[34] *Navjivan*, 5 December 1920.

[35] Raj Thapar, *All These Years*, p. 2.

[36] Aparna Basu, *Mridula Sarabhai: A Rebel with a Cause*, p. 36.

[37] Vikram Sarabhai in *India and Science Today*, a documentary produced by Michael Treguer for French television.

[38] C.J. Bhatt, 'The Boy Vikram', in Padmanabh K. Joshi (ed.), *Vikram Sarabhai: The Man and the Vision*, p. 26.

[39] Ray Spangenburg and Diane K. Moser, *Werner Von Braun: Space Visionary and Rocket Engineer*, pp. 4–7.

[40] Vikram Sarabhai in a 1966 talk reproduced in *Resonance*, December 2001.

[41] Padmanabh K. Joshi (ed.), *Vikram Sarabhai: The Man and the Vision*, p. 52.

[42] 'Implementing Change through Science and Technology', talk delivered at the International Symposium on Science and Society in South Asia at the Rockefeller University, New York, May 1966, Dr Vikram Sarabhai Archives, Nehru Foundation for Development, Ahmedabad. Also in Vikram Sarabhai, *Management for Development*, Kamla Chowdhry (ed.), pp. 118-19.

2. 'STARTING PROCESSES'

[1] J.S. Badami, 'My Student, Employer and Friend', in Padmanabh K. Joshi (ed.), *Vikram Sarabhai: The Man and the Vision*, p. 28.

[2] Padmanabh K. Joshi (ed.), *Vikram Sarabhai: The Man and the Vision*, p. 19.

[3] Ibid., Appendix.

[4] Jamsetji Tata quoted in R.M. Lala, *The Creation of Wealth*, p. 33.

[5] U.R. Rao in personal communication with the author.

[6] For more on C.V. Raman, see G. Venkataraman, *Raman and His Effect*.

[7] Vikram Sarabhai, 'Cosmic Ray Investigations in Tropical Latitudes', PhD thesis from Cambridge University, 1947, Dr Vikram Sarabhai Archives, Nehru Foundation for Development, Ahmedabad.

[8] Ibid.

[9] S. Ramaseshan reminiscing in Gopal Raj, *Reach for the Stars*, pp. 3-4.

[10] S. Ramaseshan in personal communication with the author.

[11] For more on Bhabha, see G. Venkataraman, *Bhabha and His Magnificent Obsessions*.

[12] 'Man, The Observer', a presentation at the Seminar on the Human Life Cycle, Ahmedabad, 10 December 1962, Dr Vikram Sarabhai Archives, Nehru Foundation for Development, Ahmedabad.

[13] Excerpt from a lecture delivered by Professor Bruno Rossi (Massachusetts Institute of Technology, Boston, USA) at the 13th International Cosmic Ray Conference, University of Denver, 1973, reproduced in Padmanabh K. Joshi (ed.), *Vikram Sarabhai: The Man and the Vision*, pp. 161-62.

[14] M.G.K. Menon, 'Like a Prophet', in Padmanabh K. Joshi (ed.), *Vikram Sarabhai: The Man and the Vision*, p. 61.

[15] Paper presented at the Gandhi Centenary Conference on Science, Education and Non-violence at Gujarat Vidyapith in 1969, Dr Vikram Sarabhai Archives, Nehru Foundation for Development, Ahmedabad. Also in Vikram Sarabhai, *Science Policy and National Development*, p. 166.

[16] 'Leadership in Science', talk delivered on All India Radio in August 1965, Dr Vikram Sarabhai Archives, Nehru Foundation for Development, Ahmedabad. Also in Vikram Sarabhai, *Science Policy and National Development*, p. 172.

[17] Harriet Ronken Lynton, *Born to Dance*, p. 49.

[18] Mrinalini Sarabhai in personal communication with the author. See also, Mrinalini Sarabhai, *The Voice of the Heart*, pp. 78–80.

[19] Mrinalini Sarabhai in personal communication with the author.

[20] Mrinalini Sarabhai in personal communication with the author. See also, Mrinalini Sarabhai, *The Voice of the Heart*, p. 119.

[21] Mrinalini Sarabhai in personal communication with the author. Ibid., p. 91.

[22] Katherine Frank, *Indira: The Life of Indira Nehru Gandhi*, p. 182.

[23] Appendix I, 'A Cosmic Ray Expedition to Kashmere', Vikram Sarabhai's PhD Thesis, 'Cosmic Ray Investigations in Tropical Latitudes', Cambridge, 1947, Dr Vikram Sarabhai Archives, Nehru Foundation for Development, Ahmedabad.

[24] Ibid.

[25] Harriet Ronken Lynton, *Born to Dance*, p. 55.

[26] Introduction to Vikram Sarabhai's PhD Thesis, 'Cosmic Ray Investigations in Tropical Latitudes', Cambridge, 1947, Dr Vikram Sarabhai Archives, Nehru Foundation for Development, Ahmedabad.

[27] 'Bibliography of Scientific Papers by Dr Sarabhai and His Collaborators', in Padmanabh K. Joshi (ed.), *Vikram Sarabhai: The Man and the Vision*, p. 181.

[28] 'Paradise Lost', in Joan Freeman, *A Passion for Physics—The Story of a Woman Physicist*.

[29] Vikram Sarabhai's PhD Thesis, 'Cosmic Ray Investigations in Tropical Latitudes', Cambridge, 1947, Dr Vikram Sarabhai Archives, Nehru Foundation for Development, Ahmedabad.

[30] Ibid.

[31] Padmanabh K. Joshi (ed.), *Vikram Sarabhai: The Man and the Vision*, Appendix.

[32] Joan Freeman, *A Passion for Physics—The Story of a Woman Physicist*, p. 129.

[33] 'A Tribute by P.M.S. Blackett', Dr Vikram Sarabhai Archives, Nehru Foundation for Development, Ahmedabad.

[34] Mrinalini Sarabhai in personal communication with the author.

[35] From 'A Tryst With Destiny', Nehru's speech in the Constituent Assembly, 14 August 1947, in S. Gopal and Uma Iyengar (eds), *The Essential Writings of Jawaharlal Nehru*, p. 347.

3. BUILDING AN INSTITUTION

[1] Chester Bowles, *Ambassador's Report*, p. 53.

[2] Ibid., p. 27.

[3] Ibid., p. 69.

[4] Raj Thapar, *All These Years*, pp. 45, 144.

[5] Itty Abraham, *The Making of the Atomic Bomb*, pp. 45-46

[6] See Papers, *Asian Relations Conference, March-April 1947*, Indian Council of World Affairs, New Delhi.

[7] Presidential Address at the 34th Indian Science Congress, New Delhi, 3 January 1947, S. Gopal and Uma Iyengar (eds), *The Essential Writings of Jawaharlal Nehru*, Vol. III, p. 523.

[8] Nehru to Mahavir Tyagi, 9 August 1952, quoted in S. Gopal, *Jawaharlal Nehru: A Biography, Volume Two, 1947–1956*, p. 306.

[9] Ramchandra Guha, *An Anthropologist Among the Marxists*, p. 214.

[10] Kenneth L. Gillion, *Ahmedabad*, pp. 21-22.

[11] Gita Piramal, *Business Legends*, p. 301.

[12] *Atira 1949–1974*, brochure produced by ATIRA, November 1974.

[13] Ibid., p. 1.

[14] Paper delivered at the International Symposium on Science and Society in South Asia at Rockefeller University, New York, May 1966, Dr Vikram Sarabhai Archives, Nehru Foundation for Development, Ahmedabad. Also in Vikram Sarabhai, *Management for Development*, Kamla Chowdhry (ed.), p. 118.

[15] Mridula Sarabhai's diary quoted in Aparna Basu, *Mridula Sarabhai: A Rebel With a Cause*, p. 45.

[16] Santimay Chatterjee and Enakshi Chatterjee, *Meghnad Saha*, p. 35.

[17] R.P. Kane, 'Karmayogi', in Padmanabh K. Joshi (ed.), *Vikram Sarabhai: The Man and the Vision*, p. 59.

[18] Harriet Ronken Lynton, *Born to Dance*, p. 66.

[19] Praful Bhavsar, 'There Is Nobody to Be Ruled', in Padmanabh K. Joshi (ed.), *Vikram Sarabhai: The Man and the Vision*, p. 44.

[20] 'As for Me', postscript by Nora Rossi, in Bruno Rossi, *Moments in the Life of a Scientist*, p. 173.

[21] Vikram Sarabhai, quoted in Padmanabh K. Joshi (ed.), *Vikram Sarabhai: The Man and the Vision*, p. 78.

[22] 'Role of Science in Industry', 1959, Dr Vikram Sarabhai Archives, Nehru Foundation for Development, Ahmedabad.

[23] P.C. Mehta, 'Pioneering in Textile Research', in Padmanabh K. Joshi (ed.), *Vikram Sarabhai: The Man and the Vision*, p. 85.
[24] Prakash Tandon, *Punjabi Saga*, p. 549.
[25] Kamla Chowdhry, 'Institution Builder', in Padmanabh K. Joshi (ed.), *Vikram Sarabhai: The Man and the Vision*, p. 83.
[26] Kamla Chowdhry, 'A Personal Introduction to Vikram Sarabhai', in Vikram Sarabhai, *Management for Development*, Kamla Chowdhry (ed.), p. xiv.
[27] Padmanabh Joshi, 'Dr Vikram Sarabhai: A Study on Innovative Leadership and Institution-Building', unpublished PhD thesis from Gujarat University (1986).
[28] Mrinalini Sarabhai in personal communication with the author. Also see Mrinalini Sarabhai, *The Voice of the Heart*, p. 165.
[29] Mrinalini Sarabhai, *This Alone Is True*, p. 191.
[30] Harriet Ronken Lynton, *Born to Dance*, pp. 56-57.
[31] Mrinalini Sarabhai in personal communication with the author.
[32] Prakash Tandon, *Punjabi Saga*, p. 549.

4. TOWARDS A MODERN SENSIBILITY

[1] *The Times of India*, 2 May 1960.
[2] Prakash Tandon, *Punjabi Saga*, pp. 414-15.
[3] Erik H. Erikson, *Gandhi's Truth*, p. 25.
[4] Ibid., p. 69.
[5] S.P. Pandya, 'The Physicist', in Padmanabh K. Joshi (ed.), *Vikram Sarabhai: The Man and the Vision*, pp. 52-53.
[6] 'The Two Cultures', BBC interview, 1970, reproduced in Padmanabh K. Joshi (ed.), *Vikram Sarabhai: The Man and the Vision*, pp. 38–42.
[7] M.R. Kurup in *Kerala Koumudi*, 24 January 1972.
[8] Harjit S. Ahluwalia in *Physics Today*, March 1987.
[9] P.M.S. Blackett, 'A Tribute', Dr Vikram Sarabhai Archives, Nehru Foundation for Development, Ahmedabad.
[10] Prakash Tandon, *Punjabi Saga*, p. 414.
[11] K.J. Divatia in personal communication with the author.
[12] Vikram Sarabhai, *Management for Development*, Kamla Chowdhry (ed.), pp. 57-58.

[13] M.R. Raman, 'Vikrambhai: The Man We Knew', in *Sara Pragati* (House magazine of Sarabhai Chemicals), June 1972.

[14] Obaid Siddiqui, Professor Emeritus, TIFR, in personal communication with the author.

[15] Kamla Chowdhry, 'A Personal Introduction', in Vikram Sarabhai, *Management for Development*, Kamla Chowdhry (ed.), p. xiv.

[16] Padmanabh K. Joshi (ed.), *Vikram Sarabhai: The Man and the Vision*, p. 104.

[17] Mrinalini Sarabhai in personal communication with the author. See also, Mrinalini Sarabhai, *The Voice of the Heart*, p. 162.

[18] Mrinalini Sarabhai in personal communication with the author. Ibid., p. 161

[19] Mrinalini Sarabhai in personal communication with the author. Ibid.

[20] Mrinalini Sarabhai in personal communication with the author.

[21] Prakash Tandon, *Punjabi Saga*, p. 548.

[22] Mrinalini Sarabhai, *The Voice of the Heart*, p. 96.

[23] Padmanabh K. Joshi (ed.), *Vikram Sarabhai: The Man and the Vision*, p. 38.

[24] Umashanker Joshi quoted in V. Gangadhar, 'Dr. Vikram Sarabhai', *The Illustrated Weekly of India*, 30 December 1973, pp. 38–41.

[25] Ibid.

[26] V. Gangadhar in personal communication with the author.

[27] R.P. Kane, 'Karmayogi', in Padmanabh K. Joshi (ed.), *Vikram Sarabhai: The Man and the Vision*, p. 60.

[28] M.R. Raman, 'Vikrambhai: The Man We Knew', *Sara Pragati*, June 1972, pp. 31–34.

[29] Ravi Mathai, 'Developing Professional Managers', in Padmanabh K. Joshi (ed.), *Vikram Sarabhai: The Man and the Vision*, p. 144.

[30] Ibid., p. 145.

[31] Erik H. Erikson, *Gandhi's Truth*, p. 23.

[32] Ibid.

5. LAUNCHING INTO SPACE

[1] Gopal Raj in personal communication with the author.

[2] Transcript of an interview with R.D. John, ISRO, Bangalore.

[3] Gopal Raj, *Reach for the Stars*, p. 11.
[4] A.P.J. Abdul Kalam with Arun Tiwari, *Wings of Fire*, p. 31.
[5] Transcript of an interview with R.D. John, ISRO, Bangalore.
[6] Mrinalini Sarabhai in personal communication with the author.
[7] A.P.J. Abdul Kalam with Arun Tiwari, *Wings of Fire*, p. 40.
[8] Hideo Itokawa, 'A Tribute', Dr Vikram Sarabhai Archives, Nehru Foundation for Development, Ahmedabad.
[9] Address given as Scientific Chairman of the UN Conference on the Exploration and Peaceful Uses of Outer Space, Vienna, August 1968, Dr Vikram Sarabhai Archives, Nehru Foundation for Development, Ahmedabad. Also in Vikram Sarabhai, *Science Policy and National Development*, p. 29.
[10] Vikram Sarabhai, 'Space Activity for Developing Countries', Dr Vikram Sarabhai Archives, Nehru Foundation for Development, Ahmedabad. Also in Vikram Sarabhai, *Science Policy and National Development*, p. 23.
[11] Address given as Scientific Chairman of the UN Conference on the Exploration and Peaceful Uses of Outer Space, Vienna, August 1968, Dr Vikram Sarabhai Archives, Nehru Foundation for Development, Ahmedabad. Also in Vikram Sarabhai, *Science Policy and National Development*, p. 36.
[12] Vikram Sarabhai, 'Sources of Man's Knowledge', part of the National Programme of Talks, Series: 'Exploration in Space', 1966, reproduced in *Resonance*, December 2001, pp. 89–92.
[13] Vikram Sarabhai, 'Space Activity for Developing Countries', Dr Vikram Sarabhai Archives, Nehru Foundation for Development, Ahmedabad. Also in Vikram Sarabhai, *Science Policy and National Development*, p. 23.
[14] Raj Chengappa, *Weapons of Peace*, p. 90.
[15] Prakash Tandon, *Punjabi Saga*, p. 498.
[16] M.R. Raman, 'Vikrambhai: The Man We Knew', *Sara Pragati*, June 1972, pp. 31–34.
[17] N.R. Nadkarni, 'Dr Vikram Sarabhai: A Few Glimpses of His Personality', *Sara Pragati*, June 1972, pp. 4–6.
[18] Ibid.
[19] Mrinalini Sarabhai in personal communication with the author.
[20] Quoted by Mrinalini Sarabhai to the author. See also, Mrinalini Sarabhai, *The Voice of the Heart*, p. 165.

21 Prakash Tandon, *Punjabi Saga*, p. 565.
22 Quoted by Mrinalini Sarabhai to the author. See also, Mrinalini Sarabhai, *The Voice of the Heart*, p. 164.
23 Ibid.
24 Gunnar Myrdal, *Asian Drama: Volume One*, p. 256.

6. ASSUMING BHABHA'S MANTLE

1 E.V. Chitnis in personal communication with the author.
2 Gopal Raj, *Reach for the Stars*, p. 16.
3 Gopal Raj in personal communication with the author.
4 Vikram's keenness to give Asian expertise a chance led him to seek out Hideo Itokawa of the Institute of Space and Aeronautical Sciences, Japan, as an adviser to the programme in clear preference to a US or Russian expert.
5 A.P.J. Abdul Kalam with Arun Tiwari, *Wings of Fire*, p. 48.
6 Gopal Raj, *Reach for the Stars*, p. 36.
7 Favourite phrase repeated by colleagues such as E.V. Chitnis and Vasant Gowarikar in conversations with the author.
8 Transcript of an interview with Satish Dhawan, August 1997, ISRO, Bangalore.
9 Transcript of an interview with R.D. John, ISRO, Bangalore.
10 A.P.J. Abdul Kalam with Arun Tiwari, *Wings of Fire*, pp. 48–51.
11 Ibid., p. 62.
12 Raja Ramanna, 'Chairman, Atomic Energy Commission', in Padmanabh K. Joshi (ed.), *Vikram Sarabhai: The Man and the Vision*, p. 120.
13 Axel Horn, 'Problem Solving Skills Through Science Education', in Padmanabh K. Joshi (ed.), *Vikram Sarabhai: The Man and the Vision*, p. 135.
14 Axel Horn, 'A Tribute', Dr Vikram Sarabhai Archives, Nehru Foundation for Development, Ahmedabad.
15 Mrinalini Sarabhai, *The Voice of the Heart*, p. 164.
16 Pupul Jayakar described Bhabha's death on the day of Indira Gandhi's swearing in as a 'critical blow'. Pupul Jayakar, *Indira Gandhi*, p. 183.
17 Kameshwar C. Wali, *Chandra: A Biography of S. Chandrasekhar*, p. 288.

18 Raja Ramanna, *Years of Pilgrimage*, p. 75.
19 Gita Mayor in personal communication with the author.
20 Quoted by K.R. Ramanathan in 'Peaceful Uses of Space', in Padmanabh K. Joshi (ed.), *Vikram Sarabhai: The Man and the Vision*, p. 117.
21 Prabhash Kumar Mukherjee in personal communication with the author.
22 Raja Ramanna, 'Chairman, Atomic Energy Commission', in Padmanabh K. Joshi (ed.), *Vikram Sarabhai: The Man and the Vision*, p. 121.
23 Transcript of Vikram Sarabhai's 1966 press conference, Dr Vikram Sarabhai Archives, Nehru Foundation for Development, Ahmedabad.
24 G. Venkataraman, *Bhabha and His Magnificent Obsessions*, and the author's interviews.
25 Homi Bhabha quoted on a placard at the DAE stall at the National Children's Congress, 2001, Pune.
26 George Perkovich, *India's Nuclear Bomb*, p. 33.
27 Raj Chengappa, *Weapons of Peace*, pp. 79-80.
28 Transcript of an interview with R.D. John, ISRO, Bangalore.
29 Transcript of an interview with Satish Dhawan, August 1997, ISRO, Bangalore.
30 Itty Abraham, *The Making of the Indian Atomic Bomb*, p. 41.
31 Incident narrated by K. Subrahmanyam in an interview to the author.
32 M.R. Srinivasan, *From Fission to Fusion*, p. 14.
33 Raj Chengappa, *Weapons of Peace*, pp. 88-89.
34 George Perkovich, *India's Nuclear Bomb*, p. 21.
35 See ibid., pp. 65–68, for Bhabha's broadcast and discussion of costs.
36 See National Security Archive Electronic Briefing Book No. 6 (http://www.gwu.edu/~nsarchiv/NSAEBB/NSAEBB6/index.html) and George Perkovich, ibid., pp. 90–99.
37 Raj Chengappa, *Weapons of Peace*, p. 98.
38 Itty Abraham, *The Making of the Indian Atomic Bomb*, pp. 103–06.
39 Raja Ramanna quoted in Raj Chengappa, *Weapons of Peace*, p. 82.
40 Dr Vikram Sarabhai Archives, Nehru Foundation for Development, Ahmedabad.
41 R.R. Revelle, Vikram Sarabhai Memorial Lectures, PRL, Ahmedabad.
42 Dr Vikram Sarabhai Archives, Nehru Foundation for Development,

Ahmedabad. Also in Vikram Sarabhai, *Science Policy and National Development*, pp. 154–61.

[43] Raj Chengappa, *Weapons of Peace*, p. 106.

[44] For instance, see George Perkovich, *India's Nuclear Bomb*, p. 114.

[45] Transcript of Vikram Sarabhai's 1966 press conference, Dr Vikram Sarabhai Archives, Nehru Foundation for Development, Ahmedabad.

[46] Erik H. Erikson, *Gandhi's Truth*, p. 89.

[47] M.G.K. Menon, 'Like a Prophet', in Padmanabh K. Joshi (ed.), *Vikram Sarabhai: The Man and the Vision*, p. 61.

[48] Raj Chengappa, *Weapons of Peace*, p. 104.

[49] Vikram Sarabhai in *India and Science Today*, a documentary produced by Michael Treguer for French television.

[50] Lawrence A. Babb, *Ascetics and Kings in a Jain Ritual Culture*, p. 5.

[51] Erik H. Erikson, *Gandhi's Truth*, p. 109.

[52] Itty Abraham, *The Making of the Indian Atomic Bomb*, p. 130.

[53] George Perkovich, *India's Nuclear Bomb*, p. 124.

[54] Transcript of Vikram Sarabhai's 1966 press conference, Dr Vikram Sarabhai Archives, Nehru Foundation for Development, Ahmedabad.

[55] Itty Abraham, *The Making of the Indian Atomic Bomb*, p. 143.

[56] Transcript of Vikram Sarabhai's 1966 press conference, Dr Vikram Sarabhai Archives, Nehru Foundation for Development, Ahmedabad.

[57] Quoted in George Perkovich, *India's Nuclear Bomb*, p. 73.

[58] Dr Vikram Sarabhai Archives, Nehru Foundation for Development, Ahmedabad.

[59] Pupul Jayakar, *Indira Gandhi*, p. 150.

[60] Harriet Ronken Lynton, *Born to Dance*, p. 100.

[61] Transcript of K.R. Ramnath's 1997 interview, ISRO, Bangalore.

[62] George Perkovich, *India's Nuclear Bomb*, p. 126.

[63] Ibid., p. 130.

[64] L.K. Jha, 'A Versatile Mind', in Padmanabh K. Joshi (ed.), *Vikram Sarabhai: The Man and the Vision*, p. 46.

[65] Ibid., p. 47.

[66] Ibid., p. 48.

[67] From the memorandum of conversation from the office of the assistant secretary of defence: 'Meeting between the secretary of defence and Mr. L.K. Jha', 18 April, National Security Archive

Electronic Briefing Book No. 6 (http://www.gwu.edu/~nsarchiv/NSAEBB/NSAEBB6/index.html).

68 George Perkovich, *India's Nuclear Bomb*, p. 136.

69 From the memorandum of conversation from the office of the assistant secretary of defence: 'Meeting between the secretary of defence and Mr. L.K. Jha', 18 April, National Security Archive Electronic Briefing Book No. 6 (http://www.gwu.edu/~nsarchiv/NSAEBB/NSAEBB6/index.html).

70 Address given as Scientific Chairman of the UN Conference on the Exploration and Peaceful Uses of Outer Space, Vienna, August 1968, Dr Vikram Sarabhai Archives, Nehru Foundation for Development, Ahmedabad. Also in Vikram Sarabhai, *Science Policy and National Development*, p. 37.

71 A.P.J. Abdul Kalam, 'The Aim of a Lifetime', in Padmanabh K. Joshi (ed.), *Vikram Sarabhai: The Man and the Vision*, pp. 67–69.

7. THE TOUGHEST BATTLE

1 Vikram Sarabhai Memorial Lecture by P.N. Haksar, IIM, Ahmedabad, February 1976. Dr Vikram Sarabhai Archives, Nehru Foundation for Development, Ahmedabad.

2 Ibid.

3 See A.S. Rao, 'Electronics: The Drive for Self-sufficiency', in Padmanabh K. Joshi (ed.), *Vikram Sarabhai: The Man and the Vision*, p. 125.

4 'Television for Development', paper presented at the Society for International Development Conference, New Delhi, November 1969, Dr Vikram Sarabhai Archives, Nehru Foundation for Development, Ahmedabad. Also in Vikram Sarabhai, *Science Policy and National Development*, p. 40.

5 'How Green Is Our Revolution', Lal Bahadur Shastri Memorial Lecture of the Indian Agricultural Research Institute, 1969, Dr Vikram Sarabhai Archives, Nehru Foundation for Development, Ahmedabad. Also in Vikram Sarabhai, *Science Policy and National Development*, 125-26.

6 Itty Abraham, *The Making of the Indian Atomic Bomb*, p. 132.

7 'Television for Development', paper presented at the Society for International Development Conference, New Delhi, November 1969, Dr Vikram Sarabhai Archives, Nehru Foundation for Development, Ahmedabad. Also in Vikram Sarabhai, *Science Policy and National Development*, p. 43.

8 Itty Abraham, *The Making of the Indian Atomic Bomb*, p. 132.

9 Raj Thapar, *All These Years*, p. 342.

10 'Public Management and Control Systems', in Vikram Sarabhai, *Management for Development*, Kamla Chowdhry (ed.), n.10, p. 39.

11 B.S. Bhatia and K.S. Karnik, 'An Unfinished Task', Dr Vikram Sarabhai Archives, Nehru Foundation for Development, Ahmedabad.

12 V. Gangadhar, 'Dr. Vikram Sarabhai', *The Illustrated Weekly of India*, 30 December 1973.

13 Transcript of K.R. Ramnath's interview, August 1997, ISRO, Bangalore.

14 M.R. Srinivasan, *From Fission to Fusion*, p. 107.

15 Itty Abraham, *The Making of the Indian Atomic Bomb*, pp. 135-36.

16 C.V. Sundaram, L.V. Krishnan and T.S. Iyengar, *Atomic Energy in India*, p. 46.

17 Itty Abraham, *The Making of the Indian Atomic Bomb*, p. 137.

18 M.R. Srinivasan, *From Fission to Fusion*, p. 105.

19 Itty Abraham, *The Making of the Indian Atomic Bomb*, pp. 144-45.

20 R. Chidambaram interview in C.V. Sundaram, L.V. Krishnan and T.S. Iyengar, *Atomic Energy in India*, p. 183.

21 George Perkovich, *India's Nuclear Bomb*, p. 141.

22 Transcript of K.R. Ramnath's interview, August 1997, ISRO, Bangalore.

23 M.R. Srinivasan, *From Fission to Fusion*, p. 108.

24 Prakash Tandon, *Punjabi Saga*, p. 546.

25 A.P.J. Abdul Kalam with Arun Tiwari, *Wings of Fire*, pp. 40-41.

26 'Education and Non-violence', paper presented at the Gandhi Centenary Conference on Science, Education and Non-violence at Gujarat Vidyapith, October 1969, Dr Vikram Sarabhai Archives, Nehru Foundation for Development, Ahmedabad. Also in Vikram Sarabhai, *Science Policy and National Development*, p. 166.

27 R. Chidambaram interviewed in C.V. Sundaram, L.V. Krishnan and T.S. Iyengar, *Atomic Energy in India*, p. 187.

[28] Raj Chengappa, *Weapons of Peace*, p. 127.
[29] George Perkovich, *India's Nuclear Bomb*, p. 150.
[30] Ibid., p. 151.
[31] Ibid., p. 152.
[32] Ibid., p. 559.
[33] Vikram Sarabhai, 'Foreword', *Atomic Energy and Space Research: A Profile for the Decade 1970–1980*, p. v, Government of India, Atomic Energy Commission.
[34] A.P.J. Abdul Kalam with Arun Tiwari, *Wings of Fire*, p. 52.
[35] George Perkovich, *India's Nuclear Bomb*, p. 153.
[36] Bhabani Sen Gupta and Centre for Policy Research, *Nuclear Weapons? Policy Options for India*, p. 4.
[37] Ibid., p. 7.
[38] M.R. Srinivasan, *From Fission to Fusion*, p. 108.
[39] Hideo Itokawa, 'A Tribute', Dr Vikram Sarabhai Archives, Nehru Foundation for Development, Ahmedabad.
[40] Mrinalini Sarabhai in personal communication with the author.
[41] J.P. Jain, *Nuclear India Vol. II*, pp. 201-02.
[42] Raj Thapar, *All These Years*, p. 342.
[43] P.C. Alexander, *My Years with Indira Gandhi*, p. 59.
[44] Raj Chengappa, *Weapons of Peace*, pp. 112-13.
[45] Raj Chengappa in personal communication with the author.
[46] Bhabani Sen Gupta and Centre for Policy Research, *Nuclear Weapons? Policy Options for India*, p. 5.
[47] George Perkovich, *India's Nuclear Bomb*, p. 159.
[48] Narrated by a former official on condition of anonymity.
[49] Vikram Sarabhai Memorial Lecture by P.N. Haksar, IIM, Ahmedabad, February 1976. Dr Vikram Sarabhai Archives, Nehru Foundation for Development, Ahmedabad.
[50] Mrinalini Sarabhai in personal communication with the author.
[51] Leena Mangaldas, *Akhand Divo*, p. 11.
[52] Raja Ramanna, *Years of Pilgrimage*, p. 76.
[53] Mrs Shandamma in personal communication with the author.

8. A 'HEROIC' DEATH

1. Vikram Sarabhai, 'Sources of Man's Knowledge', part of the National Programme of Talks, Series: 'Exploration in Space', 1966, reproduced in *Resonance*, December 2001, p. 91.
2. A.P.J. Abdul Kalam with Arun Tiwari, *Wings of Fire*, p. 63.
3. Prakash Tandon, *Punjabi Saga*, p. 567.

BIBLIOGRAPHY

BOOKS

Abraham, Itty, *The Making of the Indian Atomic Bomb: Science, Secrecy and the Postcolonial State*, London: Zed Books, 1998; Hyderabad: Orient Longman, 1999

Adams, Steve, *Frontiers: Twentieth Century Physics*, London/New York: Taylor & Francis Ltd, 2000

Akbar, M.J., *Nehru: The Making of India*, New Delhi: Viking/Penguin Books India, 1989

——, *India: The Siege Within*, Reprint, New Delhi: Roli Books, 2003

Alexander, P.C., *My Years with Indira Gandhi*, New Delhi: Vision Books, 1991

Babb, Lawrence A., *Ascetics and Kings in a Jain Ritual Culture*, The Regents of the University of California, University of California Press, 1996

Basu, Aparna, *Mridula Sarabhai: A Rebel with a Cause*, New Delhi: Oxford University Press, 1996

Bernal, J.D., *The Social Function of Science*, London: George Routledge & Sons Ltd, 1939

Bhavsar, Praful and Padmanabh Joshi, *Dr. Vikram Sarabhai: Visionary Scientist*, Ahmedabad: Gujarat Vigyan Academy, 2000

Bidwai, Praful and Achin Vanaik, *South Asia on a Short Fuse: Nuclear Politics and the Future of Global Disarmament*, New Delhi: Oxford University Press, 1999

Bondi, Hermann and Miranda Weston-Smith (eds), *The Universe Unfolding*, Oxford: Clarendon Press, 1988

Bowles, Chester, *Ambassador's Report*, Comet Books, 1954

——, *A View from New Delhi*, New Delhi: Allied Publishers Pvt. Ltd, 1969

Bowles, Cynthia, *At Home in India*, New York: Harcourt, Brace and Co., 1969

Brass, Paul R., *The New Cambridge History of India*, Cambridge: Cambridge University Press, 1990

Breman, Jan and Parthiv Shah, *Working in the Mill No More*, New Delhi: Oxford University Press, 2004

Chandra, Bipan, Mridula Mukherjee, Aditya Mukherjee, *India After Independence 1947-2000*, New Delhi: Penguin Books India, 2000.

Chatterjee, Santimay and Enakshi Chatterjee, *Meghnad Saha*, New Delhi: National Book Trust, 1984

Chengappa, Raj, *Weapons of Peace*, New Delhi: HarperCollins Publishers India, 2000

Choksi, M., *India's Indira*, New Delhi: Orient Longman, 1975

Chown, Marcus, *The Magic Furnace: The Search for the Origin of Atoms*, London: Jonathan Cape, 1999

Commissariat, M.S., *A History of Gujarat*, Orient Longman Pvt. Ltd, 1957

Erikson, Erik H., *Gandhi's Truth: On the Origins of Militant Nonviolence*, New York: W.W. Norton & Co. Inc. USA, 1969

Frank, Katherine, *Indira: The Life of Indira Nehru Gandhi*, London: HarperCollins Publishers, 2002

Freeman, Joan, *A Passion for Physics: The Story of a Woman Physicist*, Bristol: Adam Hilger, 1991

Gandhi, Arun, *Kasturba: A Life*, New York: Penguin Books, 2000

Gandhi, Rajmohan, *Patel: A Life*, Ahmedabad: Navjivan Publishing House, 1991

Ganguly, Sumit, *Conflict Unending: India-Pakistan Tensions Since 1947*, New York: Columbia University Press, 2001; New Delhi: Oxford University Press, 2001

Ghosh, Amitav, *Countdown*, New Delhi: Ravi Dayal, 1999

Gibson, Roy, *Space*, Oxford: Clarendon Press, 1992

Gillion, Kenneth L., *Ahmedabad: A Study in Indian Urban History*, California: University of California Press, 1968

Gopal, S., *Jawaharlal Nehru: A Biography, Volume One*, Bombay: Oxford University Press, 1976

——, *Jawaharlal Nehru: A Biography, Volume Two*, Bombay: Oxford University Press, 1979

Guha, Ramchandra, *An Anthropologist Among the Marxists*, New Delhi: Permanent Black, 2001

Jain, J.P., *Nuclear India Vol. II*, New Delhi: Radiant Publishers, 1974

Jayakar, Pupul, *Indira Gandhi: A Biography*, New Delhi: Viking/Penguin Books India, 1988

Joshi, Padmanabh K. (ed.), *Vikram Sarabhai: The Man and the Vision*, Ahmedabad: Mapin Publishing Pvt. Ltd, 1992

Kalam, A.P.J. Abdul with Arun Tiwari, *Wings of Fire*, Hyderabad: Universities Press (India) Pvt. Ltd, 2000

Kamath, M.V. (ed.), *Nehru Revisited*, Bombay: Nehru Centre, 2003

Khilnani, Sunil, *The Idea of India*, London: Penguin Books, 1998

Kothari, Rajni, *Memoirs*, New Delhi: Rupa & Co., 2002

Kothari, Smitu and Zia Mian (eds), *Out of the Nuclear Shadow*, New Delhi: Lokayan and Rainbow Publishers, 2001

Lala, R.M., *The Creation of Wealth*, Bombay: IBH Publishing Co., 1981; Reprint, New Delhi: Penguin Books India, 2006

Lynton, Harriet Ronken, *Born to Dance*, Hyderabad: Orient Longman, 1995

Malhotra, Inder, *Indira Gandhi: A Personal and Political Biography*, London: Hodder & Stoughton, 1989

Mangaldas, Leena, *Akhand Divo*, Ahmedabad: Shreyas Prakashan, 1979

——, *Vyaktichitro*, Ahmedabad: Shreyas Prakashan, 1982

Masani, Zareer, *Indira Gandhi: A Biography*, London: Hamish Hamilton, 1975; Bombay: Oxford University Press, 1976

Mathai, M.O., *Reminiscences of the Nehru Age*, New Delhi: Vikas Publishing House, 1978

Memon, Ayaz and Ranjona Banerjee, *India 50: The Making of a Nation*, Bombay: Book Quest Publishers, 1997

Menon, K.P.S., *Many Worlds: An Autobiography*, London: Oxford University Press, 1965

Monk, Ray, *Bertrand Russell: The Ghost of Madness 1921-1970*, London: Vintage, 2001

Moraes, Frank, *Jawaharlal Nehru*, Bombay: Jaico Publishing House, 1959

Myrdal, Gunnar, *Asian Drama: An Inquiry into the Poverty of Nations, Volume One*, London: Allen Lane, The Penguin Press, 1968

Nayar, Kuldip, *Between the Lines*, New Delhi: Allied Publishers Pvt. Ltd, 1969

Nehru, B.K., *Nice Guys Finish Second: Memoirs*, New Delhi: Viking/Penguin Books India, 1997

Ninan, Sevanti, *Through the Magic Window*, New Delhi: Penguin Books India, 1995

Oldenberg, Philip, *India Briefing*, New York: East Gate Books, 1995

Page, David and William Crawley, *Satellites over South Asia*, New Delhi: Sage Publications India Pvt. Ltd, 2001

Patel, Prahḷad C., *Viral Vibhuti Vikram Sarabhai*, Ahmedabad: Gujarat Vishwakosh Trust, 2001

Perkovich, George, *India's Nuclear Bomb*, New Delhi: Oxford University Press, 2000

Piramal, Gita, *Business Legends*, New Delhi: Penguin Books India, 1998

Piramal, Gita and Margaret Herdeck, *India's Industrialists: Volume One*, Washington, DC: Three Continents Press, Inc., 1985

Raj, Gopal, *Reach for the Stars*, New Delhi: Viking/Penguin Books India, 2000

Ramanna, Raja, *Years of Pilgrimage*, New Delhi: Viking/Penguin Books India, 1991

Rossi, Bruno, *Moments in the Life of a Scientist*, Cambridge: Cambridge University Press, 1990

Sarabhai, Mrinalini, *This Alone Is True*, New Delhi: Hind Pocket Books Pvt. Ltd, 1977

——, *The Voice of the Heart: An Autobiography*, New Delhi: HarperCollins Publishers India, 2004

Sarabhai, Vikram, *Management for Development*, A Collection of Papers Edited by Kamla Chowdhry, New Delhi: Vikas Publishing House, 1974

——, *Science Policy and National Development*, New Delhi: Macmillan, 1974

Sastry, D.U., *The Cotton Mill Industry in India*, New Delhi: Oxford University Press, 1984

Sehgal, Lakshmi, *A Revolutionary Life*, New Delhi: Kali For Women, 1997

Sen Gupta, Bhabani and Centre for Policy Research, *Nuclear Weapons? Policy Options for India*, New Delhi: Sage Publications, 1983

Sharma, Dhirendra, *India's Nuclear Estate*, New Delhi: Lancer Publishers, 1983

Shawcross, William, *Murdoch*, London: Pan Books Ltd, 1993

Sheth, Chimanlal Bhailal, *Jainism in Gujarat: AD 1100 to 1600*, Bhavnagar: Shree Mahodaya Press; Bombay: Vijayadevasur Sangh Gnan Samity, 1953

Singh, R.R., *History of Medieval India (1000 AD to 1707 AD)*, Bombay: Sheth Publishers Pvt. Ltd

Singhal, Arvind and Everett Rogers, *India's Information Revolution*, New Delhi: Sage Publications, 1989

Smith, Robert W., *The Space Telescope*, Cambridge: Cambridge University Press, 1989

Snow, C.P., *The Physicists: A Generation That Changed the World*, London: Macmillan, 1981

Spangenburg, Ray and Diane K. Moser, *Werner Von Braun: Space Visionary and Rocket Engineer*, Hyderabad: Universities Press (India) Pvt. Ltd, 1999

Srinivasan, M.R., *From Fission to Fusion*, New Delhi: Viking/Penguin Books India, 2002

Sundaram, C.V., L.V. Krishnan and T.S. Iyengar, *Atomic Energy in India*, Bombay: Department of Atomic Energy, 1998

Tandon, Prakash, *Punjabi Saga 1857–2000: The Monumental Story of Five Generations of a Remarkable Punjabi Family*, New Delhi: Rupa & Co., 2000

Tewari, V.N., *12, Willingdon Crescent*, New Delhi: Ajanta Publications, 1979

Thakar, Dhirubhai, *Parampara Ane Pragati*, A Biography of Kasturbhai Lalbhai, Bombay: The A.D. Shroff Memorial Trust, 1980

Thakur, Janardan, *Indira Gandhi and Her Power Game*, New Delhi: Vikas Publishing House, 1979

Thapar, Raj, *All These Years: A Memoir*, New Delhi: Viking/Penguin Books India, 1991

Tripathi, Dwijendra, *The Dynamics of a Tradition: Kasturbhai Lalbhai and His Entrepreneurship*, New Delhi: Manohar, 1981

——, (ed.), *Business and Politics in India: A Historical Perspective*, New Delhi: Manohar, 1991

Vasudev, Uma, *Indira Gandhi: Revolution for Restraint*, New Delhi: Vikas Publishing House, 1974

Venkataraman, G., *Saha and His Formula*, Hyderabad: Universities Press (India) Pvt. Ltd, 1995

——, *Bhabha and His Magnificent Obsessions*, Hyderabad: Universities Press (India) Pvt. Ltd, 1997

——, *Raman and His Effect*, Hyderabad: Universities Press (India) Pvt. Ltd, 2001

Wali, Kameshwar C., *Chandra: A Biography of S. Chandrasekhar*, New Delhi: Viking/Penguin Books India, 1991

Wolfe, Tom, *The Right Stuff*, New York: Farrar, Straus and Giroux, 1979

Yagnik, Achyut and Suchitra Sheth, *The Shaping of Modern Gujarat*, New Delhi: Penguin Books India, 2005

OTHER SOURCES

Ahmedabad District Gazetteer 1984

Ahmedabad Management Association Bulletin, December 2001

Amarnath K. Menon, 'Seeking Space', *India Today*, 5 May 2003

Annual Report 2001-02, Department of Space, Government of India

'Another India', *Daedalus, Journal of the American Academy of Arts and Sciences*, Fall 1989

Arno S. Pearse, 'The Cotton Industry of India', International Federation of Master Cotton Spinners and Manufacturers Association, Manchester, January–March 1930

'ATIRA 1949–74', ATIRA brochure, November 1974

B.S. Bhatia and K.S. Karnik, 'An Unfinished Task', Dr Vikram Sarabhai Archives, Nehru Foundation for Development, Ahmedabad

'Destination Moon', *The Week*, 11 January 2004

Documentary on Vikram Sarabhai, ISRO

Indira Gandhi, *The Years of Endeavour: Selected Speeches 1969–72*, Ministry of Information and Broadcasting, 1975

K. Kasturirangan, 'Space: An Innovative Route to Development', Fourth J.R.D. Tata Memorial Lecture, 31 August 2000

'Mirror Work' (Mallika Sarabhai profile), *Sunday Mid-day*, 19 August 2001

Nature, Vol. 174, p. 578, 25 September 1954

Papers, Asian Relations Conference March-April 1947, Indian Council of World Affairs, New Delhi

R.R. Revelle, Vikram Sarabhai Memorial Lectures, PRL, Ahmedabad

Resonance, Vol. 6, No. 12, December 2001

R.G.K. Sarabhai Profile, *The Illustrated Weekly of India*, 3 July 1966

Sara Pragati, House Magazine of Sarabhai Chemicals, June 1972, August-September 1966

'Satellite Imaging', *Outlook*, 14 January 2002

'The Ahmedabad Chronicle: Imprints of a Millennium', Vastu Shilpa Foundation for Studies and Research in Environmental Design, Ahmedabad, 2002

The Times of India, 31 December 1971–3 January 1972

The Times of India, 1–3 May 1960

V. Gangadhar, 'Dr. Vikram Sarabhai', *The Illustrated Weekly of India*, 30 December 1973

Yash Pal, 'Beyond Mere Competence', Vikram Sarabhai Memorial Lecture, April 2001

COPYRIGHT ACKNOWLEDGEMENTS

The author wishes to thank the following for photographs used in the book: Dr Vikram Sarabhai Archives, Nehru Foundation for Development, Ahmedabad; the Physical Research Laboratory, Ahmedabad; the Indian Space Research Organisation, Bangalore; Hemendra Shah; and the Bhabha Atomic Research Centre.

The author also wishes to acknowledge the following for permission to quote from previously published works:

Padmanabh K. Joshi (ed.), *Vikram Sarabhai: The Man and the Vision*, Mapin Publishing Pvt. Ltd, Ahmedabad, 1992

George Perkovich, *India's Nuclear Bomb*, Oxford University Press, New Delhi, 2000; The Regents of the University of California, University of California Press, 2002

A.P.J. Abdul Kalam with Arun Tiwari, *Wings of Fire*, Universities Press, Hyderabad, 2000

Lawrence A. Babb, *Ascetics and Kings in a Jain Ritual Culture*, The Regents of the University of California, University of California Press, 1996

Prakash Tandon, *Punjabi Saga*, Rupa & Co., New Delhi, 2000

Itty Abraham, *The Making of the Indian Atomic Bomb*, Orient Longman, Hyderabad, 1999

Dr Vikram Sarabhai Archives, Nehru Foundation for Development, Ahmedabad

INDEX